The Memoirs & Recollections of Jimmy Carl Black 1938-2008

Published by Inkanish Publications
All rights reserved

Front Cover photo: JCB family album
Back Cover art: Helmut King
Title Page photo: courtesy Helmut King

The editors have endeavored to ascertain or trace all illustration copyright holders. A table listing photographs can be found on pages 279-80. We would be grateful to hear from the photographers concerned.

Printed by CreateSpace
An Amazon.com Company
2013

Contents

The Text

Jimmy Carl Black was still working on his autobiography when sadly he succumbed to cancer. His last wish was that his book be finished and published.

The first part of Jimmy's account of his life was transcribed and edited by Roddie Gilliard from audio recordings made when Jimmy was on the road with the Muffin Men. This account, from 1938-1994, forms the "Memoirs".

When Jimmy went online at the start of this century, he wrote a 'third-person' biography for his website that he then periodically updated with news about himself and his music. In addition, he wrote extensively about the year 2000, and responded in detail for some of the written interviews he gave during these years. Elsewhere, he was writing promotional materials for CD releases under his Inkanish label or discussing his life and times during face-to-face interviews and in correspondence. The web biography, supported by text drawn from these interviews and other writings, and covering the years 1995 to 2008, forms the "Recollections".

These are Jimmy words and this is his story. He dedicated it to his family, friends and fans, for whom it was being written.

Commentary

Inevitably, there are discrepancies between accounts of the same event recalled at intervals over the years: the exact date or place, the order of events, the actors involved, and the different viewpoints of those involved. Commentary found in chapter-end notes attempts to provide answers where questions of this kind arise.

If the text has been corrected (rarely), an endnote provides an explanation. Endnotes also flag dates, explain special expressions and, when possible and useful, complement or expand on the main text.

Editing

Jimmy spoke in the vernacular and the spoken cadences of Jimmy's speech are captured in Roddie Gilliard's transcriptions of the audio tapes. So, where Jimmy's language is colloquial, it remains so. Grammatical errors, slang, expletives or redundant text have not been edited out, nor has punctuation been inserted artificially where the cadence might be altered.

[ ] brackets indicate where words have been inserted.

'...' indicate abbreviated or incomplete text.

Graphics and photos draw on ideas and listings that Jimmy provided. If an editor's license has been used, it has been to partition the book, increase the number of chapters, reorder some "episodes" to fit the sequence of events, and to provide some apposite chapter or "episode" headings for consistency and completeness. These headings are drawn from the text.

The slang or common names of drugs such as Hash, and drug expressions such as Trip and Joint are capitalized in the text to avoid confusion.

So how did the idea of the book come about? Well here's the recipe:

Put a rock 'n' roll legend in a bus with a band of blokes from Liverpool. Travel around Europe on low budget tours, sharing rooms, floors, alcohol, spices and smells. Talk, talk and talk some more, banter, chat, cuss, drink and be merry. Mix ingredients in a pot, adding additional talk, banter and spice. Someone suggests recording the old tales for posterity. Encourage Jimmy to keep talking - as if he needed it!

Much of the text was transcribed from recordings we made between 1994 and 1997 using a cheap Dictaphone cassette recorder. The tapes were recorded in the back of a bus while we - the Muffin Men - were touring around Germany, Belgium, and Holland. Jimmy was not in great shape; he nearly always had a heavy cold and his dialogue is full of swearing.

I transcribed the recordings after each tour, more or less exactly as Jimmy spoke. I made notes and got Jimmy to expand on certain incidents, people, places etc. Eventually everything was in some sort of logical order. I then set about smoothing out the dialogues to build sentences which flowed and still sounded like Jimmy talking. He was very happy with the first draft.

We expanded the original draft over the following years, both on the road and at our homes in Liverpool, Bad Boll and Siegsdorf. During that time we never thought to document the present, instead concentrating on the job in hand. But for the record, we had many adventures, ups and downs, and lots of fun.

So these are Jimmy's memoirs, transcribed directly from those original recordings. A cheap cassette in a noisy bus, engine rumbling, people talking, Jimmy coughing and spluttering, laughing and joking and swearing. It was not a particularly pleasant experience transcribing the waffling and rambling into a coherent text. The audio quality of the recordings is at best awful. But the tapes are stored in a box, in the cupboard under the stairs. I will never throw them out.

Jimmy was a social animal, a road rat. He loved being on the road playing in a band. Meeting people and talking to people were his passions. He also loved to have a drink too! Throughout our time together, I observed hundreds of mostly old bearded guys approach him with their treasured copies of old 'Mothers' LPs to be signed. Only in the final few years did I ever see him become tired of these activities. I realize now that he was saving what little energy he had left for the stage. No matter how tired or sick he was, he would always give everything to the show. I think I speak for us all of us when I say that I think of him almost daily.

We miss you Jim, you will always be The Indian of the Group.
Roddie Gilliard, Crete, February 2013

For the Memoirs: 1938-1994

Our life was not all autobahns and pensions (200 Gasthofs?). We have many people to thank for their help and hospitality over the years: Fred Tomsett for originally introducing us to Jimmy; Ulli Schaefer, Reinhard Pruess and many others too numerous to mention in such a short introduction, but you know who you are.

Special thanks must go to the original touring band of Muffin Men: Rhino, Jumpy, Bammo, Naraish, Roy, Waco, Michael and Friz. It was these people who experienced first-hand the pain and pleasures of the original recordings in the back of an old VW bus. Later, as the band line-up changed, Belge, Marty, Tilo, Sefano, Dommo, Carlo and Mike, along with our trusted recording engineer The Bean added spices to the pot. Then we can't forget Don, Bunk, Denny, Ike, Mike K and all the other "real guys" who became part of the stew. Husta, Moni, Daggie and Ruthless provided invaluable assistance along the way. A special mention must be given to Richard Ray Farrell who helped Jimmy pen his signature song, which the Muffin Men took (and used and abused) until we didn't have our Indian Boy to sing it anymore.

For the Recollections: 1995-2008

We have Jimmy to thank! His willingness to speak out or give interviews provided the reminiscences and statements that enabled the recollections to be completed, in a sense, by Jimmy. Our thanks also go to the authors, interviewers and fanzines that have graciously allowed us to quote from their transcripts in order to complete or complement Jimmy's story.

Individual thanks go to Claus Biegert, Eugene Chadbourne, Andrew Greenaway, Aad Hoogesteger, Stefan Kleiber, Calvin Krogh, Jon Larsen, Robyn Flans, Steve Moore, Horst Tolks, Ron Young and Axel Wünsch ...
(See Acknowledgements - II for a full list of acknowledgements)

Proofing and Publication

Our thanks go out to those Web sites that provide valuable research resources to the community, as a service, whatever their motivation.

Special thanks go to Roman Garcia Albertos, Monika Black, Tom Black, Bruno Ceriotti, Jerry Ford, Clark Inkanish, Sandro Oliva, Julian Smith, Horst Tolks, Art Tripp, Paul McAree, G. Stock, Charles Ulrich, and Pamela Zarubica... (See Acknowledgements - II for a full list)

To all those not mentioned here who recognize in reading the Memoirs and Recollections that they had a part to play, either materially or spiritually, in shaping Jimmy's story; for example: his American family, his remarkable friends, the musicians that he played with and those who Jimmy loved along the way!

On the afternoon of February 17, 1968 I was sitting in a motel room wondering what new and exciting things were ahead of me, having joined the Mothers of Invention. I'd just left Zappa's room where we talked about music in general, and also a little about the show coming up that evening. Frank had taken lascivious interest in revealing to me the existence of "groupies" - young ladies who liked to mingle with musicians in the bands. Frank assured me that the guy I was to room with for the weekend gigs would fill me in on all that.

As I sat there pondering all those deep subjects I heard the door open. Coming into the room was a man with hair hanging down past his shoulders, dressed in tight Levis and T-shirt, wearing a Navy pea coat, who had a huge smile on his face. "Hey man, I'm Jim Black. You must be Art Tripp. I'm REALLY HAPPY to meet you, man!" That warm greeting started a friendship that lasted 40 years.

We went on to play together in the Mothers of Invention for two years. To the band, he was "The Indian", and we loved him for it. He and I became close not only on the road and at rehearsals, but also with our families during non-band time. Jim had a fetching personality, not unlike many from his neck of the woods: that Texas lack of guile, never afraid of being thought a fool. He was assertive enough, but yet there was always vulnerability, a charm. He basically was a good old Southwestern boy with a little flower power mixed in. In fact if you were to lift up his hair, there might have been a little red on that neck.

We kept in touch a little over the years after the band broke up, and I am grateful that we started up a correspondence before he got ill. Jim was an open book to a fault, and was quick with his praise of others. I had some of the best times of my life around Jimmy Carl Black, all the while learning a little bit about rock 'n' roll drumming. I spoke with him a few weeks before his death. We talked about people we had known, and also about his health. When we hung up it dawned on me that this would likely be the last time we spoke.

As you read this book you can imagine a guy who would light up the room when he walked in. A man who, once you met him, was a friend for life. He performed for royalty, and for pub patrons. He had a wild side, but was responsible always for his family. I hope this book will give you the feel of the life and times of Jimmy Carl Black. It did for me.

Art Tripp, Gulfport, Mississippi, March 2013

Part One:

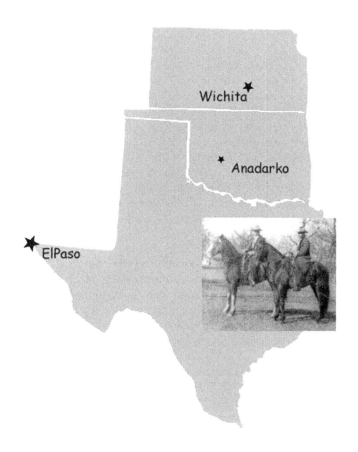

A Mother's Son

My natural father, James Inkanish, died shortly before I was born. He was a full blood American Indian[1] who worked at the Bureau of Indian Affairs as a schoolteacher. He died of tuberculosis, which at the time was fairly common on the reservation and I don't think he was much older than thirty or thirty-five years old at the most.

He died when my mom was pregnant with me. I really don't know exactly how or where they met but it was somewhere in Oklahoma. He was born someplace in southern Oklahoma. I think it was in Anadarko or near there. My sister June was also born in Anadarko. Oklahoma used to be called Indian Territory and it was one big Reservation. The U.S. government had set up this territory west of the Mississippi River in order to clear the Indians from all land east of the river. This was at the time of Andrew Jackson's presidency and when the famous "Trail of Tears" happened to the Cherokee Nation. The government sent around 16,000 Cherokees on a forced march from North Carolina and Georgia, Alabama, and Tennessee to Indian Territory. Over 4,000 died on that march, mainly from lack of food and the freezing weather. There was still a reservation system in place when my father was growing up but it was in the process of being phased out because "they" had discovered oil there! They didn't want the Indians to have all that black gold!

My mother's maiden name was Linnie Mae McLish. She was born in the year 1910 in Capitan New Mexico, on a wagon train travelling back to Oklahoma.[2] She was one-fourth Indian as her father was half Chickasaw[3] Indian and half Scottish. So I'm not what you'd call a full-blooded Indian, as I have some Caddo and Chickasaw blood in me, and some Scottish, and probably a mix of other blood[4] from my grandmother whose name was Lulu.[5]

So in 1937, after my father died and while she was pregnant with me, Mom left Oklahoma with June and hitchhiked all the way to El Paso, Texas. June can't remember exactly why Mom had decided to make the move. Maybe she just wanted to make a clean start.[6] She got a job working in a hotel called the Vogel very near downtown El Paso. After I was born,[7] she met Carl L. Black, who was living at the hotel, and they started going together. I was one year and fourteen days old when they got married on Valentine's Day, Feb. 14, 1939. He was a good man for my mother and a good father to me and my sister, June. That is the year we moved to Anthony, Texas.

Just before Mom and Carl got married, Carl went up to Anthony and bought a dry-cleaning place called the Valley Cleaners.

Anthony's a small town about 20 miles north of El Paso. It's as far west in Texas as you can go, half the town is in Texas and half in New Mexico. During the early 1940s, it was a community of about 700 people. We lived on the Texas side of Anthony and just up the street from the Valley Cleaners. So we moved up there to live and work, and Mom and Dad owned that place for over 30 years.

One of my memories of that time was the maid Juanita, who my parents had hired to take care of me until my sister got home from school. Juanita didn't speak a word of English and my parents or sister didn't speak a word of Spanish, but I learned to speak Spanish. As a young kid, it was as easy to learn two languages as it was to learn one. After two years, my parents bought their first house in town and it was even farther up the road from the Valley Cleaners.

We were the farthest house up the road from town for a long time. Up the road from town was about 1/4 of a mile. I really didn't have anybody to play with in those early days because of this, except of course when my sister got home from school.

June is the one who took care of me most of the time as a baby and even after mom and Carl got married and we moved to Anthony, she really raised me. June really was the best friend I ever had.

But I had a lot of fun in Anthony. We had chickens, a cow, and rabbits to attend to and then I got to know everybody because Anthony was a small town and I was always down at the Valley Cleaners after I started school. I was known as Sonny Black by everybody and I went under that name all through my 12 years of school. As far as I knew that was my real name. It turns out that it was my sister June who had started to call me Sonny, as it had been the name of my real father's younger brother.

In 1944 I went to Anthony Elementary School, which was on the New Mexico side of town. Nobody knew at the time that I was part Indian. All they knew was I was as dark as the Mexicans that went to school with me. The area we lived in was populated by about 85 percent Mexican families. It was a strange time for us as June was as dark as me.

Right next to the school, there was some sort of camp for German prisoners-of-war. We used to go to the back fence and the prisoners would be out there just hanging around. They were really friendly guys and seemed like nice people, but I couldn't understand a word they said. Years later, when I was living in Bad Boll Germany, I went to a bar with a friend of mine and was totally amazed to meet a man there who was at that camp in Anthony. He recalled that the people of my hometown had treated the prisoners of war with much kindness.

I remember an event that happened in 1945 in Anthony that was never explained, or at least not when it happened. Anthony is about 70 or 80 miles from one of the wonders of the world called White Sands National Monument. At the far end of the Monument is a place called White Sands Proving Grounds where the US government exploded the first two atomic test bombs. When the first one went off, it shook the ground in Anthony so much that it broke windows in town. Well, nobody knew what happened and it was thought to be an earthquake. It is strange that to this day there are so many cases of cancer in that area. It makes me wonder, as I was diagnosed in 2000 as having a weak case of Leukemia.

When I was small, I had a little "BB gun". It was an air gun that shot little ball bearings and it didn't have much power, which is fortunate. My friends and I used to have these little so-called wars with those guns. You must remember that the war was just winding down and probably the reason we played at such a stupid game as war.

Now, when I was in the first or second grade in school, my musical interests got started. I had started taking piano lessons from Mrs. St. Johns and I was also starting to sing a little bit. I used to go down to Pettit's Hardware Store and sing a song, and I'd get paid with a big pack of "bullets" for my little BB gun.

I suppose that is where my singing career actually got started. I was always a little nervous singing in front of a bunch of white farmers who thought this little dark-skinned boy was kind of cute.

I used to sing 'Don't Fence Me In', which was a very popular song at the time, and those old farts in Pettit's thought I was a good singer. In the third grade, I got to sing a solo at the Christmas Program at Anthony Elementary School. I sang 'White Christmas' which was made popular by Bing Crosby and the song went over very well. My mother was especially proud of me although she never thought I would become the kind of musician that I became later in life.

I was really having fun at school with all my friends. Most of them were white boys and I remember one in particular named Bobby Hughes. Bobby and I hung out pretty thick until all of a sudden he quit hangin'. It was my first experience with prejudice. His mother had told him she didn't want him hanging out with someone that looked like a Mexican and certainly not spending the night with me at my house. My mother and father really got pissed over that and didn't want me to see him anymore either. Later in life, Bobby and I did use to hang out and didn't care what our parents thought.

Every Saturday was the highlight of the week for the kids in Anthony. The afternoon movies at the New-Tex Theater were great. We either saw a great western, a Buck Rodgers sci-fi film, or a Laurel and Hardy film. Always before the film, there was a cartoon and a short feature like The Three Stooges or Our Gang. Man! I never missed those Saturdays and neither did any of my friends!

 In 1948, when I was ten years old, I started working at the Valley Cleaners with my Mom and Dad and my Dad filled out a Social Security form for me. Fifty-five years later, I started drawing on that Social Security. That is the American Dream for most Americans. But I could never actually consider myself retiring from music.

That was also the year my Dad went into debt and bought a new Ford two-door sedan. It was maroon with beautiful white-wall tires and it had an overdrive unit on the transmission which was suppose to give great gas mileage. Hell, gas only cost twenty cents a gallon in those days but everyone wanted the overdrive unit. I learned to drive in that car in 1950, when I was twelve years old.

That year also, my sister June graduated from Valley High School. She got married the following year to Ted Whorton and I was a very happy boy because I really liked Ted. I had a lot of fun with him, as he liked me and my brother and cousin very much. I was starting to grow up.

13

Notes to Chapter 1

[1] Jimmy believed for much of his life that his father was Cheyenne. Perhaps more interestingly, Jimmy discovered late in life that his father was part Caddo, a descendent of the Caddo-speaking Tribes that had inhabited the Piney Woods eco-region of the U.S., roughly East Texas, Oklahoma, southern Arkansas and northern Louisiana, for more than a thousand years. The Cheyenne arrived in Oklahoma much later.

[2] Born Oct. 5, 1910; Died Sept 15, 1999 in Anthony, Texas

[3] The Chickasaw also suffered the "Trail of Tears" in 1837; a trail already trodden by the Choctaw and Creek tribes; more than 500 Chickasaw died on route.

[4] Cheyenne? [See: Note 1]

[5] "Mclish, John 22 Edwards, Lulu 16 11 Jun 1905 Tishomingo/Reagan" [From: *Chickasaw Nation Marriages Register*, 1895-1907]

[6] James Inkanish Jr. died Caddo County, Anadarko, Oklahoma, in 1935. It probably did not occur to JCB that he might be illegitimate.

[7] At the Thomason General Hospital in El Paso, Texas on February 1, 1938

14

The summer before I started Junior High School in the seventh grade, myself and some friends of mine were in a club called The Junior Anthony Rangers. I didn't even have my own horse yet until about six months later. That was the summer that John Hall opened up the second movie theater in Anthony. Mr. Hall had hired a projectionist from California named Mr. Judd. Judd was also a cameraman and had made movies in Hollywood before moving to Anthony. Well, he took the Junior Anthony Rangers and made a western movie with us. Now, none of us were very good riders on our horses at that time and for sure we weren't actors.

I got the part of the Sheriff (I had to borrow a horse for the movie) and my friend Jerry Hall got the part of the bad guy. Mary Lipps, who probably was the best rider of all of us, was my deputy. The big fight scene was done at the big sand dunes outside of town and, me not being very good on a horse, I was not leading the posse but bringing up the rear. That was kind of embarrassing since I was the Sheriff and my trusty deputy (who just happened to be a girl) had to do the fight scene with Jerry. All in all, I guess that experience got me ready for my part in *200 Motels* as Lonesome Cowboy Burt twenty years later. Anyway, it was Mucho fun to do. Parts of the film still exist.

Like most kids in a town like Anthony, riding horses becomes second nature and I was no exception. During my time riding, I owned three horses but my first one was hardly what you could call a racer! I began riding seriously when I was about 12. That was when I got my first horse, Old Red. Now Red was old. He was about 28 when I got him and he wasn't that big. Red was only about 13 hands high but he was a good old boy. I had him for about a year and a half and then we sold him to another kid in Anthony. I believe he lasted another two or three years with that kid. We'd bought him for about a $100 and when we sold him we got about the same. My Dad was a real shrewd businessman when it came to wheelin' and dealin'!

So we sold Old Red and bought Dolly. She was a beautiful, dark brown bay horse and cost about $150. She was only about four or five years old. She was gorgeous and sweet and so sleek. I loved her very much.

15

I used to ride up into the sand hills and shoot my rifle from the saddle like they did in the old days. I used to think I was an Indian and I'd shoot at things like a stick or an old bottle. I'd got my rifle when I  was about 14. It was a powerful gun and it fired big 30/30 slugs which were designed for killing deer but I never tried that. The first time I shot from the horse, I almost fell off. She jumped and went crazy when that thing went off!

I had Dolly for about a year but she got a nail from the corral stuck in her knee which really fucked her up. The horse dealer didn't think she would be any good again so we traded her for Brownie, who was also bay-colored and a gelding (which means he had been castrated). Brownie was an excellent roping horse. He had been trained by a man that knew what he was doing.

Many of the local kids took their riding seriously, with aspirations to becoming Cowboys. They'd show their skills by entering into rodeo competitions. I was now in my mid-teens and decided I wanted to enter them too! Through Junior High and the first two years of High School I was a cowboy, right up until I was sixteen or early seventeen. I rode in rodeos. I had my own bucking rig for riding bucking broncos, the whole thing. I thought I was going to be a "bronc-rider". But Man! That ground is fucking hard when you hit it after you've been thrown six or seven feet [two meters] up in the air and you come smack down on your ass! I rode a couple of

bucking broncs and a couple of bulls, but after a few times I decided that that sport was way too rough for me. I got thrown off every time! I remember that the second horse I rode was called Recoil and he lived up to his name. When he came out of that chute he bucked on his front feet, then on his back feet, did this about three times and I was airborne! In the Valley Cleaners, there was a picture of me getting bucked off the first bull that I ever rode. I was leaning out with this look on my face - just about the time I was ready to hit the dirt. That picture was pinned on the wall of the Valley Cleaners for about 15 years. It was there until my parents sold the place.

So, after that, I went for the easier option. I decided that I would rope calves. Brownie was a great roping horse and I figured I was good enough to compete. I rode in rodeos for two years and reckon that I did about 15 or 20 rodeos.

You wait in the chute on your horse and when they let the calf out, that's when the time starts. You ride out, rope the calf (if you're lucky), slip off your horse, grab the calf and throw it down, put a picking string around the calf's legs and tie it and then you throw you arms up in the air. That was when the clock stops and the one who does it in the fastest time is the winner. There were some heavy-duty ropers around my area but I wasn't one of them. I really didn't care about winning that much. It was just a lot of fun for me and you know I was more interested in partying down with the guys and looking at the cowgirls with their tight jeans on.

A freak accident which occurred while me and my cousin were driving our horses to a practice arena finally brought my rodeo career to an abrupt end. I was with my cousin, Gary McLish. We had to drive the horses about 50 miles from where we lived to an arena that we could practice in. We set off in my Aunt Sybil's car, with the two horses in a trailer. We'd just had this trailer built in Houston by a friend. The guy who built it fucked up. It didn't pull right with the car and it started swaying while I was driving. The horses freaked out and started kicking the trailer gate off. My horse Brownie tried to get out of the trailer as I was stopping. I think we were probably going about 20 mph but he jumped out and fucked his ankles up on the highway. I tried for months but those ankles of his never did heal, Man! Eventually we had to have him put down and he probably went for dog meat or to the "Glue Factory". After that I just didn't want to do it anymore.

When I was in seventh grade, I started playing the trumpet. I was about twelve years old at that time. We were given a choice of what we wanted to play. For some reason I fancied the trumpet, probably because it only had three valves on it. I had taken some piano lessons when I was five and could read music so it wasn't that bad reading music. My problem was to figure out how to get the fingering of the valves right. In the seventh grade, I was just learning how to blow the thing and trying to get the tones happening and learn all the notes and fingerings.

The eighth grade was where I really started getting into the instrument properly. I practiced a lot and by the time I was a sophomore in High School I was in the first chair section, which meant I was pretty good. I eventually took over the soloist chair and I kept that position for the whole year, but believe me I was being challenged every week by somebody. So that meant I had to practice all the time! I also took some private lessons from a great trumpet player, Mr. Wadley.

In retrospect, I wish I'd have taken up the saxophone instead of the trumpet because Rock 'n' Roll music was just starting to happen and nobody was playing trumpet in that music at that time. That wouldn't start happening until the middle sixties with the bands Chicago, Blood, Sweat and Tears and of course, The Mothers of Invention.

We had a very good high school band because we had a very good bandleader, Mr. Jack Gracie. He was a multi-talented player and there were only two instruments in the high school band that he couldn't play. Those two instruments were the oboe and the bassoon. He could play the French horn pretty damn good but his main instruments were saxophone and the other reed instruments. During his college days, he had played with Tommy Dorsey and Glen Miller and was an exceptionally good musician.

MR. JACK GRACIE
Director

During the fall semester of school, the band played at all the football games. During the half-time break, we did shows which included marching up and down the field, playing John Philip Souza Marches and doing special steps at the same time.

We had to practice quite a lot and we were very good at it. We also marched and played on New Year's Day in the Sun Parade in El Paso. There were bands from all over the region in competition and our band won it two times while I was in High School.

After football season was over, the band started rehearsing for the series of semi-classical concerts we performed for the school and our parents. We also learned a lot of Mexican music to perform at these concerts, mainly because there were so many Mexicans in school. They loved it and so did we because it was interesting to play.

We had a Dixieland Jazz Band at school that also put on concerts. That was really interesting music to play when I was that young and I had to really get my chops[1] up for it. Mr. Gracie got the ten best players from the school band to make up the Jazz Band. Mr. Gracie always liked to give us a variety of music to play and I guess that is why music was always my favorite subject in school.

The rest of the subjects, like English and Math, they could keep but I always enjoyed going to band sessions.

I also played baseball during high school and I managed to make the team as a pitcher. In fact, when I was a senior in high school, our team won the New Mexico State Championships and I was the winning pitcher.

Seems that that was in the family as my uncle was a professional baseball player for twenty years, his name was Cal McLish. He was a great pitcher who played with The Cleveland Indians, The New York Giants, The Los Angeles Angels, The Philadelphia Phillies and most all the other major teams, as he was traded around a lot. I think he probably did his best with Cleveland because he was a "twenty-game" winner that season. He got to play with them in the World Series that year.

I would have liked to play professionally but I wasn't quite good enough. By that, I mean I really was a pretty skinny guy in those days and didn't have the power it required to play at that level. I did play some when I joined the Air Force a few years later and did okay with that.

Compliments of
VALLEY CLEANERS

SANITONE

Anthony New Mexico-Texas

PHONE WAbash 6-2521

When I got into High School, I started working at the Valley Cleaners. I actually started working there when I was ten years old but I didn't do that much then except help my Mom with the customers in front. Now I'd get home from school and work for about two and a half hours in the evening, five days a week, then all day Saturday. I'd go down with my dad to help fire the boiler up and then I'd work on the counter. I would take care of the front while my dad was in the back cleaning. When my mum would get there, I'd go in the back and start helping my Dad. I was the scrub boy which was a wet job and a shitty job. Sometimes the pants would be so dirty that I'd have to scrub them with a brush and soap before we could clean them properly.

You know, a lot of kids would just be out having fun all the time, but at least I got paid, which was more than most kids did and I considered myself lucky to have a job. I was making about twenty bucks a week. In the fifties, that was good money, but I earned every penny of it.

In those days, the most popular music to be heard locally, either live or on the radio, was Country and Western. I was listening to a lot of Country and Western because that's just about all they played in El Paso. Hank Williams and people like that were real big. Marty Robbins did that song 'El Paso' about Rose's Cantina. You know the one where the guy fell in love with a Mexican girl. It was a big hit.

Some of the newer country bands were beginning to draw influences from other fields. Hank Thompson and His Brazos Valley Boys were one of my favorite Country bands because they were more of a Country Swing band. They used saxophones and even trumpets. The band had wonderful arrangements. Another band called Bob Wills and His Texas Playboys were almost playing jazz. Country music with a jazz twist to it: swingin' violins, fiddle players, horn players and good drummers who played the shit out of the tubs. It was good music.

In 1952, on a clear night, we started receiving this station that was coming out of Acuña, Mexico, which is about 400 miles away. I'd be out cruisin' around Anthony with the guys and listening to the radio because most of my friends had cars - I didn't get my first car until 1955. There was this guy on the air called Wolfman Jack and his dog, Oscar.

His radio show was sponsored by Stan's Record Shop in Shreveport, Louisiana, and that's where I got turned onto to the Rhythm 'n' Blues because that's all he played. It was all black music, and I just thought to myself, "Fuck the Country music I had been listening to for years! THIS IS WHERE IT'S AT!"

I was about 14 or 15 when I started listening to all that stuff. It was artists like Howlin' Wolf, Muddy Waters, Jimmy Reed, Willie Dixon and Sonny Boy Williamson, all those greats and there it all was coming off of Wolfman Jack. I loved Lavern Baker, 'Jim Dandy' and 'Bop-Ting-a-Ling'. Those were great songs. Fats Domino was also starting to happen at that time.

Now I was wishing I'd have chosen the saxophone to learn. If you played sax you could play Rock 'n' Roll or Rhythm 'n' Blues, but it you played trumpet you had to either become a classical player or a jazz player - and my fondness was now with Rock 'n' Roll!

In Juarez, Mexico, at that time, there was no age limit for drinking. If you had money and you could crawl up to the bar, they would serve you as long as you could pay for the drinks. We used to go over there and for one dollar we could get completely blasted. Beer was ten cents a bottle and a shot of tequila was five cents!

When I was fourteen years old, I went over the bridge and for $2.00 I lost my cherry at the Paris de Noche whorehouse. I never really had a girlfriend in high school. With Mexico that close who needed one! There was a whole gold mine of pussy over there. They had live sex act shows, striptease joints and places where you could do some drinking. Besides, I knew I wasn't going to get any pussy off the girls in school. That was the America of the early 1950s - the sexual revolution was still ten years away!

There are a lot of stories about those places in the "Red Light District" of Juárez. I'd say there were at least 250 whorehouses. The Commodore was where Big Bertha worked. She was a big beautiful whore who cost three dollars. The Taxico Bar used to have the freak show where a woman let a donkey screw her on stage. It cost you 50 cents to see that. I saw it a few times too! So that's what we'd do on the weekends, but in the summertime we'd go sometimes three times a week, gettin' a lot of pussy. My budget was set up for it!

There was never really any trouble over in Juárez at that time. It was a pretty cool place although it's not so cool to go there now. But we would never go there on a weekend when it was payday for the military. You could get into a lot of trouble with those fuckin' soldiers. They could get pretty rowdy! Fort Bliss in El Paso is a big training facility for the US Army. They got paid once a month and they would go and spend all their money on the first weekend, then they wouldn't be over there any more until the next month. So we'd let them have Juárez on that particular weekend.

 There used to be a club there which was our hangout, called the Lobby Bar. That's where I first saw a black guitar player by the name of Long John Hunter, a legendary R&B player. Man! He taught us all how to play the Blues! Just by listening to him and watching. Long John was the best. He had a Mexican bass player and drummer. They couldn't speak English at all but Long John taught 'em the right way to play "The Blues" - they were cookin'. They played six nights a week at that place. He would start playing at about 10 o'clock, playing forty minutes on, then forty off, all night long. Sometimes he would play for hours without a break if he got into a groove and he had an audience that was jumpin'.

It was quite a big room with a long oval bar, 20 meters long. Hundreds of people would pack in there, seven nights a week, and it was still going at 8 o'clock in the morning. The walls had a dark wood finish so there was a real live sound to the room. I used to drink Singapore Slings there in the Lobby, they cost you 25 cents. You'd drink a few of those and you'd walk back across that bridge sideways. There must be a thousand stories about crossing that bridge back to the States,

Photo: John, Jimmy's brother

with people fighting and drunk. I remember my brother, cousin, and a bunch of their buddies ended up spending the night in jail there. It was around graduation time and they were rowdy and drunker than shit.

Long John Hunter is a legend in El Paso. He  introduced a lot of musicians to the Blues. The Bobby Fuller Four and all those guys used to go to watch him. Everybody in Juárez knew who he was and they loved him - he was the coolest guy in the whole area! I think he must have played at the Lobby for at least 10 years. Then he moved in to El Paso and played at the Kings X for another five years. My son Darrell was his drummer for a while!

My big sister June loved Country and Western music and thought the sun set on Willie Nelson. She especially liked Lefty Frizzell. He was a great Country singer. So, we used to go to Country and Western nightclubs together. Her husband didn't like Country and Western music that much; he was from Dallas! He loved R&B - that was his kind of music.

Around about 1955, I started going to the big shows which were being held at the El Paso Coliseum. One night I saw a Country and Western concert featuring Faron Young and Wanda Jackson. The opening act was Elvis Presley. I was seventeen and I saw chicks jumping out of their seats. I'm sure some of 'em were coming in their pants to this guy up on the stage. 'Heartbreak Hotel' was just breaking. About three months later, he was on the Ed Sullivan Show and that's really when the Elvis thing took over like a rocket. So, when I got to see the King play in '55, I thought to myself, "Hey Man! That's what I wanna do! I wanna get the girls doing that with me!" Although it didn't quite happen that way, I'm still a big Elvis fan.

In 1956, I saw the Fats Domino Revue when it came through town. That was even better than the Elvis show. Fats was something else! It was a big package tour and there were about 10 acts: Fats, Lavern Baker, Chuck Berry, Little Richard and Hank Ballard and The Midnighters. It was dynamite, Man! I think Big Mama Thornton was on that tour too. They had one band that was the back-up band for the whole show.

The Five Satins were on too, their hit was 'In the Still of the Night'. The place held about 5000 people and it was jam packed as not many artists came to El Paso, maybe once every six months.

So that's when I really decided to get into music. I was already having a change of heart and getting ready to change my image, to be an Elvis Presley kind of a guy, a Rocker!

I knew I couldn't play trumpet - that was out! You couldn't play trumpet in Rhythm and Blues so I started looking at the drums. I liked the drums, I liked what the drummers were doing and in R&B it looked like a fairly easy job, you just needed to learn how to shuffle!

I was eighteen when I graduated from Gadsden High School in 1956. That summer I went to work for my uncle in Houston. I worked on an oil field pipe yard. We stored pipes for the oil fields. My job was to load those pipes onto trucks and they'd take them out to the oil fields which were all over West Texas. I only worked there for the summer because my Mom and Dad wanted me to continue my education and go on to the university.

I'd had my own apartment for the first time and I met a girl from Jacksonville while there. I was 18 and she was only about 16 or 17. I asked her to marry me and she said she would but I soon moved back to El Paso, 600 miles away, so of course that one didn't last.

In 1956, I went to college to study geology at The University of Texas at El Paso. I wasn't really that interested in school anymore but my parents wanted me to go. Eventually I gave it up after two years. I really didn't have any aim so my heart wasn't in it.

One day, I was walking down the main street in Anthony with my friend Jim Coogan. I saw this girl crossing the street with a girl I knew and who happened to be seeing Jim at the time. I asked Jim who this other girl was and he told me her name was Loretta Moreno. She lived in La Mesa, New Mexico, which was about 10 miles north of Anthony, just up the valley. She was a senior in high school at the time, as was Jim and the other girl. I asked Jim if he could arrange a double date, they were very popular at the time.

After our first date, we started to see each other regularly on our own. By the time she graduated from school, we were in love so I asked her to marry me. It was fashionable to get married young in the late fifties! I was 20 and she was 18 years old.

We knew that there would be all kinds of shit to deal with from our parents so we did what a lot of kids were doing at that time. We went over to Juarez, Mexico and had a secret marriage! All you needed for proof was your driver's license. It cost 10 dollars and my friend Roger McWilliams was my best man.

We didn't tell anybody about it, we would just see each other of an evening and then go back to our parents' homes. She was a virgin when we got married. She was a sweet girl and I loved her. I'd known her about eight months when we got married. Obviously, it wasn't long before Loretta became pregnant and we had to tell everybody the news. Now that it was out, there was hell to pay! My dad was a fairly strict kind of guy and he did tend to have some redneck ideals although fuck knows why. After all, his wife was part Indian and his two step-kids were even more so. But he was very upset that I'd married a Mexican girl. Even though she was lighter skinned than me! So, let's just say that the shit hit the fan. He started shouting something about me not being able to use his last name anymore, and I didn't have a clue what he was talking about.

Notes to Chapter 2

[1] "chops" = skills, ability to play proficiently

Loretta and I had only been married about three months and it was very difficult to find decent work, especially if you hadn't done your military service. Back in those days it was mandatory to do military duty so I decided to join up and get it over with. I joined the United States Air Force on September 15, 1958. There was no way I wanted to be in the army and I certainly didn't fancy the navy. I'd always had an interest in airplanes and I thought I could obtain some electrical skills so that I could get a job afterwards.

Certificate of Birth

THE STATE OF TEXAS
COUNTY OF EL PASO

I, J. W. FIELDS, County Clerk of El Paso County, Texas, do hereby certify that
*** Jimmy Carl Black ***

was born on the 1st day of February 19 38 at El Paso,
El Paso County, Texas and is the son of James Inkanish and
Ima Dollah as appears from Vital Statistics Records on file in this
office same having been filed on the 3rd day of February 19 38 and recorded in
Book No. 34 Page No. 510 Birth Records of El Paso County, Texas.

Given under my hand and seal of office at El Paso, Texas, this 19th day of September 19 66.

(Name changed from James Inkanish, Jr. to Jimmy Carl Black
by the 34th District Court Order #91,207,filed
September 15, 1958). [SEAL]

J. W. FIELDS
County Clerk, El Paso County, Texas

By _____ Deputy

I was immediately off to the Enlistment Office to join up (like a fool) but first I had to get my birth certificate. When I got it, I saw that my name was James Inkanish and suddenly quite a few questions I'd had started to make sense. It all came out clean in the end, thanks to my Mom. Carl adopted me legally and I officially changed my name to Jimmy Carl Black.

My Air Force number was A.F.18562611. I had to go to Boot Camp for 12 weeks. I was sent to Chanute Air Force Base to attend Tech School in Electronics for B-47 Bombers.

Loretta joined me when I had finished about half of my training and we lived off the base in the little town of Rantoul, Illinois. It turned out that our marriage certificate wasn't valid in the United States because we had gotten married in Mexico, so Loretta and I had to go and get married again in Champaign, Illinois. After I graduated from Tech School, I had to go off to another place called Whiteman Air Force Base in Missouri on a three-month course in Autopilot and Compass Systems, so Loretta went back to El Paso.

THE HUB There were a couple of guys in the Squadron who really liked R&B music and of course I did too. On the weekends, we used to go to a lot of the black bars in Kansas City. It was fairly cool back in those days and there wasn't much trouble. That's where I saw Wilbert Harrison perform the song 'Kansas City' in a little bar called The Hub. It was a great experience for me to see this guy sing that song. It has become a standard for most musicians and I sure have played it a few times in my career.

While I was away in Missouri, our first son Gary was born in William Beaumont Military Hospital at Fort Bliss, El Paso on April 8, 1959. By this time, my dad had made a complete about face and when Gary was born he was over the moon. The old man really loved that boy!

When Gary was born he had what they call a "hammer" thumb which always upset my dad, so he secretly saved up some money and when he had enough, paid to have it fixed by surgery since the Air Force would not pay for the operation.

About this time, I went home on leave and went down to a place called the Green Frog in El Paso and that's where I first met Big Sonny Farlow and

his brother Rich. They were still in high school but they were already playing serious R&B music around the town. I never dreamt that I'd be playing with them 16 years later.

We moved to McConnell Air Force Base in Wichita, Kansas, and that became my permanent duty station. We were to stay there for around three years.

They trained me pretty good in the Air Force. I was in the Armament and Electronics Squadron and I was an Auto Pilot and Compass System Specialist. I would eventually, in early '61, make E4 rank, or 'Buck' Sergeant, three stripes on the sleeve of my uniform and more responsibility in my job.

There were a lot of guys in the Air Force who were musicians. I had this one friend in particular whose name was Gary Willis, he played rhythm guitar and sang. He had a brother named Ray (Willis) who wasn't in the AF, but was a lead guitar player. They said, "If you buy a set of drums, we can do Country and Western music and start playing gigs!" So I bought my first set of drums for $200 in 1959.

The drums were a real nice set of Slingerland Drums with a 26-inch[1] bass drum, a bolt-on 12-inch side tom, a 16-inch floor tom, and a snare drum with cases and cymbals and everything.

It was actually a lot of money for that set of drums as my wages were shit in the Air Force. I was making only about $100 a month although I got housing allowances and things like that. I was also working part time at a gas station for a friend of mine named Johnny Gilbert who had always given extra work to G.I.s.

Anyway, the extra money I was making at the gas station allowed me to buy the drums as, in my thinking, it would be a great investment in the future.

Them Three Guys

So we started our first band towards the end of 1959. We called ourselves Them Three Guys. On the first gig, I didn't even know how to set those drums up. We had never rehearsed, Man! I actually didn't even know how to play the drums. We use to play at Angels 37 Club. It was a dive, Man! I mean, A REAL DIVE. Angel was this big, fat lady and she fancied herself as some sort of entertainer. She used to pantomime songs. She'd pantomime racy stuff like 'Hot Nuts' and songs by Redd Foxx who was famous for making party records. I didn't sing at this point and we were doing a lot of Rockabilly stuff - songs that Elvis Presley and Gene Vincent were doing. Great songs like 'Blue Suede Shoes', 'When My Blue Moon Turns To Gold' and 'Be-Bop-A-Lula.' The band lasted for about six months.

I had this other friend in the Air Force who was a drummer and he was teaching me a little bit about how to really play my drums. By that time, I was starting to learn more and more about the drums. At least I knew how to set 'em up! This guy used to play Country and Western music at a place called Elmo's Spur Club in Wichita. The owner of the club was Elmore Barnett and he had a little house band called Elmo B and The Other Three, which was a Country Swing band. I used to go out there and sit in every once in a while for my friend when he couldn't make the gig.

 After I'd started to learn to play quite a bit better, I got rid of the Slingerlands and bought my Gretsch Drums. That kit cost me $450, including cymbals, cases and everything and came right off the showroom floor. They were a grey pearl color, and they were beautiful. I'll never forget the smell of them. I really liked that kit and we still have them in the family or at least my son Darrell does.

Our second son, Darrell, was born on August 23, 1960, while we were in Wichita. Darrell was such a different baby to Gary who had hardly ever cried. Darrell, on the other hand, cried all the time. That boy had a set of lungs on him and still does. I had a lot of fun with the boys, although I was still pretty young myself and didn't really know much about being a father - but when put in that position, you learn pretty quick!

[Photo: Darrell; Sept 1964]

I started playing with a guy named Tom Beard in a band called The Debonaires and we played under that name for about six months and then decided to change the name to The Keys.

The Keys We played mainly the R&B stuff of that time. I was starting to sing a little bit then, doing Jimmy Reed stuff like 'Big Boss Man', 'Baby What You Want Me To Do' and 'Bright Lights/Big City'. We played a gig every weekend in Wichita. The guys in the band were Johnny Holt on guitar, Larry Hurst on bass, Tom Beard on piano and me on drums.

That's the band that I cut my first single with in 1962, 'Stretch Pants'  b/w 'A Matter of Time' on Ultimate Records. The songs were written and composed by Larry Hurst, lead singer and bass player.

Tom knew this guy who had a recording studio. It was a little two-track studio because that was all there was in those days. We all sang background vocals on the songs and of course, it was recorded live with no overdubbing or anything. We financed it ourselves and it didn't cost more than about $200 to do the whole thing, including pressing 500 records. We sold them right away so we pressed another 500. Man! That little baby was selling like hotcakes! There are 1000 of those things floating around and I didn't even have a copy until a fan sent one to me.

At this time, I got a chance to play with some quite good musicians. One of them was a guy named Jerry Hahn, a guitar player who went on to play with The Gary Burton Quartet before he formed his own band, The Brotherhood. Mike Finnigan was the keyboard player, although when I first met him he had a band called The Surfs. He was only sixteen years old at the time and he really could boogie on the Hammond organ.

He went on to play with lots of people. Probably the most famous one being Jimi Hendrix on a song called 'Crosstown Traffic'. He also played with Crosby, Stills, Nash and Young for a few years, a wonderful player.

I met a band called The Exceptions who were playing in a big club in Wichita called the Star Club. I think they played for at least a month as all bands they hired did.

The bass player, Pete Cetera, later went on to play with Chicago Transit Authority and as he was already a good friend of mine, used to come to visit me in Woodland Hills[2] when I was in The Mothers of Invention.

The organ player, whose name I can't remember, later played with a band called The Rivingtons and the guitar player, a guy called Cal Davis, later played with The Illinois Speed Press. They all went on to do bigger and better things because they were great musicians.

I got out of the Air Force on September 14, 1962 and we moved back to Anthony Texas. We were living right next door to my Mom and Dad in a little rented apartment that belonged to them.

I started school again at the University of Texas at El Paso and went to work at Joe Bob's Texaco gas station.

JOE BOB BROWN
Service With A Smile
WE SERVICE ANY MAKE OF CAR
Anthony, New Mexico-Texas

Loretta started working for her dad at his food store up in La Mesa. While we were there, we found that Loretta was pregnant again!

I didn't enjoy school at all and I certainly didn't like pumping gas so, after the first semester, I persuaded Loretta to move back to Wichita. I got a job at the Kansas Gas Company working in their electrical department as a truck driver on a Line Crew. We laid the 128,000-volt electric cables that served the whole Wichita area.

I worked there for two years[3] while I was also playing in a band.

I got in a band called The Squires.

The Squires were a very showy R&B band for three white boys and an Indian. We did Ray Charles songs like 'Sticks and Stones' and 'What'd I Say'. Then we started playing a few Beatles songs. About a year before they came to the States (in Feb. '64), somebody turned us on to some Beatles records from England. We all liked them a whole bunch as they sounded really good. They used some chord patterns that were real different to what we were used to hearing in the States. We played 'Please Please Me' and some of the covers they were doing like 'Matchbox' (Carl Perkins) and 'Slow Down' (Larry Williams), the early recordings. We saw pictures of them and we started buying those suits with the little collars, and Beatle boots. Unlike my first band, we had some band uniforms. We wore tuxedo jackets and those Beatle suits.

I was with the Squires for about a year and a half. The guitarist was called Richie Hepner, who went on to play for a brief time with the early Magic Band in Lancaster, California and was a real nice guy besides being a great player.

When he left, a guy called Tom Green started playing with us. They called Tom "Rock" because he was a big, tall, redheaded, freckle-faced fucker that looked like he was whipped with an ugly stick, as the saying goes. You know, the Squires fired me because they thought I was too ugly!

By this time we had three kids. Our first daughter, Kim, was born on October 2, 1963 in Wichita and to me she was so beautiful and so different from the boys.

I had bought a brand new car while I was in Kansas. It was a 1964 Chevelle Super Sport made by Chevrolet.[4] I was so proud of that thing! I drove that car to all the gigs the Squires had until I got replaced.

That's when we decided to move to California.

[Photo: Kim, Gary, Sept 1964]

My father-in-law was telling me that I would be able to get a job out there. After all, California was "The American Dream" and everybody went there if they wanted to find work. He wasn't talking about me playing music. He was talking about me getting a real job, but by this time the only thing I wanted to do was play music. I couldn't give a shit about my qualifications. I wanted to concentrate on music and see if I could go on to bigger and better things. I actually wanted to become a Rock 'n' Roll star.

So we decided to try it out and made the move. Richie Hepner, the guitarist from the Squires, decided to move out there with me to see if we could get something going. He became disenchanted very quickly and after about 10 days, he decided to split and go back east. He had to pawn his wristwatch to get the money together and it only took him as far as Lancaster, California. That's where he met Capt. Beefheart and The Magic Band. He didn't play with them very long even though they were playing a sort of blues at the time. I suspect that Beefheart was too much for him!

Notes to Chapter 3

[1] An inch is about 2.54 cm
[2] The family Black lived there from around late April 1968 to late 1969
[3] This would take us to the end of 1964 when JCB was already in CA. The Feb 2003 draft of this text reads "a year", the Sept. 2004 has been amended to "Two year" (sic). Somewhat more than 18 months is probably correct.
[4] The Chevelle model was introduced in Sept. 1963.

Part Two:

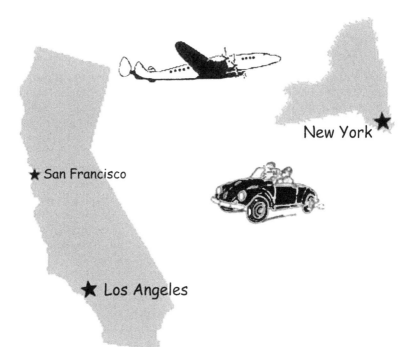

New York

★ San Francisco

★ Los Angeles

A Mother's Tale

I'd been there a couple of weeks when I went down to the West Coast Drum Shop in Santa Ana. I was getting ready to put a piece of paper up on the wall saying I was available as a drummer[1] when this great, big Mexican walked in. His name was Roy Estrada. He told me he was starting a band called the Soul Giants and that they were looking for a drummer. He said to come right now and audition, as he was going to rehearsal anyway. So I went by the house and got my drums and went to the rehearsal and they hired me. Roy and I hit it off right from the beginning.

Jim Fielder
Soon after I joined the band, I found a job teaching drums to young kids in a music store called the Woodwind Shop in Anaheim, the next town along from Santa Ana. It was right across the street from Disneyland.

The bass guitar teacher there was a guy named Jim Fielder. He was 17 years old and he was still at High School. I was considerably older than him but we became real good friends.

Tim Buckley
Every day, this little 16 or 17-year-old kid used to come in and he'd start fiddling with all the guitars. He used to bug me, Man! I'd say, "Are you gonna buy one of those guitars or are you just gonna come in and play 'em. Is that the deal?" I was kind of shitty to him at the beginning. I eventually got to know him because he was a friend of Jim Fielder. Actually, he was a nice kid and he was a pretty good little player. His name was Tim Buckley. I didn't realize it then but I'd see a lot of him in the years to come! After I found out he was Jim's friend, I started to listen to his music and liked it a lot. He really was a one of a kind songwriter and player. His band did a lot of gigs with the Mothers. When the Mothers started playing at The Trip[2] in Hollywood, he and Jim came to see us play one time and I introduced him to our manager, Herb Cohen.[3] Herb signed him after hearing some of his original material and stayed his manager until Tim's untimely death in 1975.

One day, I drove back to my father-in-law's house from the music store to get some lunch. When I came back out, my lovely new car had disappeared. I called the police and they informed me that it had been repossessed. I hadn't made the last month's payment. That was the end of that since I wasn't making enough money to catch up on the payments and besides, I wasn't suppose to take the car out of Kansas! I went and bought a 1959 Oldsmobile 98 through a finance company. It was like a boat, a real cruiser!

Roy and I always went together in my car to the gigs. He was to become my travel buddy for the next few years. Roy liked to do "Speed"[4] and I did too![5] I had been taking Speed a little bit back in Kansas when I was with the Squires. They had also been smoking "Pot"[6] but I wasn't into that then! I was into Speed and the Juice.[7] I used to like to tilt a few beers and drop a few pills, take a trip to the moon! But The Broadside was when I started smoking Pot.

The Soul Giants
The Soul Giants original line-up was I myself on drums, Roy Estrada on bass, Davy Coronado on sax, a guy called Larry on guitar and the singer was called Dave. Davy Coronado was an excellent sax player. He could play all that 'honky-tonk' stuff. In fact, he used to do that song called 'Honky Tonk' a lot.

So, we were rehearsing a little bit and playing around different places in Orange County. It was the first band that I'd been in that actually wanted to do a little rehearsing. 1964 was just mainly a period of trying to get work and getting tight as a band just by playing all the time. Then we got this job as the house band at The Broadside club in Pomona.[8] We played six nights a week, for about three[9] months. We were making $90 each a week for the six nights, which wasn't that bad. We were playing a lot of the same stuff that I'd been playing back in Kansas, like 'Woolly Bully' and 'She's about a Mover'. We were also starting to do a lot more English stuff, some Rolling Stones' songs, some Gerry and the Pacemakers'.

Ray Collins
The band was only going a few months when Larry[10] the guitar player got drafted into the Army. We found a guy named Ray Hunt[11] to replace him. Our singer Dave also got drafted so we needed to find a new front man.

A guy called Ray Collins[12] had been coming to The Broadside all the time; he liked the band and what we were doing. He would sometimes get up and do a few numbers and I thought Ray could sing Rhythm 'n' Blues better than anyone I'd ever heard. Skip, the owner of the club, said we could be the house band if we would hire Ray as a permanent member and front man. That was just fine with the rest of us since he sang much better than Dave.

The only problem was Ray Collins really didn't like Ray Hunt worth a shit. Before long, the two Rays got into an argument or rather a fistfight[13]. Ray Collins didn't like the way Ray Hunt played. He was shouting, "You ought to learn how to play R&B instead of all that Surf music!" So that left us without a guitar player and you can't have an R&B band without a guitar player!

So we asked Ray if he knew any other guitar players and he said, "Yeah, I know this guy who's just got out of jail." We said, "What was he in jail for?" and he told us, "Oh, he made some pornographic audio tapes and sold them to the vice squad but it was all a set-up." We had nothing to lose so we said, "Let's get him down for an audition, what's his name?" Ray said, "Frank Zappa."[14]

Ray told us that Frank was running a little recording studio called Studio Z[15] out in Cucamonga. They had recorded some stuff there together and some of it had even been released on a few small labels. Frank arrived at the audition in a car driven by a guy called Motorhead.[16] We liked the way Frank played. He was a strong rhythm player[17] although he wasn't a very good lead player back in those days. Little did we know what was going to happen!

Frank joined the band in April. We were playing a lot of gigs at The Broadside and Frank was very grateful to have a job that was paying $90 a week. We went over to his house a couple of times in G Street, Ontario. He was just getting ready to move out; he was getting divorced. When I met his wife Kay I thought, "God, Man! Why are you moving out of the house? She's a Babe!" I thought she was a good-looking lady but there were about nine cats in the house too! Roy's father always said to us, "Don't trust anyone that has that many cats!" So Frank moved into Studio Z. There was a woman called "Pete" (Lorraine Belcher) living there[18] and another white girl who had a little black baby.

I think Frank recorded us live one time at The Broadside. I remember that he brought the tape recorder down from Studio Z and recorded the whole night. Motorhead was running the tape. Motorhead was hanging out with us all the time, so I've known him for as long as I've known Frank.

 The first time I met Don Van Vliet (Captain Beefheart) was at The Broadside. He and Vic Mortenson walked in after they'd played a gig someplace. I didn't know anything about him at that time, just that he was a blues singer. I thought Don was a pretty nice guy and I got on with him real well. He liked the fact that I was an Indian - he had a fascination for Indians. His band was called Captain Beefheart and The Magic Band. Vic was the drummer and they had a new guitar player, Richie Hepner, the very same guy who'd left to go back east a few months ago! Richie was a great blues player, so it made sense that he was playing in an R&B band. I met Beefheart a few times after that, but I didn't see him perform until the *Trout Mask Replica* band played with us.

Davy Coronado Quits

When Frank suggested that we start to play some original material and try to get a record contract, Davy Coronado said, "No, that's the end of it for me. We'll never play in The Broadside again if we play original music." Davy was very attached to The Broadside, he liked it there, but he quit the band and moved back to Texas. So The Broadside club stopped when Davy left the band because he was thick with the management. They said, "You can keep the job but you have to get a sax player and it better be one like Davy Coronado!" Now we were without a horn player and a job. So Frank had to play all the lead lines and we were just a little concerned about that, but he filled the gap brilliantly.

By this time, Frank wasn't even thinking about that R&B stuff anymore, he wanted to do his original stuff. That was his dream and he'd finally found three other guys that were willing to go with him. You know, I liked the stuff that he was writing, it felt - good. Frank said, "Well guys, we've got to start rehearsing all the time, we've gotta really get this stuff together."

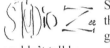 So we started to rehearse at Studio Z. I thought it was the strangest fuckin' place, Man, pretty small and grubby! Everything was painted black in there so you couldn't tell how grubby it really was. It had all these props and shit in there for making a movie. (We found out later he'd been working on something called *Captain Beefheart Versus the Grunt People*.) But he had a nice little tape recorder and I think that he recorded some of the stuff that we were doing.

The first of Frank's original songs that we learnt was 'Anyway The Wind Blows'. Then we started to do things like 'I'm Not Satisfied' and 'How Could I Be Such A Fool'. I really liked 'I'm Not Satisfied' because I could play a "Ringo"[19] beat to it.

Roy and I would get home at about four in the morning and we would have to leave again at ten in the morning to be back at the studio in Cucamonga at noon - it was probably about 40 miles from where we lived. We would rehearse about six or seven hours until we had to go play the gig. It was paying off because the band was really getting tight by that point.

We only got to rehearse in the studio for about three weeks before Frank got evicted. They were going to widen the street - Archibald Avenue. This was probably about the end of May. Frank moved to Echo Park near Hollywood to be nearer to the "scene". The "freak" scene was just getting into swing about that time and Frank wanted the band involved. His new place was a little hole in the wall, it really was. I know that that's where he wrote a lot of the songs that are on *Freak Out!*

My Father-in-law's Garage
So then we had to find someplace new to rehearse. For a while we rehearsed at my father-in-law's garage in Santa Ana. He wasn't there when we rehearsed. If he would've been there, he wouldn't have liked it, Man!

We didn't have a PA system, so Ray's dad made us a PA system - he built this really wild looking cabinet. I think we had two microphones, one for Frank and one for Ray. So that was our PA, that's what we used to take around with us every place we'd play, that big fuckin' box! We didn't really have band transport; we just used our cars. We used to go around to clubs all over the L.A. area and audition for gigs.

I remember Roy bought a brand-new 1965 Buick Riviera at the time the band was absolutely starving. I don't know how he did it - a brand-new Riviera, not just any brand-new car. He kept telling me, "Don't tell Frank that I've bought this car, Man! He'll think I have money. Tell him that my Mom and Dad bought it for me."

So Roy had the new Riviera, I had the '59 Oldsmobile. Frank had a '63 Chevy station wagon. How in the fuck he ever got his driving license I'll never know, Man! Frank was the worst driver that there ever was! At that time, we were still playing all the little gigs and we used his station wagon to haul the band's stuff around because we could get it all in. But, we wouldn't let Frank drive it. Roy or I would drive, or maybe Ray, but I wouldn't ride with Frank, he was too dangerous. It was funny to see that car because the hubcaps on it were practically welded to where the tire fits on. To stop the car, Frank would just ram it into the kerb. It was the strangest thing I ever saw, Man! His car was bright orange. Frank was having to come out to Santa Ana to rehearse in my garage and you could see that thing coming for miles.

The Mothers
By now Frank had a good idea about how he wanted the band to go. He was coming up with suggestions and we would go along with him, most of the time. We didn't really know what he was up to all the time. We lived 40 miles away so we just saw him at the gigs and rehearsals. We thought he was kind of weird, but I didn't really care what he was up to outside of the band because I had my own problems, family and all that shit.

You know, I'm from a fairly straight family. I'd always been fairly straight. I'd only just started smoking Pot with Roy and Ray - they'd both turned me on. Frank didn't do any of that shit. We thought, "Boy, this guy doesn't need any anyway." In fact, it turned out that Frank was very against using any stimulants at all.[20]

What was worse, he seemed to take a total dislike to anyone who did, something that was always going to cause problems in the future!

We changed the name of the band a few times. Right after being called the Soul Giants we were called The Batmen[21] for a while. We played one gig as Captain Glasspack and his Magic Mufflers.[22] We were auditioning all over the place just trying to work. In May, we changed our name to The Mothers. Actually, it was spelt Muthers in the beginning!

Our Band Uniform

We went and bought a band uniform. Can you imagine? The Mothers used to play in band uniforms! We had purple shirts and black pants and we each wore one of those Homburg hats. Frank was the one who wanted the hats. Then we got some lime green shirts so that we could switch, so we didn't have to wear the same stuff every night. Those lime green shirts were horrible. We used to call them our baby-shit green shirts. We bought them at Mr. P's in Hollywood - the uniforms had to come from Hollywood!

We got Loretta's brother Philip to paint "Mothers" on my bass drum skin. He was still at high school, but was becoming very interested in art. I had that skin on my drums for the whole of the time I was with the band, right up until we split.

Playing the Go-Go Joints

We managed to get a gig at the Tom Cat à Go-Go in Torrance for a month.[23] It was a real go-go joint. We had to play 'Woolly Bully' and 'Louie Louie' about ten times a night. We had to play what the girls wanted us to play. It was their show so they chose the numbers. We did five 45-minute sets a night, six nights a week. We were making $90 a week and believe me we fucking earned it.

All the time, we would try to put a few of the original songs in. We could play 'Anyway The Wind Blows' and 'I'm Not Satisfied', the girls liked those songs. Every once in a while, we would do 'Memories Of El Monte' and the reason that we got away with doing that was because everybody thought it was such a joke. It was a good song actually. I always liked it, with all the parodies in it - of The Penguins and Little Julian Herrera and The Tigers - and Ray sang those songs so nice, Man! He used to be a member of Little Julian Herrera and The Tigers before joining the Muthers.

We played around a few other go-go joints. I remember The Red Flame in Pomona, The Shack in Fontana and the Brave New World, which wasn't a go-go club and was the first gig we did in Hollywood. Frank had met some people in the Hollywood scene and had gotten us the gig. We played a few other little gigs and occasional one-nighters.

Jina
Around this time, our second daughter Jina was born on August 15, 1965, at the Orange County hospital in California. She was a lovely baby.

Alice Stuart
There was a girl guitar player called Alice Stuart on the scene.[24] I think she and Frank had a little thing going. She was a good player, but very much a folkie-type player. However, she became quite a blues player. I think Alice only played at the Brave New World and a couple of those little one-off gigs. It was a nice idea and she was a nice woman, but I didn't think that she fitted in that well and ultimately, I don't think Frank did either.

Henry Vestine
We met a blues guitarist called Henry Vestine. Henry's band had also being playing out at The Broadside, a trio. I think Larry Taylor had been playing bass with him. They'd done very well there. I don't know how we talked Henry into joining, but we did.[25] So now we had two guitar players, Henry was playing all the lead stuff. Frank played lead on very few things - he concentrated on the rhythm stuff.

We got The Broadside back because we hired Henry. We were only allowed to play cover versions but we would always try to sneak an original song in. Every time we'd sneak one in they'd say "What IS that, never heard that song before!" We would say, "It's an original song." and they would say, "Oh no, not in our club, we don't want any of that shit, no original music, what do you think you are, recording stars or something?"

Yardbirds in LA
The first time the Yardbirds came to Los Angeles, Jeff Beck was in the band. They didn't have work permits so they couldn't play their show at the Whisky a Go Go. So Kim Fowley opened his father's house up and had a big party for about 300 people, and the Yardbirds played there. After we had finished playing, we all went up to there to hear them play.[26]

We were all very interested because Jeff was doing all this feedback stuff with his Vox amplifier and guitar. Frank was very interested to see what he was doing and so was Henry Vestine. It was a great experience to see Jeff play.

Mark Cheka

We were introduced to Mark Cheka around the Fall of '65.[27] Mark was a Pop artist aged about 50. He was a real cool guy, he was involved in the new freak scene that was happening and he's the one who introduced us to the guys at the *L.A. Free Press*. Around the Fall of '65 was the time the *L.A. Free Press* was beginning to happen in Los Angeles. Now it's a major newspaper but at the time it was strictly underground. They liked us, they were quite heavily into the Mothers and they liked Frank's attitude about politics and all that stuff. Mark could see that there was something there too and I think Frank realized that Mark would be a good contact. So all of a sudden we were going to have a manager. Things started popping with that guy - well at least a little bit. Although he didn't know shit about managing a band, he liked our music. I liked Mark - I thought he was a nice guy. He didn't really get us any work, we were still playing around those go-go joints but he introduced us to Herb Cohen who did.[28]

Herb Cohen & The Action

When Herb Cohen came into the picture, he immediately became co-manager. He got us an audition at The Action club on Melrose Ave. in Hollywood. Finally, we had hit the big time!

At that audition, we played Herb some original songs and then we played the cover stuff for the club owners. They liked us and they hired us and we thought, "Man! We're in the big time now!" We still weren't up on the "Strip" yet - we were only on Santa Monica Boulevard - but we were closer. We got a month long gig there, six nights a week. The money didn't change. In fact, it might have even been less because we had to pay Herb 15% right off the top of anything we earned. Herb was involved with a couple of clubs. I think he'd owned the Café Unicorn and he managed a few bands, mainly folk acts. He had The Stone Poneys with Linda Ronstadt and The Modern Folk Quintet. He also had something to do with Lenny Bruce. I would imagine it was through Herb's affiliation with his uncle (Mickey Cohen) and the local club mafia that we got that audition![29]

The Action club was really the first place we could play some of our stuff. They didn't seem to care; it was OK. By this time, we'd learnt a bunch of other stuff like 'Go Cry On Somebody Else's Shoulder' but we were still playing mostly R&B and not many original songs.

Mark had got us a slot in the film *Mondo Hollywood* which was being produced by a guy called Robert Cohen, no relation to Herb. (Henry was in the band at the time and we had just acquired Herb Cohen.[30] We were playing at The Action at the time.[31])

That was our first encounter with real freaks, the first time that I ever really saw what the freak scene was all about in Hollywood although Frank already knew most of the freaks by then. So they filmed us playing at this party. It was in a house on Franklin Street, one of those big old Hollywood houses near Hollywood and Vine. I've never seen the movie so I don't know whether they used that footage or not. I've heard rumors that Herb had wanted too much money so they decided to cut it out,[32] but I really don't know what happened! Of course, the first "Mondo" movie was *Mondo Cain*, a strange movie.

It was totally wild at that party, like Halloween. They had a big light show and people were dropping "Acid"[33] like it was going out of style. Everybody in the place seemed to be on Acid except the band. This happened in 1965, before we even recorded *Freak Out!* and I didn't really know what Acid was at that time. We'd heard about it from some of our friends, like Ray, and some guy had tried to talk us into taking it, but mine and Roy's first Acid "Trip" was to come about six months later when we went to Hawaii.

That was the first time I met Carl[34] Franzoni, Vito Pauluka and all those people. Vito and Carl were the leaders of this movement although they were quite a bit older than the others. They were ex-beatniks, poets and artists. I had been a fairly straight guy and so had Roy and we just couldn't believe some of these people. Man! The outfits they were wearing were wild! We were wearing our black Homburg hats and we still had our band uniforms on, the green shirts that everybody had to wear. So it was kind of strange, like it was a fancy dress party and not "real"!

So right after that party we stopped wearing our uniforms. Frank told us they would have to go but sometimes we'd wear the hats. Frank punched his up from the inside and wore it like that for a while, and then the rest of us did so too. That's when we started wearing "freaky" stuff.[35] Frank told us to go to the Salvation Army Used Clothing Store and start buying the freakiest clothes we could find. I couldn't wear that stuff around the house in Santa Ana, so I had to change when I got into Hollywood. It was a dual life I was leading, like James Bond or Superman.

Politics & the Undeclared War

In 1965, the political climate was starting to change all of a sudden, not only with the freaks but a lot of other people too! Everybody was starting to wonder about the war that the US was involved in over in Vietnam. It wasn't a war - they couldn't call it a war because Congress had never declared war!

But all of a sudden there were thousands of troops in Vietnam. If you were between 18 and 26, you could count on going into the military unless you had a serious ailment, and if you went in to the military, you could pretty much count on going to Vietnam.

So there were a lot of young people at that time thinking about leaving the States and moving to Canada and places where they weren't in this war.

At the time, Frank wasn't really writing protest songs, he was writing songs about the "Great Society". So Frank was writing songs like 'Hungry Freaks, Daddy' and 'Who Needs The Peace Corps', songs that reflected what was happening socially. In fact, we used to do 'Who Needs The Peace Corps' instrumentally before Frank put the lyrics to it.

But most of the freaks were just out having a good time and enjoying all this free sex that was going on, and there was a lot of it! I think I screwed all the girls in Vito's crowd at least one time or another. The only one I wouldn't screw was his wife. She kept hitting on me, but I liked Vito and I thought he'd get real pissed off at me. I found out later that he actually wanted me to screw her and boy, she was a beauty too, much younger than him!

Frank & John Wayne

I remember one of the nights at The Action when Frank was sitting outside on the steps of the club and a whole bunch of people walked in.[36] One of the people was John Wayne and he said something to Frank about the way he looked. Before we started to play, Frank told the people in the audience that we had a special guest that night. He said that John Wayne was running for the U.S. Senate and would John get up and make an acceptance speech. Everybody in the place started cheering. Now, I must tell you that John Wayne was drunk as a skunk that night and he did try to get up and make that speech. His bodyguards threatened Frank with bodily harm if he didn't shut up quick. They got John out of there pretty quick and everyone there got a very good laugh.

While we were at the Action, they would let us rehearse there of a daytime between about 3 and 7 pm and then we would have to stop. We'd go to Pink's and get a hot dog or something that was cheap, for a quarter or something like that. By this time, Frank was slowly but surely starting to get himself more involved in the freak scene in Hollywood.

Vito's Studio

Then Vito let us use his dance studio (or dungeon of sin!) in Hollywood to rehearse in. It was a studio/gallery/workshop down in the basement of the place he shared with Carl Franzoni. Getting that place to rehearse made it a lot easier for everybody except me and Roy, as we still had to come from Santa Ana.

One night, coming home from a gig, some drunk driver hit the back of my car and fucked up the trunk pretty bad. We couldn't get the thing open so the next day we drove to Vito's place. He came out with a hatchet and chopped a big hole around the lock so we could get my drums out; luckily they weren't damaged. I drove the car around like that for another year, until it completely blew up. I left it at the side of the road someplace in Hollywood. That was the final resting place of the '59 Olds - that was a classic car.

Whisky A Go Go Every once in a while, we would get to go up and play at the Whisky a Go Go when Johnny Rivers wasn't playing. Johnny was resident there for years until he had a hit with his song 'Secret Agent Man'. So we started playing the occasional night there and we were starting to get a following around Hollywood. People were starting to like what we were doing even though I still didn't understand what Frank was up to, and wouldn't until I heard *Freak Out!* "full on" on LSD eight or nine months later.

By now, we were playing 'Motherly Love', 'You're Probably Wondering Why I'm Here' and 'I Ain't Got No Heart'.

'How Could I Be Such A Fool' was the first thing that we ever played in waltz time. Frank called it "Motown 6/8". It also later became the backbeat to 'Help, I'm A Rock'.

We were starting to do 'Trouble Comin' Every Day' about the summer of '65. Frank wrote that when the Watts riots started to happen.[37] I wish there was a recording of 'Trouble' the way we used to do it when we had Henry Vestine with us. It sounded like a John Lee Hooker song. Man! It was so bluesy! Frank was singing on it and Ray was playing harmonica. Ray didn't want to learn all those words. It was way too many words for him to learn! Since Frank wrote the words, he already knew them and so that was the first song Frank really featured as a vocalist. Mostly he only sang background, he never considered himself as a lead singer. Personally, I think he was a great lead singer.

I was still doing a few Jimmy Reed songs at the Whisky a Go Go. I would get out in the front and sing and Frank would go back and play the drums. It looked good on the stage. Frank liked the way it looked - he thought it was good for the audience to see multi-talented people changing instruments on stage and I agreed.

Finally, Johnny Rivers decided to go out on the road so they gave the job to us. We got the job because the club was owned by Elmer Valentine. He was the head of the Los Angeles mafia and Herb's uncle was Mickey Cohen, head of the West Coast Jewish mafia.[38] So we were a kind of mafia band and later on, it paid off. We had that job for 22 weeks, playing six nights a week.[39]

We thought we'd hit the big time and actually, we sort of had. The money wasn't any better - that never really changed much - but the status of the band changed.

That's when Tom Wilson came in to the Whisky and heard us. Tom was a well-respected producer who had worked with many great jazz artists and with Bob Dylan. He produced all of Dylan's early Folk stuff for Columbia Records. Tom had just moved over to MGM Verve. The story goes that Herb got him to come over to see us. He only heard the one song which was 'Trouble Comin' Every Day' and decided to sign us. He thought he was signing a blues band! We found out that he had also just signed a New York band called The Velvet Underground.

We'd get done playing at about two and the first stop would be Canter's on Fairfax Avenue or Ben Frank's up on Sunset Strip, those were the two main freak hangouts then. We would spend a couple of hours there 'til at least four. It would be packed with all the freaks. Lenny Bruce would be there, Phil Spector would be there, all those pretty little freak girls and, of course, Vito and Carl. The Byrds would be out down there too, they were big around L.A. We never played a gig with them but I knew all those guys.

We'd sit around and drink coffee, talk about what was going on in the world, maybe try to talk some girl into stepping outside to the car for a quick "wham-bam-thank-you-ma'am" before I had to head back home to the wife.

The sexual revolution was really happening and those freaky little girls all liked the Mothers and they all liked to fuck, just about any time you wanted to and just about as many girls in one night as you could handle. I've had up to four different girls in one night, just going from one room to the next. Man! If you could keep a hard on, you could keep that thing wet! At this time, I used to think that I should never have been married. Man! There was so much going on!

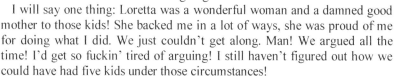

I will say one thing: Loretta was a wonderful woman and a damned good mother to those kids! She backed me in a lot of ways, she was proud of me for doing what I did. We just couldn't get along. Man! We argued all the time! I'd get so fuckin' tired of arguing! I still haven't figured out how we could have had five kids under those circumstances!

Roy and I used to get home at about 6 o'clock in the morning. That silly talking started between me and Roy during all that driving - he was "speeding" all the time and so was I!

First Demo Recording

Herb was always out trying to get a record deal for us. We started auditioning around and doing demo tapes for RCA, A&M Records and Capital Records - MGM was interested in us. I remember we did one recording, a demo recording for a producer called Billy James at Columbia Records. He liked what we were into - he was a bit of a freaky kind of a guy anyway. It was in the fall of 1965. It was only about a 4-hour session. We did two songs. I think we did 'Anyway The Wind Blows' and 'How Could I Be Such A Fool' but we might have done 'The Grunion Run', as we used to do that a lot, it was one of our instrumental numbers.

Compulsive Listening Sessions

This is about the time that Frank started listening to Ravi Shankar and Raga music. He made the whole band listen to it. We asked why and he said, "Because we're going to start doing some stuff like this!" And of course we did, not exactly like Raga but it was influenced by it, the type of time changes. That's when all that "stuff" started! Over the next years, Frank would often gather us together for "compulsive listening" sessions - anything that he thought we needed to know and understand in order to perform certain pieces. He used to play us Stravinsky, notably *The Rite of Spring* and *The Firebird Suite* which I really loved. We also listened to John Cage and Aaron Copeland, as well as some of the free jazz stuff like Archie Shepp and John Coltrane.

Music Lessons

I was having to play some beats that I'd never played before, like the Motown 6/8, although every once in a while I had played a little 5/8. They were strange rhythms to me, being an R&B player but Frank was real good about it. He'd come back on the drums and show me how to do it. Frank was never a really great drummer, but he knew how to play those weird times. It was interesting and he always took the time to show me what he wanted me to do. He had a different way of teaching me how to play his songs. He would block out the whole song, say 16 bars of 4/4 time, 3 bars of 3/4 time, 2 bars of 2/4 time, that's the way he blocked them out for me. It was interesting to see it laid out like that.

He had to teach all the guys in the band in the beginning, because nobody could read music (though I could still read music a little bit from my trumpet days). He used to teach Roy the bass line section by section. We did have good memories so we learned pretty quick, and we'd always talk about what we were doing.

By now, Frank had started to write all the parts out. He was ready for it but he just didn't have anybody in the band who could read it, not really.

Frank was at his happiest when Donny, Bunk, Art and Ian arrived, guys who could really read music.

San Francisco

In November, we went up to San Francisco for the first time and played at the Longshoreman's Hall for the Family Dog.[40] It was a co-production between Chet Helms and Bill Graham. We played with the Charlatans - Dan Hicks was the drummer with them at the time. I think it was the last gig ever to be played there. One of the songs we were playing was 'Rumble', the old Link Wray song. While we were playing it, we could see Herb at the side of the stage in some sort of fight with the promoters - probably about money – and the place got a bit trashed. Bill went on to do shows at the Fillmore and Chet set his thing up at the Avalon.

So this was our first encounter with the San Francisco scene. I met Alan Ginsberg at a poetry reading given by Timothy Leary - he was doing a reading there. Ken Kesey and a lot of other trippy people were there. Stanley Owsley was there. He came up and gave us handfuls of Acid. That first night he handed me 15 tabs of "Raspberry", they looked like little raspberry candies. I didn't even know what LSD was at that time, as I had never done it before. It would be a few more months until I took my first Trip.[41]

Meeting Don Preston

Late '65 was the first time I met Don Preston. We went over to his little studio. Frank took us all over there for a jam. He wanted all of us to go. Frank had met Don Preston at the Unicorn club that Herbie used to run right next to the Whisky. Don used to play piano there, mostly jazz stuff. He only got to do the avant-garde stuff at home in the studio. Don had all these instruments in there that he'd made, strange instruments, pieces of a grand piano that he played with hammers, all kinds of brake drums and automobile springs that he played to get these weird sounds.

This was around the time that Frank was thinking about extending the band. But he thought at that time that Don was too much of a jazz player and didn't understand the Blues or Rock stuff we were doing - he couldn't play 'Louie Louie'! It was probably nine months later that Don auditioned for the band again.

Bunk Gardner

At the time though, Don was working with Bunk Gardner. They were active within the avant-garde scene - experimenting with music and film. They have probably got hours and hours of avant-garde stuff that they recorded from that period. It was neat to see that place, I think it was in Echo Park or Silver Lake - it was actually quite close to where Frank was living.

We started to play some gigs at The Trip, which was owned and run by the same people who ran the Whisky.[42] We were playing about three or four nights a week and that's really when we started doing some freaky stuff like -

'Help, I'm A Rock'.

Notes to Chapter 4

[1] Or JCB was putting up a paper advertising his cymbals for sale? [Ref: Roy Estrada comment!]

[2] Between late 1965 and early 1966. Herb Cohen became manager Oct. 1, 1965.
[Ref: globalia.net/donlope/fz/chronology]

[3] In July of 1966 [Ref: *Guardian*, Manchester, UK, Obituary, Apr. 1, 2010]
The Mothers were at The Trip May 3-5, 1966 [Ref: members.shaw.ca/fz-pomd/giglist/]
Meeting was on Feb 5, 1966 at The Trip [Ref: timbuckley.net/bios/timeline.shtml]

[4] Amphetamine. The slang or common names of drugs such as Hash, and drug expressions such as Trip and Joint are capitalized in the text to avoid confusion.

[5] In 2002, on a visit to Europe, Roy said that the band did not do drugs when playing and that there was often no free time outside of music [Ref: Roy Estrada interview, posted on idiotbastard.com]. JCB says essentially the same – not when working!

[6] "Pot" = Marijuana

[7] the Juice = alcohol

[8] "It was a brand-new place that was just opening up...Ray Collins was working there as a carpenter."

[9] Jimmy says one month, in 1964. [Ref: Jon Larsen, *The JCB Story*, Pt. 4 (Audio)]
Jimmy may be conflating two occasions here, if the Soul Giants were first engaged around Dec. 1964-Jan. 1965 and then returned (or reengaged) with Ray Collins as the "house" band until the end of May, 1965.
1. Zappa plays the last week or so of the 2nd stint. [Ref: rockprosopography102.blogspot.de]
2. JCB says the band were going about three months when, toward the end of the third month, the changes took place that resulted in Zappa joining three days before the gig ended, "...at the end of the month". Zappa had just got out of jail. [Ref: 1972 Talking Bio]

[10] Roy Estrada recalls his name as Roger [Ref: John French, *Beefheart Through the Eyes of Magic*]

[11] Playing with the band by Dec. 1964/Jan. 1965 [Ref: rockprosopography102.blogspot.de]

[12] Playing with Soul Giants Jan. 1965 [Ref: rockprosopography102.blogspot.de]

[13] Ray Collins says he never touched him. [Ref: Interview with David Allen, for *Inland Valley Daily Bulletin*, posted May 30, 2009 at dailybulletin.com/ci_12484780]

[14] Frank Zappa claimed this was not true in an interview with Bill Reinhardt and Harry Mishkin at the Paramount Theater in Portland, Oregon, originally aired on KBOO FM in 1974.

[15] Bought from Paul Buff for $1000; contract dated Aug. 1, 1964. [Ref: Michael Gray, *Mother! The Frank Zappa Story*]

[16] Euclid James Sherwood; Jim

[17] "He was the best rhythm I ever heard. He was a great arranger." [Ref: JCB Interview with Calvin Krogh, 2007]

[18] *"When I first met Frank, I told him my name was Lorre, spelled like Peter Lorre. He never called me Lorre and went on with Pete from then on."* [Ref: Lorraine Belcher Interview on idiotbastard.com]

[19] Ringo Starr, drummer with the Beatles

[20] Except cigarettes and coffee?

[21] Or The Blackouts first? [Ref: JCB interview with Vicenza AFN, 1993]

[22] JCB also says Muffler not Mufflers [Ref: JCB Audio interview,1972]

[23] June-July 1965?

[24] Aug/Sept-Oct 1965 [Ref: rockprosopography102.blogspot.de]

[25] [Jon Larsen, *The JCB Story*, Pt. 4 (Audio):] JCB says Henry played for 8/9 months with the band. Henry officially joins Nov. 15, 1965 when the Mothers associate as a band. It was probably somewhere between four and seven months.

[26] It was at Bob Markley's house, on Sept 9, 1965
[Ref: en.wikipedia.org/wiki/The_West_Coast_Pop_Art_Experimental_Band]

[27] Apparently, Zappa persuaded Mark Cheka to go see the band play at the Broadside.
[Ref: *The Real Frank Zappa*, Frank Zappa &Peter Occhiogrosso]

[28] Herb Cohen was officially hired as Personal Manager on Oct. 1, 1965

[29] Herb Cohen was not Mickey Cohen's nephew, as he sometimes claimed to be. [Ref: Art Tripp, in correspondence]

[30] Roy Estrada has it that this is where the band met Herb Cohen [Ref: J. French, *Beefheart...*]. So does FZ.

[31] JCB statement here places the date of this party to Oct, during the interim period when the band had two managers. [But see: Note 26, which suggests a Sept. date]

[32] Not so apparently.
[Ref: "Robert Cohen Speaks at": globalia.net/donlope/fz/videography/Mondo_Hollywood]

[33] LSD

[34] Or "Karl"

[35] Clothing considered outlandish at that time

[36] Oct. 31, 1965

[37] Second week of Aug. 1965

[38] [But see: Note 27]

[39] This figure neatly covers the period between starting at the Whisky around Nov. to going to Hawaii in April 1966. JCB has the Mothers playing at the Trip 3-4 nights a week during this same period of time! The Internet has The Mothers playing Jan. 31- Feb. 2 and Feb. 5, 1966 at the Trip and that around this time is when Henry Vestine quit. JCB has the band rehearsing during Feb., starving and not getting paid? This is also when they would've tried out different replacements for Henry. So is JCB recalling a period of time here? Is it more likely that the Whisky stint was 12 weeks ending late Jan? However, JCB says 21/22 weeks on more than one occasion over the years.

[40] Nov. 6, 1965. This was Family Dog's first production.
[Ref: en.wikipedia.org/wiki/Chet_Helms]

[41] JCB also says elsewhere: "I took one of 'em when I got back home." [But see: text associated with Chapter 5, Note 18]

[42] Playing The Trip and the Whisky at same time? Did the MOI take time off from their 22-week stint at the Whisky to do The Trip gigs?

The MGM Contract

We signed the deal in January 1966.[1] The band got $500 each for signing the contract - minus 10%, that was Herb's management fee - so we got $450 each for signing with MGM.

As soon as we got the deal, Herb and Frank told Mark that he wasn't needed anymore. Before we knew it, Mark was out! We never really got an explanation for his leaving, only that he was just gone. That was the way of the future, as we should have realized then. Frank was the undisputed boss and Herb was the enforcer.

Henry Quits

The day the contracts came was the same day that Henry quit the band. We'd finally worked our way up to playing at The Trip on the Strip and were just about to sign a record contract. During a rehearsal at The Trip, Frank brought out the music for 'Who Are The Brain Police'. Henry looked up and said, "I'm not playing that shit! I'm gonna go join a blues band - you're not playing blues anymore, Frank!" Just then, Herb came down with the contract. Herb really had to do some tall talking to Tom Wilson. The band almost lost the contract because Henry wasn't in the band anymore but Herb somehow convinced the record company that we had a replacement ready for Henry, which we did in Elliot Ingber.

Steve Mann[2] and Tim Hardin were two to try out with us. Steve Mann was a great blues player, a slide player, and a good singer too. There seemed to be too many drugs around for Frank's liking and we're talking "Hard" drugs so that never happened. Tim Hardin was pretty "strung out" on heroin and that was when I smoked some in a "Joint".[3] That cured me of ever wanting to do that drug again. It was the worst feeling I had ever experienced and I couldn't figure out what people saw in it. Just as well.

Eliot Ingber Joins

Elliot had just got out the army and had started to come and watch us play at the Whisky and The Trip. He looked so fuckin' straight it wasn't even funny, and he certainly didn't look like any of us.

Frank was thinking of getting rid of Roy. He didn't like the amount of Speed that Roy was taking, so a guy called Jim Guercio was going to start playing bass with us.[4] Getting rid of Roy never happened as Frank found out that nobody could play the material he wanted played as well as Roy did it. Jim was around for a few months but he didn't like the way that things were being run by Frank, so he kind of drifted out of the scene. He went on to become one of the most famous producers in the business, especially with the band Chicago Transit Authority.

Rehearsing *Freak Out!*

We did the rehearsals for the *Freak Out!* album in January and February.[5] We spent five weeks in an old sound stage on Seward Street, in Hollywood. Frank was owed some money from writing the music to a movie called *Run Home Slow* and the producer - a guy named Tim Sullivan - couldn't pay the money so he gave us use of his studio.

During the rehearsals, we weren't making that regular $90 a week we'd gotten used to and sometimes we would make money and sometimes we wouldn't make any. MGM wasn't paying us anything yet so we were collecting and stealing bottles to get some money for something to eat. It was usually baloney sandwiches because that was the cheapest thing and they could feed us all. No vegetarians in this band.

Besides the songs we'd been playing live, we started working on some brand new songs which Frank had written especially for the album. They were songs like 'Hungry Freaks, Daddy', 'Go Cry On Somebody Else's Shoulder' and 'You Didn't Try To Call Me'.

Dr John

Dr. John[6] rehearsed with us for a while at Seward Street. He would come in and play piano on quite a lot of songs during those rehearsals. Frank was really thinking about getting him into the band until he found out that John was a full-blown junkie.

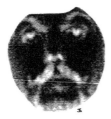

I remember Elliot asking him if he had ever done Acid and he said, "Oh, about twelve times." in his beautiful New Orleans accent. I really think he would have been an asset in the early days but would have had to split when the music starting getting a little freakier.

It is just as well since he went and made a huge name for himself.

Moving to Hollywood

Now everything was happening in Hollywood, but Roy was still living with his parents and I with my in-laws in Santa Ana. I didn't want to be there anymore because it was too far to drive all the time. Relationships at home weren't real good because the father-in-law was always bitchin' and moanin' about something or another. So I didn't like to stay around there that much. I just didn't want to hear shit all the time about me letting my hair grow out and not making any money.

Loretta was behind me, although I don't think she ever really liked the band that much. At that time, she really didn't understand what Frank was doing with the music and to tell the truth, neither did I that much. She was kind of behind me and said, "Go ahead and do it if you must." She just hoped that we would start making some money.

I moved my family out of my father-in-law's house to Hollywood as soon as we got the advance from MGM, a little before we started recording *Freak Out!* We got a place right near Melrose and Vine, in a little cul-de-sac that isn't even on the map. We only lived two blocks away from the Musicians' Union. We had to join when we started recording the album even though we didn't get paid for doing it. You had to be a union member in order to receive your recording checks. What checks? All checks from the record company went through the union. Where were the checks? In fact, anything we got went to pay the union dues, so it was like we got less than nothing.

Laurel Canyon Frank moved to a house over on Kirkwood Street in Laurel Canyon. Frank had a bunch of chicks living with him at the Kirkwood house. It was "pussy heaven" as far as Roy were concerned, just "a covey of quail"[7] to my way of thinking: Pamela Zarubica, a girl called "Pepper", "Cherry", or "Pete" who had been living at the studio in Cucumonga,[8] and Jeanette Vassoir who was, by the way, the original Suzy Creamcheese.[9] They were groupies that liked Frank a lot but not necessarily in a sexual way. They liked what he was doing and they were into the scene that was really starting to happen. I guess that they could see that there was great potential in living there with Frank.

Recording *Freak Out!*

In March,[10] we went right from the rehearsals at the sound stage into TTG Studios on Highland Avenue in Hollywood.

We recorded the whole record in three days. We only had so much of a budget for the whole album. I think it was about $12,000, but I'm not really sure since we never knew what was happening with the finances. We crammed it all into three days and nights but that wasn't a big problem. We all knew the material backwards - and forwards! We had been rehearsing so much that we could do the songs in our sleep.

The first day, we recorded all the basic tracks except the songs that had the extra players on them. The second day was when we had that bunch of session guys come in and we did those songs as one big orchestra. On the third night, we did 'Help, I'm A Rock' and the big "freak out" 'Monster Magnet' thing that takes up side four of the album. By the way, *Freak Out!* was the first "Rock" double album.[11]

The very first song we laid down was 'Anyway The Wind Blows'[12] which was a fairly safe little song. The second song was 'Who Are The Brain Police' and it freaked Tom Wilson out, Man! It shouldn't have, because Tom had produced The Velvet Underground and he'd produced Bob Dylan. We couldn't have been that goddamn freaky! But he looked just a little concerned when he heard that. He was on the phone to the head office at MGM in New York City saying, "I don't think we signed a blues band." and "At the moment, I'm not sure what we signed."

The three songs that the session guys played on were 'How Could I Be Such A Fool', 'I Ain't Got No Heart' and 'You Didn't Try To Call Me'. We had around a 20-piece band with horns, strings, and percussionists. Frank had all the parts written out so they just came in and we did most of those things in one or two takes. I remember Gene Estes was the principal percussionist and he played the vibes parts. Dr. John played piano on quite a few things on the album, although he wasn't credited.[13] I never thought that was very cool.

Roy Quits

It all became pretty tense on a few occasions and on the second night, at about 7 o'clock, we were doing vocals on 'You Didn't Try To Call Me'. I guess that Frank was pretty tired or something because he started in on Roy saying something about his singing, so Roy quit the band. His very words were "Fuck it, I quit!" and split. He just packed up his bass and amp and left.

He was headed back to Santa Ana so Frank asked me to go follow him and try to talk him out of it. I had to run out after him since we were in his car that night! We travelled all the way to Santa Ana - Roy was really upset! I talked and talked and talked and then talked some more all the way down trying to convince him:

"Roy, this is our chance right now, Man! Don't blow it! Frank didn't mean it and he told me to tell you that!"

"Well, why doesn't he tell me himself?"

"Well, you know he's under a lot of pressure right now, please let's go back!"

We got all the way back to Santa Ana, but eventually we turned around and went back, and he recorded his vocal on 'Go Cry On Somebody Else's Shoulder' and it was brilliant! We finally got respect for the "Boy Soprano"!

Sidelining Tom Wilson

I remember the third night of the recording mainly because the girls gave Tom Wilson some Acid. Frank didn't know how he would handle 'Help, I'm A Rock' and the other things we did that night.[14] That last session didn't actually start until about one o'clock in the morning. 'Return of the Son of Monster Magnet' was created in the studio. It was just a jam and, of course, the 'Who Could Imagine' section was all done in the studio.

I met Little Richard when we were recording *Freak Out!* He was doing some work in the downstairs studio at TTG. He said, "I like 'Wowie Zowie', that's a nice song." That was quite a compliment from "The Prettiest Man in Show Business".

After the album was finished, we left for a one-month trip to Hawaii on April 1st.

We played in a club called Da Swamp six nights a week, for at least four hours a night, for the whole month. Da Swamp was a dive right on Waikiki beach in Honolulu. We flew out there, just the five of us and all our equipment. We had three rooms in the building right behind the club. Roy and I had one room, Ray and Elliot shared one and Frank had his own because nobody wanted to room with him. He was writing the music for the next album in every spare moment he had.

I remember they were paying us $150 a week each and of course, we had to buy our food out of that money. We found this little Hawaiian guy called Jimmy who became a very good friend and he had a little restaurant two doors from the club. Jimmy made real nice Hawaiian Food and it only cost us maybe 75 cents a day to eat really good. It was the first time I had rice wrapped in seaweed - very tasty!

We got free drinks in the club but we didn't drink that much. Ray and I were the only two who would drink a little beer. I would have a couple of beers each night and that was about it. Frank didn't drink anything and neither did Elliot or Roy. We were a good deal for those guys - Da Swamp, that is - compared to Beefheart's band who'd been over there the month before us. Those guys tried to drink the place dry every night. The people that ran the club really hated Beefheart's band because they were so much trouble. We sure were smoking a lot of "Weed"[15] though!

We did get every Sunday night off but we rehearsed almost every day that we were there and, as a result, there were few days that we got any time off. We'd get up and we'd have to be at the club at 2 o'clock and we'd rehearse for three hours. That was kind of fun to do because we were getting into some new material and we were jamming a lot in an organized way. We were doing Raga type things and things that developed into songs later on.

Frank was busy writing new material all the time. He wrote a whole bunch of new material over there. All the basic sections which were to make up 'Brown Shoes Don't Make It' and 'Call Any Vegetable'[16] were done in that little room of his. I'm glad nobody was bothering him, actually.

The clientele of that club was a mix of sailors and locals and it was a pretty rowdy place! I'll never forget the bouncer at the place. They called him Baby and he had been a Mr. Hawaii, a former body builder. He was a little short guy but he had a set of arms on him like you wouldn't believe, almost like Hercules. He was a nice guy and handy to know because if anyone ever started trouble in the place, Baby would take care of it pretty quick. He not only was a weight lifter but he liked to knock the shit out of people if they got out of line.

Beefheart, being as arrogant as he was, got himself into some serious trouble with Baby. He almost got the shit beaten out of himself several times over there. The management really didn't like Beefheart - he was too freaky for them.

We were playing some of the *Freak Out!* songs live. Of course, it was the more tame ones. The people liked 'Trouble Comin' Everyday' and 'Motherly Love' and we did a lot of 'Louie Louie', 'Woolly Bully' and a lot of blues numbers. We even did my Jimmy Reed songs with Frank playing the drums. We did some James Brown songs like 'Papa's Got A Brand New Bag' and 'Please, Please, Please'. On real risky nights, we might start messin' around a little bit with 'Help, I'm A Rock' but only as an instrumental. We were doing a piece called 'Arabesque' which was an instrumental and that tune evolved into 'Absolutely Free'.

One Saturday afternoon, we went up and played an outdoor thing at The University of Hawaii which gave us a bit of extra money and that was nice.

We met Mama Cass in Hawaii and she used to come down to the club and hang out with us. She was on vacation from The Mamas and The Papas, just chilling and hanging out. She was a wonderful woman, a good friend to be with and a great singer.

She had half a pound[17] of Acapulco Gold she had smuggled over there. Naturally, we commenced to help her smoke it and we managed to smoke about half of it. She was there for one week and she just left the other quarter pound with us, as she didn't want to take it back to the States with her.

I remember she was trying to get into Elliot's pants and that was funny because Elliot didn't really want to have anything to do with her. He really wasn't into huge girls and as everyone knows, she was huge.

We met this guy in the club (I don't remember his name) who lived across the island over on Sunset Beach, and he invited us all out there on our day off. We all chipped in $5 each and rented a two-tone pink Jeep Surrey for the day - the night of course - taking Mama Cass with us. After the gig on Saturday night, we all took off except for Frank as he was busy writing and wasn't really hanging with us much. We got over there and the guy says, "OK, who wants to take some Acid?" Roy and I had thought about doing it before[18] but we really didn't know anything about it, except that it was supposed to be like a sixteen-hour Speed Trip. We thought about it long and hard - maybe one or two minutes - and decided that we had enough time. Sunday was our free night, so we all dropped the LSD.

Man! It was the wildest thing that I had ever taken! God, it was unbelievable, especially being in Hawaii! Can you imagine this pink Jeep Surrey bouncing down the road with six people in it - Mama Cass was on that trip! with us as well - blown out of their skulls on LSD. Luckily the guy was driving and he knew the island very well.

They were having the International Surf Contest at the time of our trip[19] and surfing on those 40-foot[20] waves. I sat on the beach and I could feel those waves, Man! It would just shake you. It was one of the wildest Trips I ever had. We were up all night and all the following day - it was a 24-hour Trip - but I enjoyed it!

So, we got back to our little place and of course, Frank wanted to know what the fuck we'd been up to. That's when Ray started telling him, "Man! You need to take LSD, Frank!" and that only added to their problems. Ray and Frank didn't get along too well. Ray wasn't the easiest guy in the world to get along with and neither was Frank. Ray didn't really like the idea of Frank running everything, doing everything. Ray didn't like the idea that he didn't have any input on anything and that was their trouble all along. That's the biggest reason why Ray used to quit the band all the time. Ray would leave for weeks at a time, but normally we could persuade him to come back.

The next weekend, we rented a little car again - a Volkswagen or something - and drove back over to Sunset Beach. This time we brought our instruments. I still don't know how the fuck we got them all in that little car. Somehow, we got lost going over there this time. I'm sure that Cass's Grass had something to do with it. We were in one of these sugar cane fields smoking that Acapulco Gold, which was pretty powerful stuff, it was hallucinogenic. Anyway - these giant spiders were jumping out across the road in different colors, Man! What a trip!

We finally got over there. It was kind of like a commune. We were going to take another Acid Trip but the guy couldn't get any LSD, so we took some Baby Woodrose Seeds.

Hawaiian Baby Woodrose Baby Woodrose Pods are very decorative little pods that florists use at Christmas time to make wreaths for putting in windows or on the front doors of people's houses. I have no idea who learned about the hallucinogenic properties of those seeds but someone did. The Trip was similar to Morning Glory seeds - the things that hippies would do just to get "out of it" were truly amazing.

Each pod has 10 seeds in so we each swallow 10 seeds. Then they tell us, "You're gonna get a little sick, but it'll pass!" We had just eaten some spaghetti that they had made for us and we had set our equipment up to play some blues for them that night. About 45 minutes after taking the seeds, I started getting very ill with bad stomach cramps. I threw up all the spaghetti and went and laid down because I thought I was going to die - at least that's the way I felt. All of a sudden the sickness went! It just went up and away and I was feeling great, the best I'd ever felt in my life. About 15-20 minutes into playing, the drumsticks started feeling like logs and I could barely lift the fuckin' things they were so heavy. The music, and us, were slowly but surely slowing down and pretty soon I just fell off the drum stool. I managed to get up against the wall and found myself just staring out into space. I was tripping my ass off. Then I'd slowly start sliding down the wall. It would take me about 45 minutes to get back up and this went on all night long. The same thing happened to everyone else in the band. Everyone in the band was there except Frank - nothing unusual there!

Roy, Ray, Elliot and I did do one other Trip a couple of weeks later, but it wasn't out there at the commune. We did it on our night off in our little hotel rooms behind the club. Most of the Trip we spent out on the beach in front of the club just laying around in the sand. That is where Roy said, "Indio, I can feel a flower growing in my stomach." He was pretty sick that whole trip[21] but I guess I was lucky because I really enjoyed it.[22]

T R I P We got back to L.A. to learn that MGM had organized a special event at The Trip to promote The Velvet Underground and The Mothers of Invention at the start of May.[23] Both bands had new albums to promote as they were both produced by Tom Wilson. The Velvets were headlining and I really think that pissed Frank off. The reason for them headlining was probably because they'd come out from New York and, of course, Andy Warhol and Nico were with them so there was a lot of hype going around.

The band seemed kind of strange to us as they were coming from a totally different angle than we were. I talked to Nico and I thought that she was nice and also I talked to Mo the drummer but Lou Reed and John Cale seemed pretty out there. I didn't see much of those guys, because they were kind of strange. At the time, they were all junkies and I didn't know much about junkies. I don't think Frank was too pleased that the Velvets seemed to be getting all the attention. Frank and Lou Reed seemed to take an instant dislike to each other that lasted most of Frank's career. I think we played three nights there with them at The Trip.

FRENCHYS About a week after those gigs, we travelled up to Hayward to play at a place called Frenchys for a couple of weeks.[24] The night before we left, I went off with Roy and Elliot to get some Pot from Elliot's girlfriend who lived not far from Frank's house. We had just smoked a Joint when there was a knock on the door and all of a sudden, Frank was there! He stood there and shouted, "You three guys, outside with me!" He gave us the rundown there and told us that he didn't want drugs on this or any other tour from now on. He said if we got busted he was going to leave us in jail! We found out later that Ray has told him what we were up to ...THANKS RAY!

We took the Pot up there with us anyway. Jeanette and Pepper came on that trip with us and they knew we had the Pot, because they'd helped us smoke some of it. We drove up the night before playing at the club.[25] Frank and Ray came up the next day because Frank stayed back to finish work on the album and there wasn't any more room in the car for Ray. It was just as well because of what Ray had done to us. So, we had to keep the Pot hidden from Frank and Elliot decided to bury it under a rock in a field next to the Motel. I think the girls must have seen us putting it there and told Frank when he arrived because when we went back for it after the gig it was gone! The whole quarter of a pound was GONE, DISAPPEARED, VANISHED INTO THIN AIR. We looked under every rock in that field, and there were a lot of rocks. I really think that Frank was looking out his window at the motel and laughing his ass off at that.[26]

Neil Diamond

We met Neil Diamond in Frenchys because he was going to do an early, one-night show.[27] He had a song called 'Solitary Man' out then and was promoting it. Being the house band for the two weeks, we were asked to back him in his one hour set. We had to rehearse with him the afternoon of the show and so we got to know him and liked him very much. We used to run into him on the road from time to time and he was always cool with us. He was a very big star by then and maybe he never forgot us playing with him at Frenchys.

Elliot somehow managed to piss the club owner off big time because he turned out to be a very patriotic guy that was all for the war in Vietnam and all that shit. He finally, after almost two weeks, figured out that we were a pretty freaky bunch of guys and more than likely dirty *RED* commies and everything else. On our last night at Frenchys, Frank had The Joke Savage

Jug Band open up for us. Those people were a bunch of heavy-duty San Francisco hippies and shit, the owner flipped out. He totally lost it and he was going for his gun because he wanted to kill Elliot. I don't know why he picked on Elliot. Maybe he had been fucking with his girlfriend or something, although by this time Elliot was the freakiest guy in the Mothers.

We were getting a lot of action up there and I was getting more than my share. There were a lot of freaky girls up there in Hayward. One night we got a chance to see Round Robin in a black after-hours club. The brothers looked at us kind of funny when we walked in there but nobody said anything. I really enjoyed that show and so did everyone in the band. It was one of the rare times that Frank went with us but I know he really wanted to see Round Robin, as he was a fan.

San Francisco & the Fillmore Auditorium

After the Frenchys engagement finished and we got out alive, we went and played at the Fillmore Auditorium in San Francisco for the first time. Once again we played with The Velvet Underground.[28]

The Fillmore was quite an interesting gig as it was in an old dancehall which had seen better days, smack dab in the middle of the black district of S.F. and pretty raunchy. It was the first time that I'd ever really seen a real big psychedelic light show. Captain Wizzo's Light Show was the wildest thing I had ever seen. He was a guy from Texas - one crazy motherfucker - who later on became a very close friend of mine.

Bill Graham had recently opened the place and he was in direct competition with Chet Helms, who was now promoting shows at the Avalon Ballroom. It seemed like the whole city was a freak scene because things were going on everywhere you looked.

I don't know what happened that night, but it seems like we got there a little late and Herb Cohen and Bill Graham were screaming at each other. I liked Bill Graham and he seemed to like us - we were pretty regular up there for the rest of that summer. He was a very straight, hard-working guy - a professional - but he could get very upset if things didn't go the way he wanted.

We were really the first band from L.A. to start playing up there on a regular basis because people from the San Francisco scene didn't think too much of the L.A. scene. That San Francisco scene was totally different to the L.A. scene - they were much more into Folk Rock and beginning to lean toward "Flower Power". They thought that people from L.A. were a bunch of dorks. People from L.A. thought that people from San Francisco were a bunch of Acid "heads",[29] which they were, but we were catching up fast!

The second time we went up to play the Fillmore, we had moved up from the opening act to the second on the bill. We played with Quicksilver Messenger Service. It was a two-night gig and, if I remember right, the

Warlocks (Grateful Dead) were the opening band.[30] We didn't play with the "Dead" that many times. Once at the beginning of the Fillmore run, in Sacramento, one time in San Jose and I think also one time in New York City. We played more with Jefferson Airplane.[31]

I got to meet some real nice people while we were up there. Grace Slick became a very good friend and so did Spencer Dryden, the drummer with The Jefferson Airplane. I used to hang out with "Pigpen"[32] from the Grateful Dead quite a lot. I liked him and the band because they were pretty "acidy" and I was starting to get into Acid quite a lot by that time. Pigpen liked the Mothers and he used to come and watch us play a lot although he was about the only one that did. I don't think that Jerry Garcia could be bothered. He wasn't really interested in Zappa as he was into a totally different thing.

Barry Feinstein came and filmed us at the Fillmore, maybe the second or third time that we were there. The movie was called *You Are What You Eat.*

The Fillmore always had three bands playing unless it was a very special occasion, like when we opened for Lenny Bruce.

Lenny Bruce
In late June, we went back up there and supported Lenny Bruce, just a short time before he died.[33] I know that Frank was extremely influenced by Lenny, with his sarcasm and the satire. As you know, Lenny liked to say "fuck" and "shit" a lot on stage. Those were things that you weren't supposed to do but Frank liked that too!

On one of those visits up there, maybe the 3rd, Ray had talked Frank into taking a hallucinogenic Trip. He told Frank he needed to try and get closer to the band, expand his mind or some shit, and gave him some Baby Woodrose Seeds.

So, after we had played the last of three shows,[34] we didn't see Frank for at least two days, he kind of disappeared! He never spoke about it afterwards because, I think, it might have scared the shit out of him.

That recording of 'Downtown Talent Scout' that was released on *You Can't Do That On Stage Anymore Vol. 5* was done at one of those gigs. It says 1965 on the sleeve notes, but we didn't go up there until 1966![35] It would have had to have been one of the shows that John Judnick did the sound on because I think he recorded a few things for us on some analogue two-track thing. I'd completely forgotten all about it, but that was Ray playing harmonica on it although I don't think he was ever credited for it! I only heard the CD years later but that was some great material recorded back then.

Elliot, Elvis & the Cover of *Freak Out!*

The album was mixed mainly by Frank, before we went to Hawaii. Frank had a lot to do with the album's artwork also because he knew pretty much everything that he wanted to do. I didn't know anything about the list of names or anything else on the cover until I saw the album when it came out.

Around that same time, we recorded a session for the single 'Orange Colored Sky' by Burt Ward.[36] Burt Ward was famous for playing Robin in the TV *Batman* series. They had decided to make a record on the back of that. There was only one session and we did the B-side which was called 'Boy Wonder, I Love You'. We even got paid for that session. We got session money for it through the union. That was kind of nice, since we didn't get session money for *Freak Out!!*

We took the photos for the album cover before we went into the studio. We went out to the beach someplace around Malibu to do the front-cover photo, the back-cover photo was taken in Ray Collins' backyard. He had a little place off of Formosa St. in Hollywood. In fact, in that picture on the back of *Freak Out!* the purple shirt I have on was from our old band uniform. I started wearing wild colored vests with it and things like that and started to let my hair grow a little bit. Motorhead would say my hair was "getting good in the back".

Elliot was starting to grow a beard again when that photo was taken. He had grown a beard when he joined the band but had to shave it off when he got a job as an extra in the Elvis Presley movie *Girls Girls Girls*. Elliot got to meet Elvis and told him he was in a band called the Mothers. When Elvis heard 'Help, I'm A Rock', he thought it was the craziest thing so he started calling Elliot "Help I'm A Blimp".

The Mothers of Invention

Freak Out! was finally released in the summer of 1966[37] and the record company executives had insisted that the band name be extended to The Mothers of Invention. It was released on the Verve label which was a subsidiary of MGM. Despite our differences, we were stable mates with The Velvet Underground.

The whole band went over to "Frank's Harem" (as we used to jokingly call Kirkwood) to listen to the album. When I first heard it, I didn't understand it at all. I knew it wasn't what you'd call commercial and I thought, "Fuck, we ain't gonna have a hit with this, Man! Are you kidding! What is Side 3? -and 4? It's just a bunch of bullshit!" I know Roy felt the same way too! It was really confusing to my wife also. She said, "What are you wasting your time doing that shit for? It sure doesn't sound like the Beatles to me!"[38]

Then a few days later I took an Acid Trip at my house in Hollywood and listened to it. Then I understood what it was about. I thought, "OK! That's cool!" Looking back, I don't think that the album could have been better for the time because it's a good album and it's the only one that I'm the only drummer on, so I'm partial to it.

The Doors
The Doors were just starting to come up. They were playing at the Whisky a lot at that time and I used to go see them play. I would always go backstage and say hi to Robbie Krieger. Robbie and I had become good mates and he was real good friends with John Densmore. John was a great drummer and Don Preston did some work with him later on. I hung out quite a bit with them but I didn't know the others in the band that well. Jim Morrison always came across as some kind of weirdo to me and as it turned out, he was that way to a lot of people.

We did a few concerts with them, mainly around the L.A. area. One time I saw the Doors get fired, thrown off the stage and out of the club! Jim Morrison said "fuck" on the stage and the owner, Elmer Valentine, just came over and stopped the show, shouting: "You've got three minutes to get all your shit off the stage and out of this club!"

Promoting *Freak Out!*
The record company put out two singles from the *Freak Out!* album. The first one was *How Could I Be Such A Fool* b/w *Help, I'm A Rock*[39] and I thought there was no way that they were going to get played on the radio. 'How Could I Be Such A Fool' was in waltz time! Nobody released singles that were in 3/4 time - the only one I remember being a hit was 'Go Now' by the Moody Blues. What chance did 'Help, I'm A Rock' have of breaking into the charts?

In July, we did our first promotional tour for *Freak Out!* We did four TV shows: Washington D.C.,[40] Detroit,[41] Winsor Canada, and Dallas. Carl Franzoni went with us on that trip! That is what I would call it, as he'd dance like crazy while we performed! Whenever we could, we would play live, but most of the time we had to mime to a pre-recorded tape. We hated having to mime and would normally end up doing something really freaky which didn't sync up with what was being played. That was the way Frank wanted it and it did make sense to us.

If these Mothers move in next to you, your grass will die!
[See Note 40]

I especially remember Dallas, Texas. We arrived by plane and, as we walked down the corridor to the baggage hall, the people coming the other way parted in front of us and just stared. It was like we had some kind of plague and they would catch it if they even breathed the air in the same corridor. The feeling was scary and the whole city felt completely "up-tight" to us. Frank kept saying that Dallas is where they shot JFK. We were checked into a four-star hotel but we didn't spend the night there. Frank got so paranoid that we changed our flight tickets and flew out of Dallas at two o'clock in the morning. Loretta wasn't happy with the situation - she had to come pick me up at the airport in L.A. at four that morning.

It was when we returned from that little tour that Frank met Gail Sloatman and almost immediately she moved into Kirkwood with him.[42] In my opinion, a big mistake for Frank but then he was a big boy.

GREAT UNDERGROUND ARTS MASKED BALL & ORGY This was the time that we did GUAMBO.[43] The Great Underground Arts Masked Ball and Orgy was the first big "freak-out trip" that happened in L.A.[44] The gig was set up by *L.A. Free Press* to celebrate their 2nd anniversary in business.

The cops were there checkin' the whole thing out. They were checking anything "underground" because they didn't understand all these freaky kids going around growing their hair, wearing colorful clothes, all this dancing in the streets and "free love" happening and all that stuff. They wanted to know what was going on and what bands were involved with all this.

So I think that's about the time when we really started getting checked out by the police. We were seen as subversives, maybe even dirty red "commies". Well, Carl Franzoni was a registered communist cardholder because he showed me his card one time. I think Vito Pauluka was too. I really didn't care because the saying at that time was "Better Red than Dead". I had served my country militarily (with an Honorable Discharge) and I had always been taught to think that anyone who was a communist had to be a low life, a no good person, but I knew Carl so well and I thought he was a real cool guy. That's when my thoughts about communism changed. That's when I discovered in my own mind that communism is nothing more than just another political party.

So, needless to say: the CIA was watching us, the FBI was watching us, the LAPD was watching us, everybody was watching us and the only really safe place to be was in Hollywood where there were many people like us. San Francisco and Greenwich Village were the only other havens at that time for the "hippies", which was the new term for freaky people.

This was the time when we had Billy Mundi join as our second drummer.[45] He had been playing with Tim Buckley and, as we were in a rehearsal room over at the Lindy Theater,[46] it was easy for him to join. After all, we both had the same manager. Billy was the first of the new guys to come into the band at the end of the summer.

Photo above: courtesy Billy Mundi

I think Billy was already in the band the last time that Elliot went to San Francisco with us. It was a six-piece band with two drummers. I don't recall but I'm told we were still billed as The Mothers even though *Freak Out!* had been released.

Elliot Gets Fired!

We played for the Family Dog at the Avalon Ballroom.[47] It was a commune thing and that's mainly where the Grateful Dead played – bands like Quicksilver Messenger Service, Country Joe and The Fish and Big Brother and The Holding Company used to play there a lot too. The Avalon is where Elliot got fired.[48]

We played there for three nights and after the show on the second night, Elliot and Roy took some Acid. They took it pretty late, or early in the morning, as Elliot was still blown out of his skull by the time we had to play our last show on Saturday night. There were some critics or some such there and it was a pretty important night for Frank and for the band. We were playing 'Call Any Vegetable', which Elliot was supposed to take a solo in. When it came to that part of the song, he was wailing away on his solo. The boy was really playing a hot solo and Frank was just looking at him like, "What the fuck is wrong with you?" Elliot was playing his solo, this blazing solo, without his amp turned on. So, when we got back to Hollywood he was fired and of course everybody was bent out of shape at Frank. We all thought, "How dare you fire him!" and "Who do you think you are anyway?" Then we were all talking about firing Frank from the band but of course nothing came of that because you can't fire the Boss.

Frank had decided that we needed a keyboard player so Don Preston came and auditioned again. This time he had a better angle on what was required and he got the job.

Don was quickly followed by his old friend, Bunk Gardner, giving us woodwinds, flute, and saxophone.

So we'd expanded the band to a 7-piece.

Frank wanted to go in another direction, although he never came to us and explained anything. We were happy to let him take us for the ride we were on. He didn't feel he had to explain anything. He knew exactly what he wanted. After all, he was the Big Boss Man.

Now we were playing one-hour shows, most of the cover versions had gone but we were still doing 'Baby Love' and some of the comedy songs. We were starting to get into more comedy stuff, and satire. We were doing most all the *Freak Out!* songs and some that were going to be on *Absolutely*

Free. Songs like 'Brown Shoes Don't Make It', 'Call Any Vegetable', 'The Duke Of Prunes', and 'Suzy Creamcheese, What's Got Into Ya'. We were also doing 'Plastic People' the new way - we'd been doing the straight "Louie Louie" beat before.

Jim Fielder Joins

About this time, Jim Fielder came into the band. I had known Jim since the days we taught together at the Woodwind Shop in Anaheim, California. Frank actually wanted to have two bass players in the band. Since he had two drummers, he thought that it would be cool to have two bass players but Jim never really got to play bass. He ended up playing second guitar and he really didn't like that. He wasn't in the band long as it turned out.

We were practicing every day but by then Frank had bought in kettledrums and gongs and percussion stuff like that, so I wasn't playing the drum set all the time anymore. I still played drums on certain songs but Billy was real hard to play with because his time was so goddamn erratic. Man! He had terrible time! He was like a roller coaster, speed up, slow down, speed up, slow down and it was driving Frank crazy too because Billy was also doing a lot of Speed.

With the new extended line up in place, Frank had a lot of things in mind that he wanted to try. We were starting to improvise a lot more with experimental stuff, and there was the Varèse kind of things that he wanted to do. We were starting to stretch out and improvise now that Don and Bunk were in and given solos. So now we had a couple of jazz players in the band!

SHRINE EXP. HALL SAT SEPT. 17 9:00. We played the Shrine Auditorium on September 17th, with Count Five, The Factory, The West Coast Pop Art Experimental Band and others. The Shrine Auditorium was very near Watts, right by the University of Southern California campus (USC) where John Wayne and OJ Simpson played football before becoming famous. It was always a little dangerous to be right next to Watts. A 7-year-old black kid called Little Gary, who was the new Stevie-Wonder-type-singer, was topping the bill not the Mothers. But he never made it, just as well for the Mothers!

The West Coast Pop Art Experimental Band recorded 'Help, I'm A Rock' and became the first band to cover a Zappa song.

Big Leg Emma

In October, 'Big Leg Emma' was recorded to be released as a single along with 'Why Don'tcha Do Me Right'.[49] That was the first recording we did with Billy, Don, and Bunk. The session was recorded at TTG studios and lasted six hours. 'Big Leg Emma' was the first song that I got to sing on properly. Although it probably only sold a few thousand copies when it was originally released, it was a great song and still is.

MOTHERS FORCED TO CANCEL OUT **oct 15** We were going to play a show in Santa Barbara at the Earl Warren Showgrounds but for some reason the original date was cancelled.[50] I think it may have had something to do with the fact that Ronald Reagan had a ranch there. Anyway, it was re-scheduled for a week or so later. The opening act was The Factory with Lowell George as the lead guitarist. He was only about 21 years old at that time but he became a real, dear friend of mine. The Factory were doing some demos for Frank.[51]

The night before we played Santa Barbara, Roy was busted in Hollywood for possession of pills. Herb had to bail him out so we could go and do the show and so Roy wasn't the flavor of the month in Frank's eyes. He was put on probation for a while and he had to go back to L.A. a few times while we were in New York City, at least until Herb signed some papers agreeing to take responsibility for him.

Violet Vodka LSD

I was at Ray's house one night and he had some "Violet Vodka" LSD in liquid form. It was a purple color, coming from Santo's Pharmaceutical in Switzerland and it was called LSD 25. Someone had cut it with Vodka. At this time, LSD still hadn't been made illegal. I'd arranged to go up to Lowell's house at the top of Lookout Mountain Road in Laurel Canyon to listen to them rehearse. I took a hit of this stuff before I left.

You had to drive all the way up this winding road to get there and just as I was starting to Trip, I had to manage driving up that road. I was so fucking blasted by the time I got up there I don't know how I made it. The house was open so I walked into the kitchen and heard the band rehearsing in the next room. They were right in the middle of some really psychedelic song so I decided to stay in the kitchen and listen.

Then WOOF! I saw the "Clear Light"! All of a sudden, they stopped playing and came and looked into the kitchen and said, "Hi, Jimmy!" They could feel that I was there. I must have been glowing like a glow-worm because I was higher than a kite!

I was with this chick I'd met up there and when we left we were going to go to Carl Franzoni's house for a while. I couldn't turn the car around. I had one of those Corvairs which was one of the first American compact cars. I had to back it all the way down that hill in reverse because there was no place to turn around. I'm sure that there had to be a place to turn around but as high as I was I couldn't see it or find it. The girl surely had to wonder what the fuck was going on. What a trip!

I never did take any Acid when I was going to play with Frank because there were just too many parts to remember in the songs. I kept LSD and playing with Frank as two separate items at all times!

Rehearsing for *Absolutely Free*
We found a little rehearsal room just by Santa Monica Boulevard and that's where we rehearsed the material for *Absolutely Free*. 'Brown Shoes Don't Make It' took a lot of work because we had to learn it in sections. Frank would say, "Do a Beach Boys thing here." and then we'd move on to another section. We also worked on 'Call Any Vegetable' and 'The Duke Of Prunes' and a thing called 'No Regrets'. That became our ending song every night and Ray used to ad-lib around it. It was a great comedy piece that evolved into 'America Drinks And Goes Home'.

Single #2
The second single was *Trouble Comin' Every Day* b/w *Who Are The Brain Police?*[52] Needless to say, both singles released from *Freak Out!* sold miserably. Consequently, they are worth a lot of money to collectors now!

After there seemed to be no action on the charts, I didn't even bother to check the charts anymore because I didn't even care anymore. If we'd have got a number one hit or even a number 50 that would've been something, but I knew we were never going to get a number one.

It was fun playing the music we played, but I was always secretly hoping the Frank would come out with an album that had some commercial potential, but of course that never happened, as we all well know.

Recording Absolutely Free
In November,[53] we started recording the basic tracks and it took about five days. We were back in TTG working on a new 8-track machine because they had the first one in Hollywood. I think the budget for recording that album was about $11.000.00. The album would not actually be completed until we went to New York.

Don Ellis was brought in to play trumpet on 'Brown Shoes Don't Make It'. He was the first trumpet player I saw who had a pick-up on his horn and he played it through a Fender Amplifier.

Although Tom Wilson was listed as producer on everything that we put out on Verve, he wasn't there most of the time. I think he and Frank had made some sort of deal so Frank could be left in charge of production and Tom would be off doing his own thing. Tom would only be around for part of the time. I really think he felt that Frank could produce the album much better than him because Frank knew exactly what he wanted to do with the songs.

The songs on *Absolutely Free* were much more complicated than the ones we did on *Freak Out!*

Lumpy Gravy

The recordings that would eventually be released as *Lumpy Gravy* were done right after we did the basic tracks for *Absolutely Free*. They were recorded at Capitol Records and Bunk played bassoon on those sessions.[54]

I am on it too, doing some talking and noise parts but exactly which parts I don't know, it was cut up and chopped about so much.[55] For Frank, it was the kind of recording that would set the stage for his future musical direction.

New York at the Balloon Farm

We made our first trip to New York in December of '66 to play some shows at the Balloon Farm. We took all our equipment on the plane. The band had a lot more equipment to carry around by then. Don had a Fender Rhodes and a Clavinet, extra amplifiers and of course, we now had two sets of drums.

The Balloon Farm was located in the lower east side of Greenwich Village. It was an old Polish dance/meeting hall on St. Mark's Place. New York was a really good place for the type of music we were doing because New Yorkers were more into it than they were on the West Coast. I liked the scene in New York because it was a lot looser than what was happening in L.A.

We only went for four or five days over a weekend, but it was important for us to impress the people of New York City. It was the end of November and pretty cold. We only played a couple of shows but we also went into Mayfair studios to do some overdubs on the 8-track tapes we'd taken with us from TTG in L.A., as we were still working on *Absolutely Free*.

Vanilla Fudge at The Beach House

We did two other shows outside of the Balloon Farm and one of them was at the Village Theater with The Fugs. The Village Theater later turned into the Fillmore East and was a very beautiful old theater. We also went out to a place called The Beach House, in Long Beach, Long Island and played a gig there with a band called The Pigeons. They later turned into Vanilla Fudge - that was out first encounter with the Fudge.

The management just flipped out at what we were doing because it was a mafia run place and they just didn't understand what we were doing at all. They thought it was a bunch of shit anyway, so they didn't pay us. They didn't give us the transportation back from Long Island to the Balloon Farm. It took about 15 cabs to get us and all our equipment back and that little excursion cost Herb about $200 - although I expect we really paid in the long run. The band didn't have any money at that time anyway.

Back at the Balloon Farm

We went back to California but decided we would go straight back to New York. We'd received such good reviews for those first shows that we went back and played over Christmas and New Year, again at the Balloon Farm.

A band called The Strangers[56] opened for us and they had a flute player called Jeremy Stieg with them. They were playing sort of jazz fusion and that was the beginning of all that stuff. I found it very interesting. We also played with a band called The Clear Light and they had two drummers too. One of them was Dallas Taylor who later played with Crosby, Stills and Nash for years.

We stayed at the Hotel Albert and that was where I got the crabs. I didn't get them off a chick either, it was off the toilet seat![57]

At the time, The Lovin' Spoonful were rehearsing downstairs in the basement of the hotel so we got to know them well.

They were playing at The Night Owl Café and had their hit, 'What A Day For A Daydream' that I thought was very good. John Sebastian is one of the nicest guys around and a great singer and songwriter.

New Year's Eve in New York

A girl that I had met up in East Lansing, Michigan, came down to New York the second time we were at the Balloon Farm and stayed with me over the Christmas holidays. Roy had picked up some girl too. We were all sleeping in the same room because it was a big hotel room. We were all getting it on and Roy was really huffin' and puffin' when suddenly he bounced out of the bed, crashed onto the floor and laid out - he just couldn't get up. His girl sat up shaking her head at him and said, "He's no good for the rest of the night, I've wiped him out!"

On New Year's Eve afternoon, we were at the Balloon Farm rehearsing and Roy was on one of his "staying-up" periods. He'd been up for days on a Speed binge. We were walking back to the hotel late in the afternoon, about five o'clock it was, and a gust of wind got up pretty hard and blew Roy over. So, when we got back to the hotel I said, "Don't fall asleep now." because I knew what it's like to wake that fuckin' guy up especially after he'd been up for days. Sure enough, he fell asleep and it was time for the gig. I was trying to wake him up, I was throwing water on him, shaking him, everything I could think of but he wasn't getting up. I just couldn't get him to move.

So, Bunk came down to the room and said, "Roy, I've got three "Uppers" here." Bingo, his eyes popped open. He was wide-awake and managed to play the gig on New Year's Eve!

Vivian

We started meeting the girls who were always hanging around at the Balloon Farm like Janet Ferguson, Lucy and Vivian. They quickly became regulars at all the New York Shows. Miss Lucy, the little dark-haired one from *200 Motels*, moved to L.A. and was already freaking out when we got back there.

To Vivian: "I'll never forget you." Bunk and Don also said the same thing to her a few years later!

Notes to Chapter 5

[1] March 1, 1966? [Ref: globalia.net/donlope/fz/chronology/1965-1969.html].
An interesting discrepancy as Steve Mann is playing instead of Henry Vestine by the end of Jan. 1966. [See: next Note]
[2] Jan./Feb. 1966 [Ref: rockprosopography102.blogspot.de]
[3] "Joint": normally refers to a Marijuana cigarette, either "straight" (pure) or mixed with tobacco. In this case who knows, but Heroin was added.
[4] Around Jan./Feb. 1966 [Ref: rockprosopography102.blogspot.de]
[5] Between Nov. and Jan. for the recordings [Ref: Billy James, *Necessity Is....*]
[6] Mac Rebennack
[7] - waiting to be flushed out! JCB sees the girls as hangers on, as the last sentence of this paragraph also suggests.
[8] "Pete" is Lorraine Belcher [who is not there] and "Cherry" (Chéri?) is Jeanette Vassoir. "Pepper" is not Pamela Z but a transient groupie [Ref: Pamela Zarubica, in conversation]. The GTOs (or a number of them) were originally referred to as the "Cherry Sisters".
[9] "Pamela Zarubica (later personified as Suzy Creamcheese)" [Ref: Billy James, *Necessity Is...*, p. 24 (SAF 2005)]. Zappa states that Pamela Zarubica was used to personify Suzy for the fans in Europe. Jeanette or Jennie was Suzy C. on *Freak Out!*
[10] Recorded between Nov. and Jan. [Ref: Billy James, *Necessity Is...*, p. 48]; but it is JCB's recollection of the recording that James quotes. JCB suggests that there was a good deal of rehearsing first which is in line with the way he says Zappa worked.
[11] Though it wasn't the first to be released
[12] Frank Zappa derides JCB's early drumming abilities in an interview with Bill Reinhardt and Harry Mishkin at the Paramount Theater in Portland, Oregon, originally aired on KBOO FM in 1974. Zappa claims that it took JCB two weeks to learn "a drum-fill" on this song. [Ref: youtube.com, willyrein, 09/2012]
[13] Quoting JCB, Billy James also mentions Paul Butterfield & Kim Fowley as sitting in.
[14] Elsewhere, JCB notes that Tom Wilson was a willing participant [Ref: unpublished JCB interview, 1997]
[15] Marijuana
[16] Though it would not yet have that title?
[17] A kilo = 2.2 pounds
[18] [See: Chapter 4 Note 39]
[19] Does JCB mean at the time of their stay in Hawaii, or the LSD experience?
[20] about 12 meters
[21] It is not clear to me whether JCB is referring here to the Acid "trip" or to the band's stay in Hawaii [Ed.]
[22] "it" means? [See: Previous Note]
[23] May 3-5, 1966
[24] May 6-26, 1966 [Ref: members.shaw.ca/fz-pomd/giglist/1966]

[25] With the band's gear in Frank's station-wagon

[26] JCB is convinced that Frank flushed the "Pot" down the toilet. But they managed to score off someone the next day. [Ref: Jon Larsen, *The JCB Story* (audio)]

[27] May 2, 1966

[28] and Nico with Andy Warhol's Plastic Inevitable on May 27-29, 1966

[29] "Acid-head": people mainly into "tripping"

[30] [Jon Larsen, *The JCB Story* (audio):] In this 2007 audio recollection of those times, JCB says they are headliners; a promotional gig coinciding with the release of *Freak Out!* that took place mid-June 1966, two weeks after their first appearance at Fillmore West. He recalls Jefferson Airplane as the third band, and that the Warlocks opened for the Mothers who opened for Jefferson Airplane. But the gig mentioned here was on the June 3-4, 1966, a week after their first visit. Quicksilver Messenger was the 3rd band. [Ref: members.shaw.ca/fz-pomd/giglist/]. [See also: Note 32].

[31] Once in July 1967 at Devonshire Meadows, Northridge CA; then not 'til June 1970 in Bath, England. [See: Internet]; [But see: previous Note]

[32] Ronald McKernan

[33] June 24-25, the weekend before *Freak Out!* was released on June 27, 1966

[34] This would make it the 1st visit.

[35] It was 1966! [Ref: globalia.net/donlope/fz/songs/Downtown_Talent_Scout]

[36] June 9-10, 1966

[37] June 27, 1966

[38] "For 1966 it was far out but it hung around 100 for three years in the charts." [Ref: JCB interview with Prism Film, Aug. 2008]

[39] Released June 29, 1966

[40] "The first TV show was in Washington, DC and we played 'Who Are The Brain Police' and really freaked out the audience as Carl Franzoni was touring with us. Those kids didn't know what to think of us and I remember that the switchboard at the station lit up like a Christmas tree with heavy complaints from irate parents all over the stations viewing area." [Ref: JCB interview with Steve Moore, 2003]

[41] "The *Detroit Free Press* claimed that 'If these Mothers move in next to you, your grass will die' and that about sums up how those people received us." [Ref: JCB interview with Steve Moore, 2003]

[42] Gail Sloatman accompanied Pamela Zarubica to the airport to meet the band. [Ref: Pamela Zarubica, in conversation]

[43] [JCB Comment:] Poster says June 23, AIAA Hall, Beverley Blvd with The Factory. Stated elsewhere as July 23, at Danish Center, L.A. It wasn't reported in the weekly *L.A. Free Press* until July 29, 1966. [members.shaw.ca:] records that the 'Ball' was moved from the AIAA to the Danish Center.

[44] Possession of "Acid" was criminalized just over three months later in the USA so it may well have been the last!

[45] Officially joins Aug 25, 1966 [Ref: globalia.net/donlope/fz/chronology/1965-1969]

[46] The Lindy Opera House?

[47] There is no firm record of the Mothers playing at the Avalon! [JCB:] The Family Dog was started by a "commune thing".

[48] Elliot was fired late Aug. 1966 [Ref: globalia.net/donlope/fz/chronology/1965-1969]

[49] [globalia.net/donlope/fz/chronology/1965-1969:] 'Big Leg Emma' was released as the B-side to 'Why Don't You Do Me Right' in April 1967, with Mar. 1967, not Oct. 1966, listed for the recording. Billy, Don and Bunk are credited on *Absolutely Free* which was recorded in Nov. of 1966.

[50] Held instead on Oct. 29, 1966

[51] [globalia.net/donlope/fz/chronology/1965-1969:] They weren't released until 1993, on the *Lightning-rod Man* album.

[52] Released Nov. 14, 1966

[53] Bunk Gardner says: "This would be late '65, early '66." [Ref: Billy James, *Necessity Is...*]

[54] Feb. 1967 [Ref: globalia.net/donlope/fz/chronology/1965-1969]

[55] On 'Another Pickup'

[56] Merle Haggard had a band called The Strangers but Jeremy Steig probably had his own band at this time called Jeremy Stieg and the Satyrs.

[57] Not possible, apparently.

Motor to Montreal

After the Balloon Farm, we hung around New York for about a week doing overdubs for *Absolutely Free*. Right after that we went up to Montreal for two weeks.

I left New York City at night with Motorhead who was driving the band truck on the way to Montreal, Canada. I had agreed to drive with him and help with the driving, as it was quite a ways to Montreal.

About three o'clock in the morning, we were pulled over by a State Trooper and I was very nervous since I had a stash of Grass on me. He ordered us out of the truck and started questioning us about where we were going. He wanted to know what all the equipment in the back of the truck was and Motor told him that we were in a band and were going to Montreal to start a two-week run of shows.

I told the cop that I had to take a piss pretty bad and he said to go up the hill and do it while he talked to Motor. I went up and took a piss and also deposited my drugs under a rock up there. When I went back down, he was searching all the equipment and then searched us. Everything passed the inspection, Motor had all the documentation on the equipment since we were going to need it when we hit the border. He actually turned out to be a pretty cool guy for a cop and let us go on our way.

I told Motor to get off at the next exit of the throughway and double back to where we got stopped. He did and I retrieved my wonderful stash because I didn't know if we could get anything in Montreal. As it turned out, we really didn't have that to worry about.

Photo above: courtesy Art Tripp

The New Penelope & Mrs. Gordon

The club was called the New Penelope. The owner had come down to the Balloon Farm to see us play and hired us for the two weeks up there - I remember he looked just like John Lennon. He was a hell of a nice guy as all the people at the club were, especially the blond girl who took the money because I had a brief affair with her that I'll never forget. Angie was her name and taking money was her game!

We stayed at Mrs. Gordon's Boarding House while we were in Montreal and she was a nice old lady. She lived in a house across the road from the annex that we stayed in and each guy had his own little bitty room. The doors to the rooms had little windows above them, so if you got up on a chair you could look into the rooms. There was a nice girl staying there and Roy got into window peeking on her late at night. He'd get a chair out there by her door, get up on it and look in on her. The girl saw him peeking one night and she reported what he was doing to Mrs. Gordon, so she promptly moved him out of that house and moved him into her house. She made him stay right next to her where she could keep an eye on him. She had him under her wing, so to speak.

We also did some recording for the Canadian Film Board[1] while we were there. I think it was for a movie or documentary.

After we finished in Montreal and flew back to L.A., Jim Fielder left the band - he hadn't been too happy playing second guitar. He went off to join Buffalo Springfield but he wasn't with them for very long before he went back to New York and joined Blood Sweat and Tears.

The Lindy Opera House

When we arrived back in L.A., the marquee outside the Lindy Opera House on Wiltshire Boulevard had a big sign advertising "The Mothers of Invention". They'd started getting phone calls from all these housewives and mothers who were inventors. They thought it was some kind of show for inventions that were made by mothers! They certainly had no idea who the band was.

Herb had arranged for us to rehearse at the Lindy for two weeks before the big show we were going to do there, as it wasn't being used at that time. I remember Van Dyke Parks would often come down to those rehearsals, as he was a big fan of the Mothers. One time, he walked in with Brian Wilson from the Beach Boys. Brian seemed like a nice guy - he was very quiet and pleasant and seemed to be interested in what we were doing.

That's when we rehearsed 'Lonesome Cowboy Burt' for the first time. God, we rehearsed that thing for about two weeks. It was exactly the same arrangement as we did later on in *200 Motels.*

Back in San Francisco

Two weeks after we did the Lindy show, we went back to San Francisco and did the Fillmore again with The Blues Project and Canned Heat. We did the debut of 'Lonesome Cowboy Burt' and Herb came up to Frank at the end of that show and said, "If you ever play that song again, you can forget me as manager!"

Those shows[2] were sort of "debuting" the new band on the West Coast and introducing the new material that we were doing.

I also met Charlie Manson in San Francisco. There was a guy called Bobby that I knew who had been part of Vito's crowd in L.A. before he'd moved up there. I was over at his place and it was kind of like a commune. Manson was hanging around there and I was introduced to him briefly (thank God for that). I noticed that everyone was calling Bobby "Cupid" and there seemed to be a strange vibe going on around the place. Little did I know what those people were going to get up to not too long in the future. As it turns out, Bobby (or Cupid as he was now known) is the one who killed that music teacher in Topanga Canyon on orders from Manson. It was very hard for me to believe that he could do that because he was always such a nice guy. He had just been part of a non-violent group of people, hanging around the Hollywood freak scene. It seems that Manson had brainwashed him, along with several other hippie kids.

In March, we were finally ready to leave for New York and it was a major move. We had to get out of California because we couldn't get much more work there and on the East Coast there was a lot of opportunities to do so. There were so many big cities within a two-hour drive from New York and we had a contract to play at the Garrick Theater in Greenwich Village for two weeks over the Easter[3] holiday.

The band bought a big new Ford Econoline van for the equipment. Roy and Motor drove the van with all our equipment plus Tim Buckley's gear to New York. Herb was now Tim's manager and so it's going to be Tim's first visit to New York as he had a new album out on Electra that he was promoting. Now we had a Vega PA system, which were two of those big A7 speakers but I don't know whether it was leased or what. We might have bought it for all I know, but I don't think so.

It took those guys about three days to get across the country and somehow they managed to wreck the new van or at least managed to put the first big dent in it. Neither of those two Californians was used to driving anywhere

where it was icy. I think Roy was driving and of course, wired to the gills on Speed. Roy had scored a massive jar of Uppers - at least a thousand of them! They looked like M&M candies with four different colors and each color was a different strength. That jar lasted him only a few weeks!

The Garrick

The Garrick was situated on Bleeker Street, Greenwich Village, NYC and right above the Café Au Go Go, which was hosting a whole bunch of new "happening" bands. The whole building was being leased by Howie Solomon and he had quite a little scene happening there. The Village was buzzing, I must say. There were stairs backstage that went right down into the kitchen of the Café Au Go Go. As we had the run of the place, we could go down and get coffee and things whenever we wanted.

All the students were out of school, because of the Easter holidays and were coming into the city. There were lines of people wanting to get in and sometimes, especially on the weekends, we were having to play three shows a night because the theater only seated about 250 people. Richie Havens[4] would open for us and play about 35 minutes and then we'd play for about one hour. They would empty the theater out after the first show and there would be about a thirty-minute intermission. Then Richie would start playing all over again and on and on. It was $3 admission on a weekend and I think $2 during the week. Some guys would get in line and buy tickets again - it seemed to me that they couldn't get enough of us.

Right after Easter, we shut down the theater for one night and took a bus to the University Of Maryland to play an audition[5] for the college circuit.

Eventually, we would get some good work out of it because later on we played Princeton, Colgate and Harvard Colleges. During the Garrick run, we'd close for the occasional night and would go and play one of those gigs.

Staying in NY

After we had done the Easter run is when Frank and Herb decided, "Well, if it's going this well, let's do an extended run for as long as we can do it!"

About a month later,[6] I had my wife and the four kids get on the plane and move to New York.

We had all been staying at the Hotel Albert but now we all started looking for flats, which in New York City are not easy to find. You'd go

Photo above: courtesy Art Tripp; Jimmy & Frank Zappa

down on Friday and buy the Village Voice and try to be the first one to the phone to get a flat. Bunk, Don and Roy got a flat together.

Dick Barber and Bobby Zappa came out from L.A. to join us after we had decided that we were going to make the Garrick Theater our base for a while. Bobby was responsible for taking the money at the ticket booth and Dick became kind of like the road manager, like the bouncer, like the gofer, but a little bit more. Herb was grooming him to really become our road manager, which he did and did it great. Dick had been a semi-pro football player who had just graduated from college, and him and Bobby were old school chums. Bobby was a nice guy and stayed with the band for the summer. Dick stayed with us. Dick had known Frank for many years and so when it became clear that we were going to need someone to organize us all on the road, Dick was the man. He was also responsible for the "snorks" that you hear on a lot of those early albums.

By now we were getting a salary or rather, a "draw" as they would call it because we were all still partners, supposedly. While we were at the Garrick we were receiving $200 a week each. At the end of the run, we were supposed to divide up the profits but of course, at the end there were no profits. In fact we owed them money! Somehow, we always owed Frank and Herb money. No matter how successful the band was, we always owed them money! I still don't know what for because they never would prove what it was for.

Richie Havens
Richie Havens did the support for almost the whole run and every once in a while he'd bring in a Tabla player to play with him. Sometimes he would have another gig in some other place so we'd bring in The Gary Burton Quartet. At that time, he had Larry Coryell on guitar, Joe MacDonald on drums and Eddie Gomez on bass.

On a couple of occasions, Tiny Tim opened for us, until 'Tip Toe Through The Tulips' got too big.

Playing the Trumpet Again
After we had decided to stay on, Frank started changing the arrangements to some of the songs and we started to improvise a lot more too. That would be about the time that we started doing a lot more of the extended things like 'King Kong'.

Frank persuaded me to go down and buy a trumpet. I hadn't played it for many years but I got my "chops"[7] sort of back. I bought a bass trumpet because it was easier to play and had a bigger mouthpiece. So, he was writing trumpet parts for me and I didn't have any problem with them as I could still read trumpet music. For a time, Bunk and I were the horn section when I wasn't playing the drums.

Every once in a while I would bring my two boys, Gary and Darrell, down to the theater to watch us perform. They would sit on the edge of the stage and watch with great interest what was going on - maybe one of the reasons that the boys are now professional musicians and very good ones.

At least, that is what they always tell me.

Don's Comic Book

Don had acquired a couple more keyboards and so now he was surrounded by keyboards. One time, we were playing a song and Don didn't have anything to play until a certain place. I can't remember what song it was but when we got to that part of the song, nothing happened. Frank looks around and there's Don sitting back with his feet propped up on the keyboard reading a Dr. Strange comic book. Frank just stops the band; we were stopped for a few minutes! Don was still reading because he didn't even realize that we had stopped and Frank was waiting for him to look up. Eventually Don looked up and his eyes got about as big as saucers. Frank was shooting daggers at him. He was saying with his eyes, "You've fucked up Don! Put that fuckin' comic book away, Don!" This all happened right in the middle of the show.

Café Au Go Go

We started meeting a lot of the other bands who were playing downstairs at the Café Au Go Go. People like Blood Sweat and Tears (with my old pal, Jim Fielder) were just getting together, and The Blues Project with Al Kooper and all those guys. The Paul Butterfield Blues Band would come up and listen to our show, and while Richie was on, we'd go down and check them out.

I used to go across the street to a bar called The Dugout with Elvin Bishop and we would have a few "Boiler Makers". The ingredients for one of those drinks is a glass of beer and a shot glass of Beefeaters Gin, and you would drink the beer down a little and then drop the shot glass into the beer. A couple of those drinks and a person could be flying pretty good. Elvin was a guy that was really living the blues. He was also a great guitarist.

Photos above: Gary, 1st Grade; Darrell, Kindergarten; 1965-66

When the Grateful Dead were playing down in the Café, we used to go and hang out with them. Of course Frank knew what those guys were like and normally up to, in regards to drugs, and he knew what we were like as well, so he was always on the prowl checking on us!

DMT & LSD

I smoked some DMT one night just before a show and decided immediately that I would never do that again! It felt like I had two rockets attached to the side of my head. I went way past the fuckin' moon for about 45 minutes. Man! That was a fuckin' intense Trip and I had to play at the same time! I decided then that this music of Frank's is not that easy and so I had better not get that high when I'm playing. Of course Acid was happening and we were doing Acid at the time, but I never did Acid when I was gigging. I used to smoke Pot before playing but it really didn't affect my concentration that much.

Motorhead & Joni

Motorhead had found himself a girlfriend by then. She was a nice girl who used to come and hang out with us and her name was Joni Mitchell - a very nice, little, hippie chick from Canada. Hell, we didn't know that she could even sing, especially the way she did.

Sandy Hurvitz

A girl called Sandy Hurvitz (who became Essra Mohawk) started to hang around the Village. She was a songwriter from Pennsylvania and was also a very good pianist and a good singer. She used to come to the Garrick and watch the shows we were doing. That is where she first met Frank and they became good friends. Sandy introduced Frank to an artist friend of hers called Cal Schenkel. Frank saw all his work, liked it and hired him right away. Sandy started to play with us a little bit. She was very young at that time and was still in her teens. She was given the stage name "Uncle Meat". She liked to hang with us quite a lot, especially with Don and Bunk!

Frank started to produce some sessions for her because she'd signed with Herb and Frank to do an album. We recorded some basic sessions, but it seems that Frank changed his mind, so the job was passed over to Ian [Underwood] - after he joined the band - to produce the material that was released on her album, *Sandy's Album is Here at Last*. Don and Bunk both trading off with her might have created a few problems.

Frank and Gail were living in a flat in the Village. Cal ended up living there, along with Dick and Bobby. I think Motorhead was there part of the time and Pam (Suzy Creamcheese) was also staying there too. She had just come back from England and was full blown pregnant.

The Garrick Audience

All these freaks were starting to come out of the woodwork. We gave them all names like "Larry the Seal", "Louie the Turkey" and "Loeb and Leopold" because these crazies hardly ever missed a show. Frank used to get Loeb and Leopold up on the stage. They loved to get down on the floor of the stage and have Frank spit coke all over them. They liked that although I don't know why, except maybe it made them feel like they were part of the show, which they were in a way.

One guy had just come up from Mexico and his name was Sal. He was from San Francisco, but he'd been living in Mexico for a couple of years with the Indians and he looked like a guy right out of the bush. I mean, this guy's hair was out there and he was as wild as shit, with buckskin clothes on. He kind of worked with the band for a while during our shows. We would send him out into the audience for volunteers to do stunts on stage. If no one would volunteer, he would just go and get girls, yank them out of their seat, throw them over his shoulder and carry them (kind of cave-man style) up to the stage and Frank would make them do things up there. After all, the show was officially listed as an Off-Off-Broadway Production!

One night, Sal got a volunteer up there that wanted to fuck Frank on the stage. He was really trying to keep her away with his guitar and then she started fucking the neck of his guitar. He had to get Dick Barber to come up and get her off the stage because she was going to do him. "You want to fuck around with this stuff? OK, let's fuck around with it, Man!" were her exact words. I think she was there to teach him a lesson and it was pretty interesting. That was the first time that it ever backfired on him at the Garrick but not the last time that it was to backfire. That is another story for later![8]

We ran this thin wire cable from the projection room. Motorhead ran the sound from up there because he was a sort of our soundman, amongst the many other things that he did. In the middle of 'Call Any Vegetable', he would send vegetables down on this pulley. They'd go right across the people heads and straight onto the stage. Then we would throw them into the audience.

There was an old upright piano at the side of the stage and we used to hide all our toys and things behind it. When I wasn't playing drums and Ray wasn't singing, we used to do puppet shows and things like that from behind that piano. While the music was going on, we had a chance to be extremely creative!

Hand Signals & Stage Directions

The hand signals had started by then. We had different ones for silly vocal noises and some were for time changes. We would be in the middle of some song and Frank would take us off someplace and then he would jump up in the air and we'd come right back in were we'd left the thing. It was like he was doing simultaneous cutting, like he would cut tape in the studio.

The Giraffe gets into the Act
Then there were three very beautiful girls from Long Island who went to private school and were probably from very wealthy families. They looked as straight as three arrows but they weren't that straight. They became regulars at the theater and that's when they brought the stuffed toy giraffe to us. That afternoon, Ray and I got this length of clear plastic tube and did some alterations, then went down stairs and got about 10 cans of pressurized whipped cream from the Café Au Go Go.

We got the giraffe and set it up right in the middle of the stage. Actually, right by where Frank was standing with his guitar. We ran the tube right up the side of the giraffe and cut a hole right under the tail where the asshole would be. Frank didn't have any idea what was going on because he didn't pay any attention to what we were up to. The band was doing one of those solo, improvised sections and Ray and I got behind the piano and started filling the tube up with whipped cream. We got that baby full and then got a brand new can inserted into the tube. When we hit the button on that can, the giraffe exploded and the cream went everywhere. It just splattered people. Man! That shit was all over them! I tell you, it nailed the first three rows. Frank just couldn't believe it. He was laughing so fucking hard that the music stopped and he was on the ground rolling. He couldn't believe it, Man! Neither could anyone else, especially the audience! We had topped him on anything that he could have thought of to do with the audience. We beat him to the punch on that one, Man! That's one of the most famous stunts that happened there during the whole Garrick run. I'll never forget that one.

This was getting on into June and it was starting to get sort of warm in the theater at night. The air conditioning had seemed to work fine until that night. But the thing is, when the air conditioning went off that night, that cream was all over the seats and nobody cleaned it up. About a week later, that theater was starting to smell like vomit. I mean, it stunk! Nobody would sit in the first three rows but it didn't stop people from coming to the shows, probably because they wanted to know what we would do next for their entertainment. The people still came and we'd fill the place - except for those first 24 seats there in the front!

Absolutely Free Released[9]

Frank was really pissed off at MGM because it took a long time to get *Absolutely Free* released. What he wanted was total control over his products, which is what they were promising with the Bizarre Records deal. Frank wanted to be able to complete an album/product then simply hand it over to the company for the agreed fee.

MGM held the album up because they weren't happy about the words "she's only 13 and she knows how to nasty" they wanted to change it to "she's only 16 and she knows how to nasty". Had the album not been held up, it would have been the first album with no spaces between the tracks to ever be released.

As it happened *Sergeant Pepper's Lonely Hearts Club Band* came out first. At that time, I thought it was just about the best thing I had ever heard. I wore out the first copy in about three weeks. I still think fondly of that album.

 In June,[10] we decided to re-promote the Garrick. The album was finally being released and so they wanted to do a big promotion thing. We started advertising it as an "Off-Off-Broadway Show" although we had already been calling the show that. So, on the marquee outside the theater it said, *"Absolutely Freeee"*.

We got all the newspapers down to review the show and needless to say they were mixed. That's when the *Wall Street Journal* called us "Hells Angels without their bikes" and said it was nothing but a bunch of noise. "These guys are too weird for us." But, in the *Village Voice* we got an excellent review and in the *New York Times* too. After that, it started getting packed again and so the shows were doing quite well. People started to call us the innovators of "The Theater of the Absurd".

Frank had an old hi-hat pedal right next to his guitar and he took a glove with the middle finger sticking straight up so he could give a FUCK YOU sign to anybody and everybody and that's when he got his first Wah-Wah pedal.

Frank was really trying to get the audience involved in the show because that was one of his main goals. He wanted to get them to feel like they were part of the show. He used to get people to come up on to the stage and he'd make them do little skits and things like that while the band would be playing improvised music.

I seem to remember we did a TV show in New York City, but I can't remember which one it was. We did do an audition for The Ed Sullivan

Show, but of course Ed didn't want to have anything to do with us. I am sure that we were way TOO FREAKY for him.

 In June, Cal was working on the cover design for *We're Only In It For The Money*. He had a little workroom above the theater where he was putting all the mannequins and things together for the cover. When he had finished them all, we went to Jerry Schatzberg who was a famous photographer on Park Avenue and that's where we shot the actual pictures.[11]

Jimi Hendrix was in the Village that week we did the album cover. He was back in America for the first time since he'd made it big in England. He'd come back to headline at The Monterey Pop Festival. He's not a cardboard prop on the album cover because he was actually with us at the shoot. For the record, the other black guy on there is Tom Wilson, the guy with my high school letterman's sweater on.

Jimi was hanging around his old haunts in the Village and he used to come down and he'd be wearing his silk jackets, plumes and all that. People flipped out over that because it was not until a few months later that we started wearing all that stuff. He jammed with us on a few things and he played on Frank's guitar - he just flipped that big old Gibson upside down!

Ian Underwood
You know, that summertime was really great there in the Village and we'd be outside on our break because it was cooler outside than in that fuckin' theater. I'd gone outside one evening on our break and that's when Ian Underwood came up to me and said, "Hey Man! I play sax and keyboards and I want to play with the Mothers!" He had just graduated from Berkeley School of Music in Boston and had been coming to the shows. I said, "Well, you'll have to talk to Frank." He asked me if he could meet Frank so I went and found Frank and told him about Ian.

Ian auditioned at one of the rehearsals and Frank said, "What can you do that's fantastic?" and Ian whipped it out. Then Frank put some music in front of him. I am sure it was something pretty difficult, that I think he'd just written. It was the introduction to 'Absolutely Free'. Ian just sight-read that thing and Frank just said, "You're in the band."

Ray & Don Quit
In July, Ray and Don quit the band and went back to L.A.[12] As usual, Ray quit because he couldn't take Frank anymore. Don also quit because he couldn't take it anymore and he said he'd been away from his wife, Rowena, and the two kids for too long.

I think that's when Sandy was sitting in with us and Ian was playing a little bit of keyboards as well. It really was a loss to have Don leave the band because he was the guy who did all the electronic stuff. Ian really didn't understand all that shit but Don, even with the limited equipment that he had in those days, was amazing.

When Don arrived back in L.A., he went to the house, knocked on the door and there was this big black guy, living there with his wife. Don just turned right back around, marched out of the house and went straight on the phone to Frank, "Do you mind if I rejoin the band?" So Don was only gone for about a week.

I think Ray was gone for longer than three or four months[13] because he didn't record on *We're Only In It For The Money*. When he did come back, we had already done *...Money* and Frank didn't want or need Ray's vocals as we had already sussed them out. At least he was there to do the vocals on *Ruben & The Jets* - which I believe Frank did especially for Ray - and for *Uncle Meat*. We were learning lots of new material.

I think Herb had secured the deal with Warner Bros or it was at least in the works, and it was looking good because *Ruben & The Jets* was the last album we owed MGM.[14]

Tom Wilson would often turn up at the Garrick and he was often around during the recordings but he understood that Frank knew exactly what he was doing. He pretty much left him to get on with it because he knew how important it was for Frank to do his own production.[15] Tom was a really spot on dude, in my opinion.

Rehearsals

Frank had delegated the job of rehearsing the band to Ian as he had now become second-in-command. I used to think of him as the musical director and he was very good at it.

Don was a little resentful about it because he thought he could have done the job and had been in the band longer than Ian. I thought it was better the way it was.

Frank was still at all the rehearsals and he was getting better and better on the guitar. He was becoming a premier guitar player, one of the best in the world in my opinion.

The Marines at the Garrick

The first time that *Time* magazine did an article on the Mothers was at the Garrick Theater. The afternoon before they came to take pictures of us playing a theater show, three marines came to Frank and said that they wanted to do something on the stage with us that would get them kicked out of the Marine Corp. We staged a skit for them where we would start playing some song and they would mutilate some dolls on the stage and while doing it would be singing "Kill, Kill, Kill" to the beat.[16]

After the article came out, they got their wish. They all received a Dishonorable Discharge which is the worst you can get. At least they didn't have to go to Vietnam and that is why they did it in the first place.

Mayfair Studios
Around August, we were only doing about three nights a week. We had cut it down to Thursday, Friday and Saturday because the rest of the week we were in Mayfair Studios recording a bunch of the new material for *We're Only In It For The Money*. Herb and Frank took a four-day trip to London and started setting up the press reviews for our first European tour which was going to be in September.

The First Woodstock Festival
We finally finished our run at the Garrick in the last week in August[17] and were getting ready to leave for Europe. I moved my family out of the Hotel Albert and we moved up to a little town called Woodstock in upstate New York. We rented a house up there. The town is situated about 90 miles directly north of New York City, up in the Catskill Mountains, near the Hudson River. At that time it was mainly a community of artists, musicians and sculptors. There were a lot of bands and musicians living there also: Bob Dylan, The Band, and Peter Paul and Mary were living up there. Dylan's manager, Albert Grossman, had his Bearsville studio up there. Barry Feinstein (who had filmed us at the Fillmore in 1966), was married to Mary (Travers) at that time.

We kind of had a little two-week holiday so we just hung around up in Woodstock. Billy Mundi had moved up there also. I believe that Frank went back to England to do some more press for the forthcoming Royal Albert Hall show. An interesting fact was that Frank never took a holiday, he didn't believe in holidays. I believe that that is one of the reasons why he died as young as he did, Man!

That's also the time that Frank and Gail got married. It was just before we went to Europe and just before Moon was born. My wife Loretta was also pregnant with my youngest son Geronimo at the time.

I helped this guy called Jacko put on a little festival up there and you could say it was the very first Woodstock Festival. We had Richie Havens, Jake and The Family Jewels - Jake was the bass player from The Fugs - and Don Preston did "Electronic Music". It was held in a big church and it was actually called "The Woodstock Festival". I tried to get the Mothers to play but Frank was busy in the studio getting ready for the tour to Europe and besides, he didn't want to go up there with a bunch of fuckin' hippies.

Our First European Tour

Everything was arranged for our first European tour. Billy Mundi and I left Woodstock on 13th September and everybody met at Frank's place on Charles Street.

Besides all the guys in the band, there was Dick Barber, Sandy and Pamela, Herb and his wife Suzy, Howie Solomon and his wife, and Tom Wilson. They'd chartered a bus to take us to the airport with all our equipment. Dick Barber was now officially our road manager and he had quite a job because it was quite an entourage. Fifteen of us went to Europe.

Frank, Tom, Pam and Herb, Howie and their wives all check into the London Hilton or the Palace or whatever it's called there on Hyde Park.[18] The rest of us checked into a little hotel which was only a couple of blocks away from the Royal Albert Hall. They didn't want us to stay too close to where the interviews were happening.

Frank told us, "I can't stay with you guys because we have to have a nice suite to do interviews in!" and he was probably right because they were doing a lot of press at that time, just tons on interviews. The rest of the band weren't allowed to do any interviews and that's one of the reasons why Dick Barber was there. His job was to keep the press away from us because we were always told: "Do not do any interviews!" and "Don't talk to anyone from the press!" That was fine by me because we were having a lot of fun tripping around London, going to all the neat shops and looking at the new English "Mod" clothing. We were wishing we had some money to buy something. Every third day, we would get £30 each "per diem"[19] and they were paying our hotels and meals and that shit, so we had some pocket money.

We didn't take much of our own equipment on that tour. Frank took his guitar and his Fuzz and Wah-Wah pedal, Roy had his bass and the guys took their horns. I think Don may have taken a couple of his keyboards but all I took was my sticks. Billy and I played Premiere drums and I think Frank and the guys played through Vox amps.

The Royal Albert Hall

I think we were the first Rock band to play at the Royal Albert Hall. We did the show and I thought it was a huge success. I don't know how many people were there but the hall looked pretty full to me, the balcony was full.

We played two sets and we had a ten-piece orchestra who played on a few things. They probably played on the songs we'd done on *Freak Out!* They may have played a little bit of an intro before we played and I think Frank may have written something special for them to do.

There were a lot of famous musicians who'd come to see us. I know that Jagger and Richards were there and some of The Beatles too, although I didn't get to meet any of them. There were scores of other musicians there like the Animals and I think that's where it came out in the press that Eric Burdon called Frank "a little Hitler".

Jeff Beck was there and that's where I first met Graham Nash because he came backstage. I remember I went around to his house one time and took some "Purple Owsley".[20] He was still in The Hollies at that time.

So, after the show, we had a big backstage party and, of course, we took the remnants of the party, which were the girls, over to the hotel. That's where I got my first piece of "London Ass" and it was great.

Amsterdam

The next day, we flew to Amsterdam to play a gig at the Concertgebouw and we stayed in a really beautiful hotel that was attached to the hall. We had a night off and we went to the Paradiso Club which had just opened up. It was an old church that had been converted into this club and was somehow supported by the state. When we walked in, there was a little table with five different kinds of "Hash"[21] that you could buy. It was totally amazing - it was legal to smoke it although you couldn't take it out of the building. I remember I bought a big piece of Hash for five Guilders and a Heineken beer on tap cost one and a half Guilders. Needless to say, we hung out there all night. That was my initiation to Holland and I've enjoyed going back there ever since!

Denmark & Sweden

Then we flew to Copenhagen and we had four or five days off, so we were just there checking the scene out: meeting lots of musicians, going to clubs, getting laid, taking Acid and all those kinds of things. Frank and Herb flew to Italy for a meeting with Roger Vadim as he was making the *Barbarella* movie. There were some discussions about using some of Frank's music in the film.

We travelled to Gothenburg where we were meeting back up with Frank, to play the first gig in Sweden. The gig was in a beautiful hall, all painted white with plush velvet green chairs. We played the gig and noticed that Frank wasn't feeling too good. He had eaten some food while he was in Italy and developed food poisoning.

The next day we flew to Stockholm and by this time Frank was getting really ill. By the time we did the sound-check, Frank was very weak and we didn't know what was going to happen. We didn't know whether we would have to cancel the show. He played the first half of the show but he was so fuckin' ill that he couldn't go back on, so we went out and did the second part without Frank.

Ray wanted to be the leader but Ian really took over as musical director and directed the whole thing. Frank made a set list of what to play. Pam had to take him to the hotel and she took care of him. I think Sandy played with us for the second half of the show.

The next day we flew back to Copenhagen to play at the Falkoner Theater. Frank had been to the doctor and maybe even had his stomach pumped. He was very weak but at least he was OK. Motorhead was travelling with the gear and a Dutch truck driver we had hired. Something happened to the van. We got there in time for the gig but the equipment wasn't there. We ended up using equipment borrowed from John Mayall and The Blues Breakers. They had played the night before and were staying at the same hotel. At that time, they had Mick Fleetwood and John McVie on drums and bass and they also had Mick Taylor with them on guitar. He was only about 17 years old and a young kid but a great player. They were promoting their *Crusade* album and he gave me a copy. I got them all to sign it. I've still got that album, although I think my family has it in Texas.

So, we did that show using their equipment and Billy played on Mick Fleetwood's drums. We somehow found a trombone player who had a valve trombone, which is very similar to a bass trumpet, so that's what I played. We didn't have the kettledrums or the other percussion stuff that we usually played. Luckily, the horn players had their horns because they would never leave them with the equipment. Frank had his guitar and Roy had his bass but I don't know what we did for keyboards. However, we played the show and it was a success.

There was one more show left, so we took the ferryboat back across to Sweden and played at the University of Lund. We travelled back on the ferry, spent the night in the hotel and went to Copenhagen airport to fly back to London. That's where we met Peter Sellers, in the airport, and Billy Mundi almost came unglued because he was such a big fan. We flew on the same plane with Peter to London. Then we flew on to New York and I went straight back out to Woodstock. I will say that the first European tour for the MOI was a total success.

BITTER END About a week after we got back to New York, we did the *Bitter End* TV show. We were going to be playing 'Suzy Creamcheese, What's Got Into Ya' but they wouldn't let us play it live, they made us lip-sync it. Frank was so fuckin' pissed off about that. As we were about to go on he said, "Listen, instead of mouthing the real words, mouth "motherfucker" all the way through the thing!"

When the show was broadcast they censored it. The picture went off. You could hear the music but they cut out the picture of us mouthing "motherfucker". My wife was watching it up at my house in Woodstock when the picture just went off the air.

HIPPIES *Welcome* *Always* Ray, Don and Bunk moved up to Woodstock, so over half the band was living up there. We were only playing about two gigs a month. Mainly, we were back in the studio finishing *We're Only In It For The Money*. Everybody hung out in the Tinker Street Café up there. The Band were always in the place drinking coffee. They were cool dudes and we jammed a little bit up at their house - The Big Pink - which was in the next town along called Saugerties. They had a little studio in the basement and they were playing all the time. They'd been playing with Dylan, but he'd had that motorbike accident so they weren't doing that much. I was a big fan of their music.

Mister Dylan lived about a quarter of a mile further up the hill from me on Upper Byrdcliffe Road, where he was recuperating from his motorcycle accident. I used to see him go by everyday in his station wagon and then every Sunday he went by in his Limo. I never knew him but we used to wave to each other. He was a bit of a recluse. We had a sled run that ran down from our house and stopped very close to the road. One day, my son Darrell was hauling ass down that hill and slid out into the road just as Bob was coming down. He threw on the brakes and almost hit Darrell. 'E just got out of his car and said, "Watch it, you little fucker." and got back in the car and continued on his mission. That, for my son, is a claim to fame.

There was a band called The Ultimate Spinach who later turned into Steely Dan. They never toured or anything, they just made albums and seemed to be writing all the time. I really liked those guys and was a big fan of their music. The Blues Magoos and The Electric Prunes were living up there too. Richie Havens used to come up a lot and sometimes he'd stay with me (I knew him from the Garrick days, of course). He is one of the nicest guys I ever met and I appreciated his wonderful music.[22]

Uncle Meat

Uncle Meat was the first album on Reprise and we got $29,000 to do the album. Actually, it was released on Bizarre Records, which was distributed by Reprise Records.[23]

We weren't working that much because of the studio commitments and I was having a hell of a time paying my rent in Woodstock. During one of those recording sessions, Frank and I had our little discussion about "If We'd All Been Living in California…"[24] I had absolutely no idea that it was going to end up on an album. I couldn't believe it when it came out. I said, "This was a band meeting - What's it doing on here?" and Frank just said, "Well, you know, I thought it was interesting and I thought it needed to be on the album!" End of conversation! I didn't even get any writer's credit for that because the albums cover states that everything was written by Frank Zappa.

Now, how can you write a band meeting? There wasn't even a script to follow. It was the same as when Frank told me to get on the microphone and start talking. I said, "Hi boys and girls, I'm Jimmy Carl Black and I'm the Indian of the Group" - that was on the album *We're Only In It For The Money* a few months earlier.[25]

Lean Meat

Right after we had that band meeting, Ray Collins quit the band again and went back to California.[26] Once again we were without a lead singer, so that's when all those songs from *We're Only In It For The Money* were arranged into larger instrumental medleys.[27] So many of the songs we had recorded were played as instrumentals when we played live. That was the time when 'The Son of Orange County' came into existence. It still is a great medley.

I think we played Rochester.[28] And we played up in Boston at the Psychedelic Supermarket which was our first time in Boston.[29]

When Ray wasn't around, there were really only three of us in the band that were singing. Roy, Frank and myself and, of course, Roy and I were doing mainly background vocals. Frank had his own style of singing and really I liked what he did. I thought he was hilarious because he kind of made a joke out of singing and he was more of a rapper - way before rap music was invented. Frank never thought that he was a singer but I have to differ with him on that. I thought he was one of the best singers around. He had his own style just like Ray Collins had his.

Back on the West Coast[30]

We flew back out to California and did three nights at the Fillmore West,[31] and shows in Pasadena and Santa Monica[32] and we even went back and played at the Whisky[33] one night which was more of a favor to Val[34] than anything else. We would often see Mark and Howie from The Turtles sitting out in the front because they always like to come and see the Mothers. We did play a gig with The Turtles one time in Allentown, Pennsylvania.[35]

Just before Christmas, we played at the New York Town Hall,[36] which was a block away from Carnegie Hall - the closest we were ever going to get to playing there! The opening act for that gig was The Hamilton Face Band, which featured Ruth Komanoff on drums. That was the first time that I actually met Ruth and I thought she was very sweet and I loved her. She was a great gal and still is as far as I'm concerned.

She and Ian were starting to go together at that time and the following year would get married.

The day after Christmas, we left for Philadelphia where we played for five nights at the Trauma club ending on New Year's Eve. I remember that I sure got a lot of pussy in Philadelphia. I think I had a different groupie every night because the Mothers were actually sort of becoming rock stars, so to speak.

by Geronimo Black

At that time we were getting $200 a show, so if we did four shows a week it was real good money - but that was short-lived!

Notes to Chapter 6

[1] *Ride for your life*, directed by Robin Spry
[2] MOI also played at Fillmore with Otis Rush and Morning Glory two weeks later in early March, before moving to the Garrick in NY.
[3] Easter Sunday was March 26, in 1967
[4] Tim Buckley opened for the first 7 nights, Richie Havens the last 5.

[5] For the 20th National Students Congress being hosted at Maryland Uni. Aug. 13-16, 1967?
[6] Early May
[7] "chops" = skills, ability to play proficiently
[8] Toronto, Jan. 1968
[9] June 26, 1967
[10] The band re-opened at the Garrick on May 24, 1967
[Ref: "Mothers of Invention at the Garrick", *New York Times* Archives, May 25, 1967]
[11] Jerrold Schatzberg, on July 18 [Ref: globalia.net/donlope/fz/chronology/1965-1969]
[12] Though Ray quit around this time, Don most likely quit late Sept./early Oct. '66
[Ref: globalia.net/donlope/fz/chronology/1965-1969]
[13] Probably no more than three months, from late June to early September
[14] Not recorded until sometime between Dec. 1967-Feb. 1968
[Ref: globalia.net/donlope/fz/lyrics/Cruising_With_Ruben_and_The_Jets]
[15] Tom Wilson doesn't feature after *WOIIFTMoney* where he is credited as Executive Producer
[16] Perhaps, inspired by Arlo Guthrie's 'Alice's Restaurant Massacree'?
[17] First week of Sept. [Ref: members.shaw.ca/fz-pomd/giglist/1967]
[18] Kensington Palace Hotel?
[19] "per diem" = daily, so in this case £90 for three day
[20] LSD
[21] Hashish
[22] Died April 22, 2013
[23] Recorded between Oct. 1967 and Feb. 1968 but not released until April 21, 1969
[24] On *Uncle Meat* recorded between Oct. 1967 and Feb. 1968
The dialogue suggests that the session was around late October. The sketchy gig listings for this period confirm one gig in October following the band's return from Europe. [See: Jimmy's comment in the dialogue to having worked one gig this month.] The narrative speaks of Ray leaving the band again after this meeting, ergo late Oct. early Nov. 1967.
[25] Recorded mostly during the first week of Aug. 1967 "...a few months earlier" suggests the recording session discussion took place late in the year. [See: previous Note]
[26] Ray quits the band again sometime in Oct. 1967.
[Ref: globalia.net/donlope/fz/chronology/1965-1969]
[27] Recorded At Mayfair Studios, NYC Aug 2-9, 1967
[Ref: globalia.net/donlope/fz/chronology/]
[28] War Memorial Theater, Rochester, Oct. 28, 1967. Another venue around this time was the Eastern High School in Baltimore, Nov. 3, 1967 [Ref: members.shaw.ca/fz-pomd/giglist/]
[29] Nov. 24-25. JCB is apparently wrong in saying this was the Band's first trip to Boston. They had played the "Annual Festival of Music" at the Commonwealth Armory, April 20-23, 1967, featuring Jefferson Airplane amongst others.
[30] This may have been when Ray returned to the fold.
[31] The Fillmore Auditorium, known also as the Fillmore West now, to distinguish it from the newer Fillmore East.
[32] Pasadena on Dec. 9, Fillmore West on Dec 14, Winterland on Dec 15-16, 1967. No record of Santa Monica has popped up yet but the previous week MOI had been in Michigan, at the Ford Auditorium in Detroit and at the Fifth Dimension in Ann Arbor (home of the University of Michigan).
[33] An impromptu gig?
[34] Elmer Valentine, L.A. Mafia boss according to JCB - more than just a favor?
[35] April 26, 1969
[36] Dec. 22-23, 1969

The first three months of 1968, were spent either in the studio or out on the road playing gigs.[1] The majority of the material that was released on the *Uncle Meat* album, all of *Ruben & The Jets*, and sections of *Weasels Ripped My Flesh* and *Burnt Weeny Sandwich* were recorded during this highly prolific period.[2] We also finally finished everything on *We're Only In It For The Money.*

Ruben's Return

I really enjoyed doing all those Doo-Wop songs because I really love that music and I know that Frank did too! You know, in a way, I think that Frank had decided to do a lot of those things for Ray because Ray sang that kind of music so well. *Ruben & The Jets*[3] is still my favorite of all the Mothers albums that we did. We'd been concentrating on instrumental music for quite some time because, when Ray had left, we didn't have a lead singer and had to do more instrumentals. Ray had left us a whole bunch of times[4] and so maybe Frank felt that it was time to do some stuff that featured him. Ray sings those songs so well, Man! 'I'm Not Satisfied' is one of my all time favorites.

Ruth Komanoff came and did some percussion overdubs on *Uncle Meat* that sounded just wonderful. She and Artie [Tripp] were so talented as readers and, of course, players.

Dick Kunc

Most all that material that came out on the next bunch of albums was being recorded at the same time because we didn't just go in and record one album. It was all being done over a three/four month period, mainly at Apostolic Studios.[5] I remember[6] doing the sessions for 'WPLJ', 'Valarie',[7] 'Oh No!'[8] and 'The Eric Dolphy Memorial Barbecue'.[9] The engineer there was a guy called Dick Kunc and he was a great guy. When we moved back to the west coast, he upped and moved with the band, as he was now the official recording engineer for Frank.

Toronto Glue

In late January, we went up to Toronto.[10] We were in for a big surprise. The freaks up there had heard all about our escapades at the Garrick, with the vegetables and all that stuff. Half way through one of the shows, a bunch of them in the front row started throwing cooked spaghetti at us with no sauce, just the cooked spaghetti. I know it took me a couple of days to clean my

---

Photo above: courtesy Art Tripp; Woodstock, at Jimmy's place

fuckin' drums up, because when spaghetti gets on something and goes hard, it's like glue - I had to scrape that shit off my drums!

While we were on the little tour up to Toronto, Loretta went into the hospital with false labor pains so my fifth child Geronimo was almost born on my birthday, February 1st - that would have been cool!

I'll never forget when he was born, Man! On February 21, 1968 at the hospital in Kingston, New York which was about 20 miles from our house at Woodstock. I was so proud and he was so cute, the cutest baby I've ever seen! I named him Geronimo Inkanish Black.[11]

Playing Alone Again

Billy Mundi was so pissed off by this time that he [had] quit. When *Absolutely Free* came out we were each given our complimentary copy. Billy melted his copy, made it into an ashtray, showed it to Frank, and said, "I'm quittin' the band!" So he left and joined a band called Rhinoceros.

We played a gig in Providence, Rhode Island with the Charles Lloyd Quartet.[12] He was a black jazz flute player. It was the first gig that I played back as the only drummer. I hadn't been playing drums that much so I had to learn a whole bunch of things that I hadn't been playing drums on. You have to remember that I'd been playing trumpet and percussion and I'd also been singing a lot. So, we got a message that Ian was coming up to Woodstock and we were going to rehearse at Don, Bunk and Ray's house. They said, "Jimmy, you gotta learn to play the drums on all these songs and you have one day to do it!" I knew the songs but I hadn't played drums on them, so my chops weren't that good but we did the show and it was fine. Frank said, "You did great, Man! No problem!"

So then we got Art Tripp in the band to replace Billy.[13] Art had majored in Music and he was really what you'd call a prodigy.[14]

That was when two drummers made a lot of sense to me, because Billy and I played too much alike and it sounded just like having a big drum set. Art was a great percussionist although he didn't know much about Rock 'n' Roll when he came into the band.

[Photo left: courtesy Art Tripp]

I was told that I was going to be playing drums all the time. He concentrated on the percussion stuff and I played the main beats. That was the best two-drum thing I've ever done and it was a fuckin' pleasure to play with him. I learned a lot from Art. We became very close friends and still are. We used to hang out together a lot and he used to like to say, "We're gonna have a little LUSH, a little BRUSH and a little Leaper tonight!"[15] Artie was a little freaky anyway - he had a freak streak in him!

Ivy League!
We did a small tour. These were the first gigs that Art Tripp played in the band. It was "cold as a witch's tit in the Klondike" as we used to say in Texas. The first gig was at Colgate University in upstate New York and we didn't even have a rehearsal.[16] We played in a basketball gymnasium so you can imagine what it sounded like, really funny. Frank had all the parts written out for Art. I was back into playing the drums full time so I carried all the beats. All Artie had to do was read his parts and listen to me. It worked quite well for us. Frank was extremely excited then about the prospect of the two drummers and the possibilities of what we could do, a lot more so than when Billy was in the band.

Art's Wedding
I was the best man at Art's wedding in February. His girlfriend Adrienne was pregnant at the time and they came up to Woodstock and had their wedding in the little chapel. I thought it was quite a nice ceremony and we had a great party that day. All the band members were there except for Frank because he was always too busy. He was always more interested being at 54 Charles Street (his home then), where he was writing music like crazy and planning the strategy of the whole band.

Grammy Awards Dinner
Of all the bands to play at the Grammys, I couldn't understand why it was The Mothers of Invention. It was a Pre-ceremony Dinner held in some hotel[17] and I think we played for about 30 minutes, and I'm telling you Man, we went all the way on that one! We really got out there!

I don't know how or why we got to be on their show as we have never been nominated for any of their awards and never would be.

I'll never forget that trip back home to Woodstock. It took me nine hours to get back to Woodstock in a blazing blizzard and it's only 90 miles - it took me all fucking night to get back! I was driving at 15 mph behind some big truck, which was plowing the snow off the road. When I did get home, I couldn't drive up the hill because they couldn't plow it, so I had to park at the bottom and walk up to the house.

Done with MGM

We're Only In It For The Money was finally released[18] after being held up because of problems and legalities with regards to the cover and, of course, always the music or I should say here, the lyrics. MGM edited, cut up and changed the lyrics in 'Mother People' and 'Harry You're a Beast'.

We gave *Mothermania* and *Ruben & The Jets* to MGM to finish the contract with them. It was in our contract that we had to give MGM something like two albums a year and three singles a year. When Frank gave them *Mothermania*, the company didn't check it so the first pressings of that album have the correct, uncensored versions on - so Frank snuck one in on them there!

It was good that we were finished with MGM. They were fuckin' around with the royalties. They said that all their accounts, everything, was lost in a fire so they got out of paying us any money.

THEE IMAGE We went south and played in Louisville, Kentucky[19] and at Thee Image in Miami[20] which was an old converted bowling alley.

I remember a band called Blues Image opened up for us at Thee Image and that is where I met a guy named Joe Lala. Joe introduced me to Colombian Pot and he gave me an ounce[21] of the stuff to take home with me! Would you believe my suitcase got lost by the airlines between Miami and Louisville? I had to wear the same fuckin' clothes for about three days! About two weeks after I got home, a cab pulled up in front of my house in Woodstock. It was from the airline company because they were returning my suitcase. Everything was in there except for the Pot and nothing was said, which was just as well. I was very happy about that although I wasn't too happy about losing the Grass, just happy that the police weren't with the airline people.

ELECTRICFACTORY We went back and played in Philadelphia, but this time we played at the Electric Factory.[22] Since Dick Kunc was working for us then, we were recording every show we played. That is where Frank got so much material that even today, still keeps coming out.

When we got back to New York after the west coast tour, Frank announced that we were moving back to California.[23] So I had to pack my family up and send them out to stay with the in-laws and for Loretta to find us a place to live. Ray had come back into the band again, so he came and stayed up at Woodstock, in Don and Bunks' house. Ray was like a revolving door, in one day and out the next it seemed. Actually, I was always happy to see him back because it meant we had a singer in the band that just sang.

The Fillmore East & Leonard Bernstein

March is also about the time that Bill Graham opened the Fillmore East. We were one of the first bands to play there. We were starting to play more concerts and, of course, finally making a lot more money than we had been making - which was practically nothing! The Fillmore East was where we all met Leonard Bernstein at our last gig in New York.[24] His daughter was a big fan of ours and she'd talked him into coming to the show. When Frank found out the Bernstein was in the audience he pulled out all the stops for the classical stuff or at least, our interpretation of the classical stuff - the way we did it! We played a 3-hour show and after the show he came backstage to meet us. He congratulated us all and said, "That was a wonderful show!"

 We did another photo session for *Life* magazine because they were doing a feature on rock bands. They chose us, the Jefferson Airplane and The Velvet Underground.[25] So, we get down to the place where we're going to shoot the picture and there are about 15-20 mothers down there with their babies, that we called "renta-babies". What a fiasco that was. We had to pose with all these babies screaming their little heads off because they'd just been plonked into our arms and were obviously scared shitless! Several of us got covered in baby piss and I'm sure the one that Frank was holding actually shit on his arm.

Jina Speaks

Little Jina, my youngest daughter, who was about three years old at the time, had never spoken a word, which had always been a worry to me. I was always worried that she might have a problem but Loretta was always telling me not to worry. Roger the lodger was playing and joking with the kids up at the house one day, as he often did. He turned to Jina and asked why she didn't talk and she just turned to him and said, "I don't have anything to say!" That really cracked me up!

Moving back to California

We moved back to California in April but it wasn't a direct journey because we played some gigs along the way. Half the guys in the band had cars and so we made our plans to travel back. Don had a Triumph and he set off but only made it as far as New Jersey before his car blew up. He ended up going on the plane with the other guys that weren't driving. Bunk had a Chrysler which was a nice fifties thing. Roy was sharing the driving with him but Bunk had forgotten to change the oil pump and clean the sludge out of the motor so they only got as far as Springfield, Illinois before it blew up. He had four new tires on it. I think he got $400 for it because the tires were worth $100 apiece.

I drove back with Art Tripp in my VW convertible. My car was the only one that made it all the way across the United States. Loretta and the five kids and Art Tripp's wife, Adrienne, had left two weeks earlier and they  were staying with Loretta's father in Santa Ana. She and Adrienne were looking for a place for us to live. I was left with my dog, Lady, and her six puppies which were only a few weeks old.

That trip from Woodstock to L.A. took two long weeks because we played five shows along the way. We loaded up the little VW car: me, Artie, Lady, and the puppies, and took off for Cincinnati where we had a gig. On the way, we spent a night at Art's parents' house in Pittsburgh.

Next morning, we drove straight to the dog pound and offloaded the puppies - a sad time - but there was no option. Then we drove on to Cincinnati[26] and stayed with a friend of Art and he agreed to look after Lady for a few days. We left my car there for a few days and joined the rest of the band on the plane, while we played some shows. We played with MC5 as the opening act in Cincinnati.[27] From there, we flew to Chicago and played a gig with Cream.

The Cream

That was the last show Cream ever did.[28] It was a Trip! As we pulled up outside the Chicago Coliseum[29] in two station wagons, Cream pulled up in three limousines! They had a limo each because those guys weren't even speakin' to each other by that time. I'll never forget watching the roadies carry Ginger Baker out of his limo. He was so fucked up he couldn't walk. They carried him onto the stage and sat him down on the drums. I don't know how he could even play but he sure surprised everyone there and played his ass off as if nothing was wrong. He played one of the most incredible 20-minute versions of his drum solo 'Toad' and he broke two drum pedals. The roadies were up there trying to change them and he never missed a lick. When the show was over they had to carry him off the drums.

Cynthia Plaster Caster

We also met Cynthia Plaster Caster at that show. She was becoming quite a celebrity at that time. She used to travel around after rock stars persuading them to have their dicks cast.[30] Eric Clapton had been talked into being cast. You know, Cynthia was a pretty-good-sized girl, I'd say she was pleasantly plump then. Her friend was the sexy one and she's the one who would get the guys aroused so that Cynthia could do her work.

As far as I know, none of the Mothers got cast. I know that I didn't. Somehow, Herb ended up with all her casts. I don't know how that happened, but there was a lawsuit or something and she has only recently got them back.[31] You know, for a straight guy, Herb turned out to be quite a kinky freak. He always had a little weirdness in him. He must have, to take on the Mothers!

 The next day, we flew to Detroit's Grande Ballroom with MC5 supporting again. That turned out to be a great show as the Detroit audience really always loved the Mothers.[32] After that, Art and I caught the plane back to Cincinnati and picked up my car and Lady. Then we drove 800 miles west across Indiana, Illinois, and Missouri, passing through Indianapolis, St. Louis and Kansas City to Wichita, Kansas, where we got a motel room for two nights. I still had a lot of friends in Wichita so we went and out did some serious partying with Gary Stevens who I'd played with in The Squires.

The Kingsmen of 'Louie, Louie' fame were staying in the same motel as us and it turned out they were huge Mothers' fans. So we had a nice chat and sang a few choruses of 'Louie Louie' with them, except Artie and I sang 'Plastic People' to it instead. They really got a kick out of that.

So then we continued west on Interstate 40, which runs parallel to the old route 66. We'd scored some Uppers from the guys in Wichita, so we were driving straight through to Phoenix, Arizona.[33] As we were driving through Gallup, we picked up the strangest radio station I'd ever heard. It was broadcasting in the Navajo language, which I'd never heard before. We headed on to Phoenix and found somewhere to board Lady because we had to meet the rest of the band again in Denver, Colorado.

LUCKY DOG Chet Helms, from the Family Dog, had just set up a new venue in Denver.[34] I remember that well because we had a night off before we played so we got to go out and have a little fun. I met a beautiful chick there and she was about 17 years old and she was gorgeous. She was a big girl and I was a dirty old man. I had another encounter with her when we played at the Mile High Stadium with Jimi Hendrix the following year.[35]

Meeting my Mom

After the show the next morning, we flew back to Phoenix and got off the plane. I had my shades on, the same ones that I'm wearing in the booklet from the *Uncle Meat* album. I'd had a quite a night before and had a little bit of a hangover. I was walking through the airport when someone grabbed me by my ponytail and pulled it pretty hard. When I turned around, I saw that it was my Mother. She said, "And you're not even going to talk to your own mother, is that the deal?" I just didn't see her and they'd driven all the way from El Paso: my mother, my brother, his wife, my nephew and niece to see us play. They hadn't seen me in at least two years because my family had been living on the East coast.

So I had a real nice visit with my Mom and when she came to the show that night, Frank calmed things way down and dedicated the show to her, to Mrs. Black. She got a front row seat, Man! The Spiders were opening for us - they turned into Alice Cooper later on. My mum said the Mothers were nice boys: she liked Bunk especially and always had a fondness for him, she liked Roy and she liked Frank a lot too. Frank was really nice to her and he talked to her for a long time that night.

So, the next day I said goodbye to my Mom because we had 400 miles[36] left to go, to end the trip. We got to just outside of Indigo, California and ran into a sand storm. We're not talking about any kind of a storm - we're talking about a real fuckin' sand storm! That sand blasted the front of my car; sandblasted my windshield so I could barely see out of it. It was blowin' about 60 miles an hour so we finally had to stop and wait the storm out. It almost blew that little car over.

Back in LA
We came back and played at the Shrine Exposition Hall in L.A. and that's where Eric Clapton sat in with us and naturally we jammed some blues.[37]

My wife had found a house in Woodland Hills. We had a couple of weeks off to settle in. It was a beautiful place and it only cost $250 a month. I was doing pretty well by then and there was plenty of money for everything, no problems. Woodland Hills was a good time for my family, even though I was gone on tour a lot.

I had no other payments except for groceries and we were actually saving money. There was some money in the bank account finally, after all those years. The next thing we know is that we're being put on a salary but we were told it was [still] called a "draw". We were getting $250 a week each, before taxes, whether we were on the road or not.

The Log Cabin in Laurel Canyon
Frank moved into the Log Cabin in Laurel Canyon.[38] It used to be owned by the cowboy actor Tom Mix. It was a very trippy place. It was a huge place built out of logs and we had a rehearsal room down in the basement right next to the small bowling alley that was down there. It had a lot of ground around it with a tree house. Cal had his studio in the tree house and mostly it's where he stayed. Cal was always busy because Frank kept him busy doing album covers and things like that. He was on a salary just like the band was. Loretta's brother Phil was living with us and he'd started to do quite a bit of work with Cal, as his assistant, so he would stay over at his

place too. He was also doing a bit of babysitting with Moon for Frank and Gail. They moved to the house on Woodrow Wilson Drive at the end of 1968.[39]

Dick Kunc had moved from New York and was now on the payroll and he was also living in Woodland Hills. Dick had become our sound engineer and was to stay with Frank for many years. So now there wasn't much studio stuff going on, but what we were doing was recording everything we did live. By now, we had a Uher recording machine and Dick had these little boards so he could mix everything as we played. It still went down to two tracks but he could get some very good recordings and he did.

That is when we went back to rehearsing at the Lindy Opera House. They had a small studio there that we rented. Now that we were on our so-called "draw", we had to be in that room about eight hours a day and for five and sometimes six days a week. Otherwise, you'd need a doctor's note to say why you weren't there! Frank had passed the job of rehearsing the band over to Ian, who was OK at what he did. Sometimes Frank wouldn't even show up, if he was too busy working on something else for the band or ultimately, for his own career.

The Miami Pop Festival
We played at the Miami Pop Festival in May.[40] It was quite a bill and the rest of the line-up was Chuck Berry, Buddy Miles Express, The Blue Cheer, John Lee Hooker, The Crazy World of Arthur Brown and The Jimi Hendrix Experience. We had about 35000 people at that concert.[41]

I remember on the first day we were right in the middle of our show when Hendrix came and landed in a helicopter behind the stage. It was so loud that we had to stop playing and wait for the thing to quieten down. The band just stopped and as soon as it was all over, we just continued where we'd left off.

Most of the bands stayed at the same hotel called The Castaways and there was a bar in there. After the last show of the night, the place was full of musicians and groupies. The resident band had already done their thing, so they let us use their equipment and we just jammed some blues.

I got to play with Hendrix again which I always enjoyed. Man! He had a foxy lady with him that night!

That's the first time I met Arthur Brown and saw him set his head on fire. After they played their show, his drummer jumped off the bandstand, landed on a railing back stage and broke his fuckin' leg. In order to continue their tour of the States, they sent for a young drummer called Carl Palmer[42] to come and fill in!

More Gigs!
The next little tour we did, we played Salt Lake City at Lagoon.[43] I believe the next tour after that was a three-day tour that we did. It was a bus tour and we rented a Greyhound bus. Loretta went on this tour with us. We played Santa Barbara in a big outdoor theater[44] and then...

...we played the Swing Auditorium in San Bernardino, which was also our first time in that city.[45] The next night was in San Diego and it was our first time there.[46]

...there were so fuckin' many gigs happening that I have trouble remembering them because I never kept a diary. I don't think any of us did.

The Jefferson Airplane
During the summer of 1968, we did a recording project with the Jefferson Airplane at RCA Studios on Sunset Boulevard.[47] I can't remember that much about it except that it was an evening session and it was for their *After Bathing At Baxter's* album. I'll never forget travelling to that session, because Art and I were with an old friend of mine from my home town of Anthony, who was visiting me. Stanley Bartlett was just a country boy and he couldn't believe what was happening in Hollywood - he was hanging out with a couple of the Mothers!

We were driving down the Ventura Freeway in the San Fernando Valley and just getting ready to get off and go over the hill to Hollywood. All of a sudden there was a cop car pulled alongside of us. We were doing about 60 mph and, of course, they were having a good look at us. Just about that time, the convertible top popped back and it popped back real quick. At 60 miles an hour, mine and Art's hair went straight up in the air. Those cops' eyes got about as big as saucers and the driver just stomped his foot on the gas and off they went. I'll never forget that. He must have thought, "I'm not even gonna fuck with these guys."

I finally sold my little VW bug. I'd paid $75 for that car when I bought it because it had 4th gear out, so for an extra $90 I had them put another transmission in. I'd driven that car from New York and I ended up selling it for $500 in California so I made money off that car. I went down and bought a 1966 VW camper, with a refrigerator, a bed and stove in it. It was definitely better for a family of seven, which is where The Blacks were then.

Bobby Kennedy
Right after that, we went back up to San Francisco and we did two nights at the Fillmore West and one night at the Winterland with the Chambers Brothers and Tim Buckley.[48]

Frank hired my friend Stanley to help Motorhead but I think he was only paid about $10 a day. I don't think he really give a shit about the money, as he just wanted to go with us. Pam was also on the trip with us. We all roomed together: Stanley, Pam, Roy and I and, as usual, we had a great time up there.

Stanley took his first Acid Trip and for three days we thought we'd lost him. I thought, "Shit, this country boy has come up here and got lost, we'll never find him again!" but he did come back happy as a lark.

The gigs almost got cancelled because we got up to San Francisco the night before and it was the night that Bobby Kennedy got assassinated.[49] It just threw the whole country into turmoil. It had only been five years since his brother had been assassinated. Bill Graham decided to do the shows anyway and as it turned out they were jam-packed.

The people were out anyway because they wanted to mingle and talk about what had happened.

The Cheetah
In July, we played a three-day gig at a placed called the Cheetah, which was right out on the beach in Santa Monica, because it was the 2nd anniversary of the death of Lenny Bruce.[50] It was a little festival, and the bands played right outside the Cheetah on the pier in the afternoon and then we moved our equipment inside and played that night again. We played with Chicago and Spirit and that was the first time I'd heard Chicago play.[51] They blew me away and actually blew the whole band away. Remember I had met Pete Cetera in 1962 in Kansas.

After that, we played one or two nights at the Whisky and Frank had it recorded by Wally Heider on his new 8-track mobile studio.[52]

Ray's Last Days
Ray's last stint was during the summer of 1968. It was a tour of the Midwest. Him and Frank weren't getting along, nothing new. He used to challenge Frank all the time and Frank would get pissed off and then Ray would be pissed off and so on…

First, we played in Milwaukee at The Scene,[53] and that's where the inspiration for 'Rudi Wants To Buy Yez A Drink' happened.[54] We had a visit from the local Musicians' Union, checking to see if our cards were up to date. The Scene was run by the local mafia and Rudy was the boss. Rudy had a beautiful daughter and she was coming on to me pretty heavy.

I really wanted to lay her but I thought that cement boots weren't my style and the lake was very cold even if it was summertime.

Chicago & the Democratic National Convention
Then we had five nights at the Kinetic Playground in Chicago.[55] It was the time of the National Democratic Convention,[56] and the place was swarming with FBI, CIA and Secret Service because there were big demonstrations planned to happen. On the next to last night, there was a bomb scare during

the show and we had to evacuate for a little bit but then we went back in and finished playing.

We were getting hassled pretty bad ourselves around the hotel just for having long hair. Neil Diamond was staying in the same hotel and of course, he still remembered us from the time we had backed him up at Frenchys, but by this time he was a BIG star.

That's where Frank gave us the music to a piece that was called 'The Hunchback Duke' which later became known as 'Little House I Used To Live In'.[57] He had been writing a lot of new music on the road during that tour. We rehearsed it every day before the show and we were just starting to get acquainted with it. As with lots of the pieces he was writing, we would learn them in sections. I think the song 'Agency Man' was written around the time that the Convention was happening.

During that tour Ray got Hepatitis and of course he turned yellow, a sort of gold color. He was really ill but he managed to finish the tour.[58] There was a really heavy atmosphere all over town. We flew home straight after the last show because Frank said, "I'm not staying in this town one hour longer."

We got back to L.A. early morning. When I got up and watched TV, I saw all the stuff about the Chicago Ten,[59] all those guys who had gotten arrested and there was all sorts of shit going on. There had been a lot of police brutality, as we all know. We all had to go to the doctor and get those hemoglobin shots because we'd all been exposed to whatever Ray had. They were very painful shots!

More & More Gigs!
Then Seattle[60] and then Vancouver, British Columbia,[61] then Dallas[62] and Houston[63] - it was the first time we'd been back to Texas since the TV show in 1966.

We were in Houston for a few days because we played a festival at a big place called the Catacombs, with Country Joe and The Fish, and **CATACOMBS CLUB** AUG. 31 SATURDAY AUG. 31 Canned Heat. The opening act was a band called The Moving Sidewalks which later on turned into ZZ Top. They had a keyboard player back then.

Wild Man Fischer
We played at the Rose Bowl in Pasadena, and had "Wild Man" Fischer join us on stage.[64] That's where that picture was taken that's on the back of his album, the one where he's jumping up in the air with me and Art in the background. He was a crazy man and that is why they called him Wild Man Fischer and not Larry Fischer. Frank had been doing some recordings with him for Straight Records (which was Frank's label) but I'd only met him on the street outside the front of the Whisky when he was trying to sell me a

song for a dime. I used to go out and see other bands playing at the Whisky as I never had a problem getting in there. The doormen all knew me very well and were friends of mine.

Wild Man was an interesting study in "freakiness". I remember one of the songs he wrote on a later album called 'Where's the Money, Frank?' I saw him in 1981 in San Francisco in front of the theater the Grandmothers were to play that night. He was still wild and still selling songs - for a dollar.

I guess inflation had set in.

Europe 1968: Customs & Habits

In September, it was time for us to leave for our second European tour. I seem to remember I took an Acid Trip on the plane over as we had a couple of nights off before we had to play. I don't remember who took it with me that time. Maybe it was Bunk. I never carried any illegal substances through customs and I was never stopped, although when we came back from that tour they searched Don and found some Hash taped to his balls. They could have really stuck it to Preston but they let him go. He was very lucky, like Roy was - coming back through customs in Boston. He had a pipe that had some residue in it and they detained him for a while, but they let him go.

Frank never liked to sit by any of us and we made sure we got well away from him. At that point, he was writing all the music for the orchestra pieces we were going to do at the Royal Festival Hall and so he would normally sit at the back someplace and work.

We flew from New York to London and then to Dusseldorf. We had a two-hour break in London before changing planes and I bought some nice shades there in the airport. The ones that I have on in the little booklet that comes with the *Uncle Meat* album. That picture of me with my cigarette hangin' out of my mouth, sitting on a stool.

We were well taken care of on that tour. $250 a week went to our families back home, so my wife and kids were taken care of finally and Loretta was very happy about that. The band was getting per diem everyday so we had money to spend.

First Stop: Essen Germany

Our first ever gig in Germany was at the University of Essen.[65] The university was paying for the hotel and everything and we had about three days off before we had to start playing. We were hanging around in Essen and all of a sudden these two sisters show up, Bonnie and Laura. I had met Bonnie a few weeks before in Chicago at the Kinetic Playground and had a brief affair with her. I didn't know at the time but I was second choice - she had really wanted Bunk! Bonnie is Bunk's wife now and the mother of his two lovely daughters and a wonderful friend of mine.

106

The Fugs were also on this bill. They came over and hung with us so I had my old Texan drinking buddy Ken Weaver back to hang out with and get it on. It was a three or four-day festival with different bands playing each day. I went and saw Guru Guru and The Nice for the first time and we had a great time.

The place we played was in a big auditorium with bleachers going up on each side and a big stage at one end. The German bands would go on and start singing their political songs and one side of the audience would be cheering and the other side would be throwing beer bottles at them. Then the next group would come on and they'd start singing political songs and the side who'd been throwing beer bottles would start cheering for them. The other side would start throwing the beer bottles and it was then that I thought to myself, "I wonder what's gonna happen when we go on?"

So we went on and it was great because the Germans loved us. They threw toilet paper at us. They'd hold the end and throw it so it formed a streamer. We found out later that it meant they liked us, but we weren't sure when it was happening! At least they weren't throwing beer bottles at us.

Next Stop: Frankfurt
The next gig was in Frankfurt and about half of the audience was American GI's.[66] It was almost like playing in America. The promoters threw a beautiful fuckin' party for us after the show in a big restaurant and they really gave us a good spread. We pigged out at that thing and basically had a good time.

We were staying in a hotel someplace in Frankfurt that was right across the street from a whorehouse so Mister Horny here, the "Indian of the Group", decides to take a walk over there. I got to the front door and the Madame stopped me, she just backed me right out and says, "This is for boys only. Get outa here!" I said, "Well, I'm a boy, check the moustache!" and she says, "Well, look at the hair!" So, I got thrown out of my first whorehouse in Germany before I'd even got to look inside at the girls. I think she was afraid that the GIs were going to kill me if I went in there.

We'd scored some Hash in Essen. Bunk had been stationed in Germany before so he knew how to speak a little bit of German. He had made some connections while he was stationed over there so we got some Turkish Hash and stayed up all night getting stoned. We sat by the window in our room and watched the whores coming in and out, getting hornier and hornier, but we kept getting more and more stoned so it was OK.

Better Late Than Never
Of course, Roy and I were roommates. We had to get up at 9 am to catch the plane for Sweden so Dick Barber gives the call in the morning. Unfortunately, Roy answered the phone and said, "Yeah, OK." then hung up

and went right back to sleep. The next thing I know the fuckin' door to our room came crashing in. Dick had been pounding on it and couldn't get any reaction from either of us so he knocked the fuckin' door down! I flew out of bed and had that piece of Hash ready to chuck out the window - I thought we were being busted! Barber was just cracking up, Man, when he saw our faces and so he wasn't mad at us anymore! He got a good laugh and that made his day.

So we threw our clothes on and luckily[67] our bags were already packed. Everybody was waiting down stairs for us and Frank just says, "Where have you guys been?" There was nothing I could say, but when I got in the car next to Roy I said, "I don't trust you anymore." We left that hotel with one broken door.

We got to Sweden and it was very, very foggy. We were coming in to land and all of a sudden the pilot gives it the gas because he'd missed the runway. We barely pulled off and ended up landing in Helsinki. We had to wait for about five hours, until the fog lifted in Stockholm so we could go back into the airport.[68] It was scary, Man!

Stockholm

We had the day off in Stockholm, before we played at the same place that we'd played the first time we were there.[69] That night I roomed with Don, as I was still pissed off at Roy because of the door incident. I said, "I'm not staying with you tonight. You get me in too much trouble!"

Don had gone to the subway looking for girls or something, I don't know. But anyway, he came back to the room with these two girls and we started talking to them. We then started smooching it up with them and before we knew it we had them in bed. It was still early, only about 6 o'clock, and Don was kneeling down on the floor eating this girl when he said, "You know, this pussy looks familiar to me!" It was the girl that he had made it with in Gothenburg the year before. He didn't recognize her face but she knew who he was. I fucked the other chick and then I said, "Fuck this, I'm going out. See you later."

I met Marianne that night - phew, what a beauty! A classic Scandinavian six-foot tall blonde, an absolutely gorgeous woman but she wouldn't let me in her pants - although I could eat her all night if I wanted to!

Don some way or another lost his passport in his overnight orgy and so the next day Don and Herb spent the whole fucking day at the American Embassy getting him another passport and, believe me, Herb was bent out of shape.

Obviously, Frank was also.

Copenhagen & Don Cherry

We did the concert the next evening in Sweden and the next morning we flew to Copenhagen. We had a night off, so we went out to a jazz club and saw Don Cherry. We got to talking to him and found out that he had heard about us through Archie Shepp, from when we were playing at the Garrick Theater.

He was living in Copenhagen at that time so Frank invited him to our concert to sit in with us. He came down but didn't play his trumpet and instead played the African flutes. We just started improvising in a kind of 9/8 feel, real spacey, and that improvised piece of music really soared and went on for quite a while. I really wish that piece would come out on one of the various CDs that the Zappa Trust puts out.

Don Preston recorded a lot of those things because he had his Uher portable tape recorder with him and he would just set up two mikes. He recorded just about all the shows on that tour but Frank confiscated most of his tapes. By the way, the show was at the world famous Tivoli Gardens in the heart of Copenhagen.[70]

Photo by Peter Mackay

Hamburg

From Copenhagen we went to Hamburg and played at the Market Hall[71]; and they really showered us with toilet paper there!

We were staying by the Reeperbahn, so naturally we went to check out the Top Ten Club and the Star Club and then we went and did a little sightseeing. I met a wonderful girl that had known the Beatles back when they were playing in Hamburg. She was a beautiful hooker and we got on very well. She is the one that took me sightseeing.

Bremen: The Beat Club

On the Sunday, we drove to Bremen and did the Beat Club TV show.[72] The two girls you can see dancing on the video are Bonnie and Laura because they followed us around on that whole tour. Once again, we taped that show with The Nice. I really enjoyed hangin' with those guys and also listening to them play their kind of strange Rock. After that show, we went back to Hamburg and took up where we left off the night before. I was really beginning to like Germany by this time. I do think that is when I decided that I wanted to live there someday.

Oktoberfest in Munich

The next day, we flew down to Munich.[73] It was during the world famous Oktoberfest and there were no hotel rooms to be had anywhere in the city. We stayed about 20 miles outside Munich in the little village of Erding. That is where Roy discovered that if you went into a pharmacy in Germany you could buy Speed across the counter. That was a very dangerous thing for that boy to find out, very dangerous.

Photo by Peter Mackay

We just hung out in this little village playing cards and drinking their very good beer. We were actually relaxing and we had a nice time at that little "Gasthaus". It was a five-week tour but we were only playing about two or three gigs a week. We were sure having fun in Europe and experiencing things that we didn't even know existed.

I decided that I would try the whorehouses again and see how they are in Munich. So, I went to walk in and they just turned me right back around and once again they'd say, "This is for Boys only!" I wasn't going to buy any pussy in Germany, not with my long hair. The only place that they didn't kick me out was in Amsterdam, when we went down Canal Street but that's another story.

I drank about five pints of that Oktoberfest beer that everybody had warned us was pretty powerful. I was sitting down thinking, "Fuck, I don't feel anything and shit, this beer isn't that strong!" Then I decided that I needed to go and take a piss so I got up. I'd walked about half way to the toilet there when all of a sudden I was drunker than a fuckin' skunk.[74] After that, it was all downhill. The next stop was Vienna.

Don on Brown Rice

We flew to Vienna to play at the Concert Hall.[75] Once again we had about three days before the gig, but this time we had rehearsals because Frank had written a piece for a six-piece chamber group that he had hired from the Vienna Symphony. It was kind of like a scaled-down version of what would happen at the Royal Festival Hall in London.

We checked into the Hotel Carlton[76] and we got a three-roomed suite. It had one living room, two bedrooms and a bathroom. Don, Bunk, Roy and I were staying in that suite and, of course, we were getting pretty blasted every night. We'd bought some very good bottles of white wine and cheese, you know, "Hey cool, Man, nice party area!" But by this time Don Preston

110

was really in bad shape. He was having a lot of trouble with his ulcers because of the pressure of the tour. Frank was on his case a lot. He had been getting the daggers from Frank all along and the pressure was on him. He couldn't eat on the whole tour. He'd been on a macrobiotic diet of brown rice. He had his little rice cooker, his little stove, everything he needed. So finally, in the Vienna hotel, he was at the peak of his illness and every chance he had he was taking a hot bath to stop the cramps.

Vienna: The Konserthaus

On the night of the performance, we found out that there was some kind of strange rule that any member of the symphony orchestra who played with anybody other that the orchestra had to wear these special robes. It was some tradition. They looked like Ku Klux Klan outfits with big pointed hoods with two eyes and the hole for breathing and they were made out of cloth, neatly ironed and all the way to the ground. So, these guys went out with their robes on and played their opening piece that Frank had written. In the meantime, we were backstage looking around when we found the room where the robes and the hoods were. Six of us put robes and the hoods on. These guys finished their piece and got a real big applause as they came off the stage. The audience were screaming for an encore. The six of us walked out on to the stage and took the bows, waved at the people, the whole thing. Then we just turned around and started packing each other, like a bunch of dogs, doing all these crazy things. Then we all got on our instruments, ripped the robes off and started playing. So that was the beginning of our concert.

I met this beautiful actress there, and believe me she was gorgeous, Man! She kind of liked me but she wouldn't fuck me. She just wanted to take me around to all these parties with all these actors and actresses and say, "Look what I've found, I've found a real Freak!" I got a chance to do a lot of drinking at parties and eat a lot of good food, but…I wasn't getting any action off of her!

Shooting Film in Vienna

We had been doing some filming during that tour, supposedly for the *Uncle Meat* movie that Frank was planning. We were being filmed doing all those little stupid things that you'd get to do when you're in a group. One of the most popular antics at that time was packing! "Packing" is a term that Motorhead had given to the way that dogs come up and start fucking your leg. So as the tour progressed, without warning, someone would come up to you and start packing you.

We got in two VW buses and drove to the outskirts of Vienna and we went to a castle and filmed a lot of crazy stuff there and then we went into the woods and did that stuff that eventually appeared in the movie. It was the part with us all packing Don Preston. One of Don's little antics was transforming and he used to have his cloak on and do this whole werewolf thing where he transformed into a monster. Don was doing his transformations for the camera when everybody just ran into the shot and started packing him.

Roy, Bunk, Don and I were in one bus with the two American girls. Everybody else was in the other bus. They didn't want to ride with us because they knew we were smoking Hash. I'm very happy we had such a cool driver. He didn't say anything about our smoking.

 One of those other little things we would do was the "brownout". This was showing our asses out the bus window, it's also called mooning. So, we wanted to brown them out in the bus behind us. Bunk and I kept yanking our pants down and sticking our asses against the back window of the bus and giving them a real good brown shot. But we never could catch their attention and only the Austrian bus driver saw us. He didn't know how to tell them, so nobody saw us do this brownout except for the bus driver. He looked at us kind of funny when we stopped.

The next morning, we were getting ready to check out of the hotel when one of the American girls locked herself in the bathroom. We couldn't get the fuckin' bathroom door open so we went down and got the hotel manager. He came up there but they still couldn't get the door open. They finally had to axe the door open to get that girl out and they were all bent out of shape at us. They asked, "What are these girls doing up here in this room in the first place." So, the four of us had to pay about 50 marks each.

We also had to buy a new door for that bathroom. We bought two doors on that tour, one in Frankfurt and the other in Vienna.

 Next stop Berlin. We checked in to the hotel, found out the happening places in town and went out that night. This was the time that the wall was all the way around Berlin, big time. Roy and I went out and we met these two chicks. After a while, we talked them into going back to the hotel with us. I started messing around with one girl and Roy tried to mess around with the other girl but she wasn't having anything to do with it. We found out that the chick I was with was bisexual and the other one was a lesbian. So, all four of us are in the room and I got down and started fucking the chick I was with. We'd fuck for a while and then roll over and rest for a while and that is when the other chick would just immediately dive in and start eating her pussy. Roy was trying all the time to get this girl to go with him but she wasn't having any of it. She was slapping him around saying, "Get away from me!" and all that shit.

112

Berlin: City of Radicals

In the afternoon, it was time to go down to the Sports Palace where we were going to play the gig.[77] We were all feeling real good and everybody was in a very jovial mood. We were saying, "What a great town Berlin is and this is so exciting." During the sound check, I saw Frank over at the side talking to a bunch of guys. There were about six or seven of them but I never thought anything of it.

In the dressing room just before we went on, Frank said, "Guys, I want to talk to you for a minute." So we all got around him and he explained that those guys he had been talking to were members of the SDS (Students for a Democratic Society). They'd said, "We want you to get the audience all stirred up and tell them to go down the street and burn down the Allied Supply Dump." He'd told them we were a musical group and were just here to play a concert and they'd started saying stuff like: "Yeah, but all the lyrics to your songs indicate that you guys are fairly radical." and "You're definitely left wing revolutionaries." and "If you don't do this we're going to destroy your concert!" So Frank says, "I don't know what's going to happen tonight boys, but be prepared for anything!"

The band went out there and started playing and we were a little nervous but not too bad. We thought, "What the hell could they do, make a bunch of noise maybe? We can play louder than their noise anyway." The place we were playing was a round building and the stage was right in the middle of it, so we were surrounded by at least five thousand people.

We played for about 15 minutes when, all of a sudden, here came the fuckin' eggs. They showered the stage with raw eggs and we noticed that Frank got hit two or three times and one time his guitar got egg all over it. Then they started with the hard green pears that were like baseballs. I got hit on the shoulder a couple of times and they nearly knocked me off the fuckin' drum stool, Man!

There were maybe 800 SDS people there causing the trouble. So, they did the pears, then ran up to the stage and threw a gallon of green paint onto the stage and all over us. Roy had a pair of white pants on that turned instantly spotted-green and I had green paint all over my drums. Then they rushed the stage. Around the stage was a metal railing.[78] They ripped that fuckin' thing off the floor and about 25 of 'em lifted it up because they were going to throw it out on top the stage and us.

Herb Cohen, Dick Barber and Fritz Rau, the promoter of the whole German part of the tour, ran to the front of the stage as these guys held it up in the air. They just put their feet on it and kicked it out at them. It caught all of them off guard and it threw them back so this thing fell on them and wiped the first rows of chairs out. There were people under that fuckin' railing!

So, we got off the stage and went to the dressing room, or tried to go to the dressing room. That's where all the security cops were. All of them were in our dressing room.[79] Herb got really pissed off at those guys and threw them out of the dressing room shouting, "God Damn, you're supposed to be down there protecting us, and stopping all this shit!" They said they didn't want any part of it!

We get up into the dressing room and by this time everybody is shaking, and shouting, "What the fuck is going on here?" Then word was sent up to the dressing room that if we don't come back down and finish the show they would come up and get us. We were on the second floor and the only way out would be to jump out the window. All our equipment is down there and everything!

So, we went back down and played the second show, with about 200 SDS on the stage and surrounding all of us. We couldn't even see Frank and we didn't know what the fuck we were going to play. We just played anything that came to mind. The show was destroyed by that time. We tried to keep playing and then they started lighting those fuckin' M80 Cherry Bombs and throwing them on the stage. One went off right by Don Preston and burned the fuck out of his leg. They were like giant firecrackers going off. People were getting hit with them too and they were running all over the place.

Finally, Motorhead and Dick Barber just started carrying equipment off the stage while we were still playing.[80] Pretty soon all of Don and Arts' equipment had gone and it wound up with just me, Roy and Frank on the stage. They had taken my cymbals and all that was left was my bass drum, snare drum and hi-hat. Then I stood up and they took that stuff and we got off the fuckin' stage. As we were doing that, they were loading the equipment straight into the back of the van and we were out of there.[81]

They stole all my sticks, except for the ones I was holding, my wristwatch because I had taken it off and left it on my drum box where I keep all my hardware and my Indian ribbon shirt. Everything was gone, Man!

Right after that Frank wrote the song 'Holiday In Berlin'. If we could have got a flight out of there that night, we would have gone directly to the airport.

Amsterdam: My Favorite City
The next morning, we went straight to Amsterdam for our next gig.[82] It was a pleasure to get out of Berlin as we couldn't get out of there quick enough. It was a real pleasure to be back in the West. Once again we had a day or two off before we played and we just generally tried to chill out, but Frank had to do a lot of press stuff about what had just happened in Berlin. All our shows on that tour had been sold out. I think that Frank got awarded a gold record in Holland that time.

That Amsterdam gig was the only time in the band's existence that the fans actually tried to rip our clothes off, like they used to do to the Beatles. When we went into the hall, they started yanking at our clothes and we thought, "Fuck, what's happening here, this has never happened before."

Smashing Cars in Paris

From Amsterdam we went to Paris and did a television show.[83] As part of the session, we smashed some car. I can't remember what type but they wanted us to destroy it. I know there is footage out there from that, but I have never seen it. Someone must have seen Frank do it on the Monkees' TV show.

They paid us in cash for that session, the equivalent of $200 each. Obviously, there had been some mistake. As soon as we'd been handed it, Herb Cohen was there with his hand out saying, "Hey Man! Turn that money over. You guys are on salaries, remember?" I remember everybody was PISSED OFF at that! God, we can't even make a little extra money. Some of the guys were very reluctant to give that money back, me being one of them. Once it's in your hand, it's yours - that's the way I looked at it. Herb said, "I don't want to hear that shit, turn the money over. After all, me and Frank are fronting this whole fucking thing." I thought, "Sure you are, playing to sold-out houses, don't give me that crap!"

Looking back, I guess it did cost a lot because we didn't play that many gigs on the tour and we were over there for a long time - but that wasn't our fault!

THE MOTHERS OF INVENTION
ROYAL FESTIVAL HALL
Friday 25th October

We flew to London to get ready for the big show at the Royal Festival Hall.[84] We had a week[85] to get ready so we rehearsed in a Granada bingo hall somewhere on the outskirts of London. That's where Frank presented us with the first glimpse of a script and he explained what we were going to do at the show.

We rehearsed all week for six hours a day. Artie, Ian and Bunk would spend three hours a day with the orchestra players, while we would rehearse our lines. We got our stage costumes there. I got my Jimi Hendrix costume with the feather boa and all that. Artie, Ian, and Bunk had tuxedos to wear. Roy was going be dressed as "The Boy Pope" and Don had his cape, lurking around and transforming. We played the show and it was a wonderful hit and the audience flipped out and they just loved it.

As part of my act, I had to run out into the audience to find some pussy for the rest of the guys. I grabbed one of the usherettes, who was standing in the aisle, and she shouted to me, "You're the most disgusting thing I've ever seen in my life!" and it was perfect. I guess I scared the hell out of her because I really think she meant it.

This was during the part with all the classical players. After the intermission, the band came back and played our regular concert and for the first time since recording it, we played 'Brown Shoes Don't Make It'.

Colour Me Pop

We recorded a BBC session during that week of rehearsals and so we went over there one evening.[86] I remember at the end of the session, one of those big studio lights that hang up in the ceiling came undone and it came crashing down and nearly hit somebody in the band. If it would have, it would probably have killed them. The whole session only lasted for a few hours, but we actually recorded about 30 minutes of material.

Paris Nights

After London, we went back to Paris for the last concert, which was a midnight show at the Olympia.[87] We had one night off in Paris before we played the show and we were staying on the Left Bank in a little cheesy hotel. We met some nice girls there though hardly any of them could speak English, or would speak English. I noticed in France how hard it was to get anyone to give you directions or anything. The people would not speak to you if you spoke English like an American. They really hated Americans in France at that time.

This was the end of one of the best tours The Mothers of Invention ever did while I was in the band. Hooray! Hooray! Hooray!!!!!

A New Deal

When we got back from the 1968 European Tour, just before the elections for the president in 1968, we had a big meeting with Frank and Herb and signed a new contract with Bizarre Records/Warner Bros. We got $1000 each for signing and they also paid us $500 each for the recording sessions we'd done for *Ruben & The Jets* and *Uncle Meat* - which was nothing compared to the time we put in!

Lowell George Enters the Picture

Lowell George joined the band right after we got back from Europe. He was playing in Elliot Ingber's new band, The Fraternity of Man. Elliot was still friends with all of us, including Frank, as he used to come up to the house at Kirkwood and hang out before we left Hollywood.

We had been playing a new song then called 'Oh No!' The Fraternity of Man covered that song and they actually recorded it before we did.[88] Elliot, Lowell, Richie Hayward, Stash Wagner and a guy called Marty Martin were The Fraternity of Man. Marty was the bass player and he was married to Natalie Cole. I knew her pretty well and she was so sweet a girl. She wasn't doing any singing then that I knew of. As we all know, she sure did afterwards.

116

Frank hired Lowell because we needed a singer and he was a great singer and also a great guitar player. Lowell was so fuckin' proud to be in The Mothers of Invention and Roy and I were happy about him joining because we liked Lowell a whole bunch. He was only about 5'6" tall,[89] a short guy, but kind of heavy set with his little feet like flippers. He was a very funny guy.

Lowell added a lot to the band as he could play a mean slide guitar. We started doing more blues things and more boogie stuff like 'Pachuco Hop' and also started doing 'Here Lies Love' and 'Lonely, Lonely Nights' which was a Johnny "Guitar" Watson song.

Lowell only lived a few houses away from where Captain Beefheart and The Magic Band were living and rehearsing in Woodland Hills.

Frank's Other Projects

You have to understand that we didn't hang out with Frank very often. It was only when we were rehearsing or on the road. I hung out with Roy and Artie Tripp and Dick Kunc because we were all living over the hill in the San Fernando Valley. So we didn't always know what Frank was up to because he always had so many projects on the go at any one time. He had started Straight Records so he could produce other musicians, other than just The Mothers of Invention.

Frank was now working with Captain Beefheart & The Magic Band on a new project, because they had signed a deal with him and Herbie on Straight Records. I used to run across Beefheart here and there because their house was only a mile from my place in Woodland Hills. I went over there a few times with Dick Kunc, who was going to be engineering their recordings. But you know Beefheart didn't like people coming around much, he thought they would steal his ideas or something. I never stayed very long because I felt like I was in the way. I couldn't hardly listen to what they were doing because it was so fucking weird. I don't know exactly what they were taking up there, maybe some Acid, but they were just out there anyway.[90]

There were all kinds of strange stories about what was going on up there. It seems that he had the band under a very strict regime. I used to go over there sometimes just for a laugh, to go and see the circus because that was what it was like to me. I heard that they would rehearse at all sorts of weird hours and he would get them up in the middle of the night if he had an idea. If they didn't get up, he'd beat the shit out of them. I also heard that once a week, one of the guys got to go out for groceries. "Be back soon!" was all Don[91] would say.

It took me a few years to get into *Trout Mask Replica* when it came out and I still don't completely understand that great album but after that I thought it was just the greatest. I do remember that it only took those guys about five hours to completely record the whole album.[92]

Frank couldn't believe it since he had booked a month in Whitney Studios for the project. So he rounded the GTOs up and told them it was time for them to record their album. Roy and I got a call to go down to Whitney Studios to do a session with them. The Jeff Beck Group went in and did some overdubs when they were in town a few weeks later.

The GTOs - Girls Together Outrageously - were a bunch of the groupies who were on the scene. They used to hang out at Frank's house in the canyon and they babysat for Gail a lot. Miss Lucy was one of the girls that we had met in New York City during the Garrick Theater days. Miss Lucy had started hanging with a bunch of other chicks, all young between 18-20 years old. The others were Miss Sparky, Miss Cinderella, Pamela De Barres and so on - none of the Kirkwood girls. The girls really became part of the whole scene, you know, being groupies and fooling around. They developed their own kind of language and lifestyle.

There were also a bunch of young guys who started to call themselves the BTOs - Boys Together Outrageously. They were all hanging out around Hollywood being very silly.

We played a show at Fullerton College in California.[93] Ian Underwood wasn't at the gig because he had caught the Flu pretty bad. "Wild Man" Fischer played with us on that show and Dick Kunc gave me a copy of that show. Some years later, that tape seemed to disappear. Later, I saw a bootleg album which contained exactly what was on that tape.[94]

In December 1968, The Mothers headlined at the Shrine Exposition Hall.[95] The GTOs opened and Roy and I were the girls' rhythm section because we had played on their new album. It was the first concert for them and was a nice concert. I think that Don [Preston] played piano and Lowell played guitar. Lowell produced two of the tracks on the GTO's LP *Permanent Damage*, on Straight Records.[96]

The Medal

For Christmas that year we all got a medal. That's what Frank gave us for Christmas because that is what Pam (alias Suzie Creamcheese) told him he should do! On the front of mine was a baseball player. It was a really nice bronze medal. On the back it had engraved "Berlin Survival Award 1968" I've still got it but it's with my family in El Paso. Oh yeah, I wore that medal proudly, Man!

The previous New Year, we had been busy playing but this year we just had the time off. We'd been working very hard this year. I had a Christmas Party and John Mayall, Mick Fleetwood and John McVie came. John Mayall was kind of going out with Gail's sister.

118

All the Mothers were at the party - except for Frank.

Photo courtesy Art Tripp

Notes to Chapter 7

[1] Studio: Early Jan. to mid-Feb. excl. Toronto visit
[Ref: globalia.net/donlope/fz/chronology/1965-1969]
[2] This period stretched back to Oct. 1967
[3] Recorded between Dec. 1967 and Feb. 1968
[4] But only for two extended periods so far
[5] From Oct. through Nov. 1967 and early January through to early Feb. 1968
[6] JCB is credited on the version of 'Oh No' as well as other songs recorded at this time, notably 'Handsome Cabin Boy', 'Wedding Dress Song' and 'Dog Breath'.
[7] On *Burnt Weeny Sandwich*, 1970. 'Valarie' was not recorded before June 1969. 'WPLJ' was recorded in July 1969; JCB is not credited on this track.
[8] *Weasels Ripped My Flesh*, 1970
[9] The recording on *Weasels Ripped My Flesh* dates from June 1969
[10] Convocation Hall, Toronto University, Jan. 28
[11] Pamela Zarubica was in Woodstock for Christmas 1967, staying with Jimmy. Roy, Ray (or both) was also there. The inspiration for the name "Geronimo" was Pamela's. [Ref: Pamela Zarubica, in conversation]
[12] The Mothers play in Fall River MA on Feb. 18, 1968. The third act is Vanilla Fudge. The Mothers don't play in Providence, RI until Aug 8, when Vanilla Fudge are again on the bill. [Ref: members.shaw.ca/fz-pomd/giglist/]
[13] February 1968. "In actual fact...my invitation to play for Frank was something of an audition." [Ref: Art Tripp, in correspondence]
[14] [Frank] "brought me into the band as soon as he heard me play. We toured the next day..." No wonder! After majoring in Music at the Cincinnati Conservatory of Music, Art had played

with the Cincinnati Symphony Orchestra for three years before he got a scholarship to finish his Masters degree at the Manhattan School of Music in 1967. Frank had found Art through Dick Kunc, Frank's recording engineer. [Ref: Art Tripp, in correspondence; Prism Films: Art Tripp]

[15] Something to drink, some Marijuana, and an Amphetamine

[16] JCB also recalls playing in Syracuse. This was Feb 25, at the War Memorial Theater the day after Colgate Univ. [Ref: members.shaw.ca/fz-pomd/giglist/1968]
"Artie played a drum solo to start the Syracuse show." [Ref: Art Tripp, in correspondence]

[17] At the Statler Hilton Hotel on Feb. 29, 1968

[18] Mar. 4, 1968

[19] Mar. 17, 1968 at the Kaleidoscope

[20] The Mothers of Invention "opened" Thee Image on March 15/16, 1968

[21] An ounce ≈ 28 grams

[22] Mar. 22-24, 1968

[23] If so, it took another four months to make the move.

[24] April 19-20, 1968. The recently formed James Cotton Blues Band played with MOI.

[25] This is the first mention of *Life* magazine by JCB. The feature was printed in the June 28, 1968 issue but did not include Velvet Underground. It did include J. Airplane and five other bands – Who, Cream, Country Joe, Doors and Big Brother & The Holding Company.

[26] Woodstock – Cincinnati is around 740 miles

[27] April 26 1968, with Ravi Shankar? [Ref: members.shaw.ca/fz-pomd/giglist/1968]

[28] Cream decided to break up in May 1968, but in July announced a final tour of the States followed by two final gigs in London in late Nov. 1968 [Ref. Wikipedia, April 2013]

[29] April 27, 1968

[30] Cast in plaster to make a model

[31] The case came to court in April, 1993

[32] April 28, 1968

[33] 1050 miles away!

[34] Called The Dog

[35] June 27, 1969

[36] Making a journey of about 3400 miles by land and not including the air miles!

[37] May 10-11, 1968

[38] [The Zappas] "...had already rented it before the band got back to L.A. Jimmy and I drove over to it the next day after we got back to L.A." [Ref: Art Tripp, in correspondence]

[39] Seemingly they moved out on Sept. 6, 1968, just before the Europe tour.

[40] The festival JCB refers to here was held in Hallandale in Florida at the Gulf Stream Racetrack May 18-19. It rained the second day and the festival was cancelled that day. The jam session is famously remembered. Buddy Miles is not on the bill but other bands such as Steppenwolf, Pacific Gas & Electric, Three Dog Night and Blues Image were.
[Jon Larsen, *The JCB Story* (audio):] JCB describes a 3-day affair and includes Jefferson Airplane in the line-up. However, the codicil he adds to the story is most interesting as it recalls the run-in Herb Cohen had there with the promoters.

[41] 100,000 [Ref: en.wikipedia.org/wiki/Miami_Pop_Festival]

[42] Of E.L.O. fame

[43] In Farmington Utah, about 17 miles from Salt Lake City, on May 29, 1968. Part of this tour might have included a trip to Fresno on May 25, to the Selland Arena.

[44] No confirmation of this event

[45] May 31, 1968

[46] June 1, 1968

[47] June 4, 1968

[48] June 6-8, 1968. The line-up recalled here for these three nights is the line-up that played Dec. 14-16, 1967. The line-up for this event included BB King and Booker T. and The MGs. One night was at the Fillmore, two at the Winterland.

[49] Shortly after midnight June 5, 1968

[50] The Cheetah Club, June 28-30, 1968. On July 14, the MOI again played at the Cheetah.

[51] July 14, 1968 GUAMBO #2; JCB may be conflating two events [See: previous Note]

[52] July 23, 1968

[53] Aug. 9-10, 1968

[54] "The bartender had come over to Dick Barber (road manager) to tell him that Rudi (the club owner) wanted to buy him a drink. Dick said he'd have a ginger ale. When the bartender went to tell Rudi what Dick had ordered, there were a few short words, then the bartender came back to Dick and said, 'Rudi wants to buy you a DRINK.' Dick apologized, and ordered a highball." [Ref: Art Tripp, in correspondence]

[55] Four nights: Aug. 14-17, 1968

[56] Aug. 26-29, 1968

[57] JCB clearly contradicts the record here as apparently this "piece" was performed in Denver, May 3, 1968! [Ref: globalia.net/donlope/fz/songs/Little_House_I_Used_To_Live_In]

[58] "It was during the Chicago tour that Ray announced that he was quitting... He was fed up with the new music direction." [Ref: Art Tripp, in correspondence]

[59] This may be an anachronism here, as at this time it was the "Chicago 7" (or 8). JCB may also be condensing events here as the MOI were to play in Seattle and Vancouver before the Convention started.

[60] Aug. 24, 1968

[61] Kerrisdale Arena, Aug. 25, 1968

[62] Aug. 30, 1968

[63] Aug. 31, 1968

[64] Sept. 15, 1968 with Joan Baez, the Byrds and others

[65] The Grugahalle, Sept. 28, 1968

[66] Kongresshalle, Sept. 29, 1968

[67] or wisely?

[68] Presumably, JCB means they had to wait out the time on the plane in Helsinki.

[69] Konserthuset Oct. 1, 1968

[70] Oct. 3, 1968

[71] Musikhalle, Oct. 5, 1968

[72] Oct. 6, 1968

[73] Played at the Deutsches Museum Kongressaal on Oct. 9, 1968

[74] Beer averages around 5% in Germany

[75] Konserthaus, Oct. 12, 1968

[76] Carlton Opera Hotel?

[77] Sportpalast, Oct. 16, 1968

[78] The fencing was about three feet [about one meter] tall made of vertical one to two-inch [3-5 cm] tubing. The stage was only three feet off the floor. [Ref: Dick Barber - Interview Part 1, killuglyradio.com]

[79] Dick Barber says there were 200 police there with dogs and implies that they were held back deliberately so as not to inflame the situation!

[80] Dick Barber recalls that as equipment was removed from the stage, band member by band member, their amps were re-plugged into Frank's guitar amp so he kept getting louder and louder and helped to keep the SDS back.

[81] "By the skin of our teeth, man! It was a very frightening time. But we finished the show. We played two hours and the last hour was with 200 SDS members on the stage with us, making sure that we played... and the thing is they liked us. It wasn't that they didn't like us but they were very political at the time, in the 60s, especially in Berlin and I can understand why. I mean, the city is surrounded by a wall and the only way in or out is to fly. I can understand that part of it, the frustration those people must have been feeling but ... did they have to take it out on us?" [From: JCB interview with Radio Ohr, Offenburg, Germany, 1993]

[82] Concertgebouw, Oct. 20, 1968

[83] History reports the show going out on Oct. 23
[Ref: soundcolourvibration.com/2012/04/21/lds-058-frank-zappa/]
[84] Oct. 25, 1968. [See: the Internet, which says not Oct 28 as stated in the cover notes to *Ahead Of Their Time*!]
[85] Four days at most, unless the Internet is wrong! [See: previous Note]
[86] Oct. 23, 1968, for BBC2 TV Show: *Colour Me Pop*
[Ref: en.wikipedia.org/wiki/Colour_Me_Pop]
[87] Probably Oct. 28, 1968
[88] Released on ABC Records, 1968, produced by Tom Wilson
[89] 5 feet 6 inches is about 1.68 meters
[90] "Beefheart or The Magic Band didn't do any drugs." [Ref: Art Tripp, in correspondence]
[91] Don Van Vleet, Captain Beefheart
[92] The instrumental tracks of 21 of the songs [Ref: J. French: *Beefheart...*]. JF also says that FZ only gave the band six hours in the studio to complete everything.
[93] Nov. 8, 1968
[94] Reputedly Lowell George's first gig with MOI [Ref: *Rock & Roll Doctor*, Mark Brend]
[95] Dec. 6-7, 1968
[96] Released the day following this venue, on Dec. 8, 1968
[Ref: globalia.net/donlope/fz/related/Permanent_Damage]

The Shrine & the Children of God

We played a big show at the Shrine again.[1] Fleetwood Mac were on second. I knew John McVie and Mick Fleetwood from that gig we'd played in Denmark when they were with John Mayall. Now they were working with Peter Green and Jeremy Spencer. Not long after that gig, Jeremy disappeared with the "Children of God". I remember those people because they were always hanging around on the Sunset Strip. They were a pretty strange bunch of fanatics and they liked to brainwash people into joining their sect. They really were kind of freaky.

A Second Surprise for Frank

That's also the gig where Frank had worked out a little skit for the stage which he was famous for. It was arranged for this girl named Gigi to come onto the stage. She was one of the chicks who hung out with The GTOs and she liked to be whipped with a belt. She was going to come on when we did 'Pachuco Hop' and get a little mocked whipping.

There was this guy called Skippy Diamond who was a friend of ours. The "Gentle Bear" was what we called him and he was a pretty-good-sized guy who used to be a wrestler. He had heard about what was going to happen, so he was standing over by Gigi. When it was time for this to all happen, he grabbed the belt and ran on to the stage and started wailing into the girl and the audience was going wild.

Kim Fowley, who just loved the limelight, was right in the front row and of course, he thought, "Hey, this is too good of an opportunity for me to pass up!" so he jumped up on the stage. As soon as Skippy saw him, he started wailing on him too because Skippy never really liked the guy!

The next person he started on was Frank and he managed to whack him a few times. I mean he was wailing on everybody you know, kind of temporarily insane. Frank was trying to get away from Skippy but there he is in front of five thousand people.

Skippy said, "Come on Frank, you started this so take your fucking medicine!" Now that's the second time when one of those little things that Frank liked to do backfired. I was glad that I was behind the drums and so was Artie.

Boston Jazz & Roland Kirk

We played at the Boston Globe Jazz Festival with Dave Brubeck and Roland Kirk the night of my thirty-first birthday on February 1st.[2]

Roland sat in with us for a jam and we played a song called 'Behind The Sun' where Roland, Bunk, Ian, and Motorhead were all on their backs honking away just like the old days.

16-Track in Miami

We stayed in Miami for about four ... days and went into Criteria Studios to record. Criteria was one of the first 16-track studios in the country at the time and Frank wanted to use the extra tracks. We recorded 'My Guitar Wants To Kill Your Mama', 'Little House I Used To Live In' which was still called 'The Return Of The Hunchback Duke' at that time, and a bunch of other stuff as well.[3]

After that session, I think we played one night[4] at Thee Image before we left Miami. It was a big place which used to be an old bowling alley and that they had turned into a concert hall. Jim Morrison pulled out his dick on stage there and got himself arrested - what a dork![5]

You Can't Do That On Stage

That tour was built up around a 200 miles radius of New York City. On those tours, the equipment would all go underneath the bus and so it all went with us.

Those tapes from *You Can't Do That On Stage Anymore Vol. 5* came from that tour. We did the Electric Factory in Philadelphia.[6] We played The Factory in the Bronx.[7] We did gigs around the East Coast which included colleges like Yale.[8]

Of course, on all those east coast tours we always played at the Fillmore East, as we were regulars there.[9]

1969-02-21
Late Show
Fillmore East
New York City, NY

FZ, Lowell George, Roy Estrada, Jimmy Carl Black, Art Tripp, Ian Underwood, Don Preston, Bunk Gardner, Motorhead Sherwood Buzz Gardner

The One Fifth Avenue Hotel

Roy and I were with Lowell the day he bought his Stratocaster from Manny's music store. He had asked us, "Will you take me to Manny's?" It was his first visit to New York. He bought a new black "Strat" and I think that was his axe for most of the time after that with Little Feat.

We stayed at the One Fifth Avenue Hotel in Greenwich Village. Lowell, Roy and I stayed together and we had a suite with two bedrooms, a living room and a kitchen. It was $30 a day so it only cost us $10 a day each.

I had gone down to a bar called the Tin Angel that was across the street from the Garrick Theater. It was one of our hangouts then and we kind of knew everyone there. It was a popular musician's place to try and pick up PUSSY. Well, I picked up some pussy and took her back to the hotel and we proceeded to get it on since the boys weren't there.

After we had balled for a couple of hours, we took a break. About that time, the boys arrived with a new little practice amp that Lowell had bought. The girl was giving me a blowjob as they arrived and didn't seem to care if they were there or even the Pope. Lowell couldn't restrain himself and just got down and started eating her out, while Roy played a bass solo on that new amp. That was the feeling of the 1960s.

 At the end of 1968, I bought a Sony reel-to-reel tape machine. Bunk and Roy bought one each too. Dick Kunc told us which one was the best to buy. It was stereo and it had two microphones with it. I mainly used it to record LPs. If I recorded at low speed, I could get about four hours of music on one reel. I had that machine for years - I used it until cassette recorders became popular.

We had an old upright piano in the house which was handy for when the guys came round. Early in 1969, Roy and Lowell brought their amps round for a jam. Lowell had been writing some songs, so we recorded some of them. That's when we did the first recording of 'Willin''. I never thought anymore about the song until I heard it on the first Little Feat album. I wish I still had that tape. I do know that the song was written at the One Fifth Avenue Hotel in Greenwich Village on one of our visits to New York City. I really had a lot of fun with Lowell as he was a super guy and a great musician.

I recorded some Geronimo Black things with that machine. I don't know what happened to it, it was probably left somewhere to gather dust. That old machine just became too bulky to move around.

THE L.A. FREE CLINIC We played a show with Captain Beefheart & The Magic Band at the Aquarius Theater in Hollywood and that was the only time that we ever played with them on the same bill.[10] The opening act for that concert was Jethro Tull who were on their first tour of the States.[11] Lowell was in the band and I think Buzz was too. The Magic Band had just finished the recordings for *Trout Mask Replica* and I couldn't believe what those guys were playing, they just blew me away. I thought it would be impossible to follow them, and I know that Frank was really impressed with them so we had to really play our asses off that night.

As it turned out, Beefheart was just too far out for most people at that time, especially with *Trout Mask Replica*. Most people couldn't understand where he was coming from and still don't.

A Hitch in the New Chevy

Every time I would leave town, the VW Camper would break down. Loretta had so much trouble with that car because she never could get it started. It was always like that until the day before I got back off the road and then the fucking thing would start running again. I never could find out what was wrong with it because it was always running when I had it. I'd be home for a couple of weeks and it would run perfect. Then soon as I'd leave, it would go fucked again.

I got fed up with listening to Loretta bitch and moan about everything and especially about that camper, so I went down to the Chevrolet place in Woodland Hills. They knew who I was when I walked into that place because The Mothers were pretty big in the L.A. area. They gave me the royal treatment and so I made a deal that day. I traded the VW camper for a brand new 1969 Chevrolet Caprice. The payments were $125 a month and the car cost me $4500 total. It was loaded with power-everything.[12]

Right after I bought that car, Frank gave everybody a two-week vacation and that was about the middle of May.[13] I packed up the wife and the kids and headed for El Paso, Texas. I hadn't been home in a few years and I

really wanted to show my parents that I was a Rock Star. I really had a blast on that visit, just hanging out with my old friends, who really thought I was a star.

We left to go back to L.A. after two weeks of fun. When we got outside of Tucson Arizona, we saw two young boys hitchhiking in the direction of Phoenix. We stopped and gave them a ride and they realized that Jimmy Carl Black, "The Indian of the Group", had picked them up. As it turned out, they were big fans of the band and had seen us play there the year before. They said that they were young musicians and they wanted

Photo: Kim, Darrell, Gary, Jina

to do what I was doing. I would see those lads about six years later at The Roxy in Hollywood playing with a band called The Tubes, which at that time were pretty big in the rock scene. I still can't remember their names but one played guitar and the other played bass.[14]

On the next tour, we played Detroit,[15] Toronto,[16] then Appleton WI,[17] and then back in Toronto at the Rock Pile a second time.[18]

126

Lowell's Gone!
The next thing we hear is that Lowell won't be coming to England with us! Frank had cut him loose. Frank told him it was time he started his own band and it broke Lowell's heart because he wanted to go to England so bad. Man! It just devastated him! We were never given a proper explanation for it because he wasn't fired - he was just cut loose! Frank had never kept a second guitarist in the band for any length of time. I believe that Frank really didn't want another guitar player in the band. He was also doing most of the vocals by then. Lowell was cool about the whole thing and he did what he was told - like everybody did in the Mothers!

Lovin' an Elevator & Roy
We had two days off before we left for England and we had to change hotels the next morning.

I met the guy who invented the drug MDA which I find out years later is the basis of Ecstasy, called the "Love" drug. It was invented in Toronto, Canada by some chemistry guy who was looking for an alternative to LSD. It was in powder form when I had it and this is just before we left for England. It actually was a pretty nice drug that I got off to in a big way. I came back to the Four Seasons Hotel, and I got in the elevator and - I was way out there, I was totally blasted - I couldn't get out! I had fallen in love with that fuckin' elevator! I just kept going up and down, for about two hours!

So, I finally got out of the elevator and walked into our room and there was Roy sitting on the floor with the air conditioning unit completely dismantled! He said, "It was making a noise, so I decided to take it apart and fix it!" He had taken it apart after he had taken his bass guitar apart - he was trying to adjust it! The bass was so fucked up that he had to take it to a shop the next day and get them to put it back together.

Someone had given Roy a half ounce of "Crank", Speed, pure Amphetamine, some of the nastiest shit that you could ever think about doing and I still don't know how he could do that shit.

So, after all that, he decided that he was going to go to sleep because he'd been up for about four days and when he crashed, he crashed big time. I had to get Bunk to help me carry him out of the hotel when we changed hotels. I know that they - the hotel - thought it was kind of funny with us dragging this guy down the stairs because we couldn't wake him up. He was sort of walking but he was holding on to us and when we got to the other hotel he was sleeping so we just dumped him in his bed.[19]

I still had a little of the MDA powder left when we flew from Toronto to England. I took another little MDA Trip because it was at night and a lot of the guys were asleep. I fell in love with the stewardess and the chair and everything around me.

THE MOTHERS ARE COMING!

We had a few days off in London, because every time we went there Frank would always have a few days of interviews and promotion stuff.

The band was staying at the Winston Hotel which was on the opposite side of Hyde Park from where Frank was staying. We partied a bit - we went to the Speakeasy Club every night and met girls. I met this chick there who I was doing a thing with, but back in those days I didn't want to restrict my love to just one woman, when there were so many who seemed to want it.

After a few days, Artie took over from me and she didn't seem to care as long it was with a member of the Mothers.

We took a bus for that tour and the first gig was Birmingham, which was a great gig and now famous as being where the track 'Weasels Ripped My Flesh' was recorded.[20]

TOWN HALL, BIRMINGHAM

FRANK ZAPPA
and the **MOTHERS OF INVENTION**

We went to Newcastle[21] which was famous for its beer and that was my first experience with Newcastle Brown Ale! We had two or three crates of it backstage, that they gave us. We played the gig, which was a huge success and got invited to a party afterwards. I had drunk about four of those beers at the gig. I drank one before the show and the rest after the show. I drank about four more at that party and I thought it tasted like dad's root beer because it didn't taste strong.

When it was time to leave the party, I headed for the door and ran into the wall. I could see the door was there, I could see it, but I couldn't get through it. I could see the light in the other room, but I kept running into the wall. It took me quite a while to get out of that place. I slept in my jacket that night because the boys just threw me into my room. I was down for the count and that was my first experience with Newcastle Brown Ale but certainly not my last!

PALACE THEATRE
MANCHESTER

The show in Manchester[22] was on a Sunday and there was a law in the theater that had been in place for a few hundred years. Bands were not allowed to sing any vocals on a Sunday and if you did you were subject to arrest.

So we had to play an instrumental show but that was not a problem for us since we weren't singing many songs anyway at that time.

From there we went down to Bristol and played a wonderful gig there.[23] I bought me a beautiful pair of Beatle boots there, which were nice leather boots, and I met a lovely girl there also!

The Mothers and their inventions please their fans
Colston Hall, Bristol

We drove down from London to Portsmouth to play a show [24] and drove back again that night, then had three or four days to work on the show for the Royal Albert Hall.[25]

THE GUILDHALL
PORTSMOUTH
THE MOTHERS OF INVENTION
IN CONCERT
THURSDAY, JUNE 5th at 8.50 p.m

The show was very interesting because we did our first ballet. Kansas[26] and Dick Barber were the carriers and Motorhead and Noel Redding were the ballerinas that night!

The next day we flew to Paris and played two shows at the Olympia.[27] In the middle of our second show, the whole of the cast from *Hair* came running down the aisles and got up with us. We played 'The Age Of Aquarius' - It was a wild show!

New York: Back at the Fillmore

We flew back to New York and had about three days off to get over jet lag. Then we played the Fillmore East again and I remember the bill: The Mothers Of Invention, Jesse Colin Young & The Youngbloods and Chicago Transit Authority. Now that was a fuckin' bill.[28] We did that particular bill about two of three times and we actually played quite a lot of gigs with Chicago.[29]

Then we went back to California and had a couple of weeks off that were needed. I managed to lose my wedding ring when we played The Fillmore East. As soon as I would get on the plane, that wedding ring would come off my finger as I didn't want anybody knowing that I was married, especially the girls. I wouldn't get any pussy that way and, after all, that was what touring was all about!

I had to go and buy another ring before I came back from the tour, which was expensive since I had to buy her one also. I told Loretta that I thought that it was time for us to have new rings, but I wasn't fooling her because she knew exactly what the fuck was going on. I never really fooled her but I don't think she cared that much as long as the money was coming in and it was.

Then the touring started over again very heavy.

Mile High Pop

We went on a tour which started at the Denver Pop Festival which was held at the Mile High Stadium with Jimi Hendrix. It was a three-day festival and we headlined on the Friday night.[30] Three Dog Night, The Iron Butterfly and The Flock (with Jerry Goodman on violin) opened. Hendrix headlined the following night, but we couldn't stay to see him because we flew out the next morning to Charlotte, North Carolina for the jazz part of our tour.

Duke Ellington

It was our first time in North Carolina and it was a jazz festival, with Gary Burton, Roland Kirk, The Mothers and Duke Ellington and his band headlining.[31] It was held in the Charlotte Coliseum which was one of those big halls where they play basketball. It was a beautiful concert and what a pleasure it was to play with Duke Ellington, who I had admired for years. I got to meet him briefly and told him I was a big fan of his. He told me he thought that The Mothers where a great band and that he liked what we were doing. Roland sat in with us again there.

THE MIAMI JAZZ FESTIVAL

Miami Jai-Alai N.W. 36th St. at 36th Ave.

The next day we flew to Miami, Florida, to play another gig with the same line-up as the previous night.[32]

After the gig, we all got invited to a party by the promoter which was being held for all the bands. We did a little smoking at the hotel before we went down and we were planning to do a little juicing on the free booze. So when we got to the party, I went over and got myself a glass of champagne from the punchbowl. It had a real nice taste so I got another glass, and that's when I looked in the glass and saw a tab of "Orange Sunshine" Acid, that was melting in the bottom of it. The promoters had put a hundred tabs of the stuff in the punchbowl. So, when the walls started melting, I knew what the fuck was happening but those old guys from Duke's band sure didn't know what was happening because they were "Juicers". I am pretty sure they'd never taken that stuff before and they were blasted out of their heads, Man!

So were the rest of us! I remember that Motorhead and Dick Barber had drank some of that punch and were totally blasted, since neither one of them had ever done Acid before.[33] The next morning, those two guys had to go to Fort Lauderdale to take a physical for the Army. Both had received their draft notices before we had left California. Needless to say, they were both classified as 4F, which means they weren't Army material. That was probably the only good thing that came out of that Acid Trip for those guys.

I remember seeing Frank and Roland walk into the party room just before the walls started melting. As soon as they saw what was happening, they just turned around and split quick!

We left the party as the sun was coming up and of course there was no fuckin' way that we were going to go to sleep. When I got back to the hotel, I walked up to the lobby desk. The time was about nine o'clock in the morning and lo and behold, the assistant manager was Kurt St. John, a guy from my hometown that I had known all my life. I'd taken piano lessons from his mother when I was a very young boy. He wanted to bullshit with me for about three hours about Anthony but I was so fuckin' blasted on this LSD that I was just reeling. Trying to talk to this goddamn straight guy, with a flat top haircut, was almost too much for me. I finally got away from him because we had to change Holiday Inns that morning. When we got checked into the new Holiday Inn, I started hanging out by the swimming pool and drinking beer because I really wanted to come down off that Acid. I got to talking to this good-looking receptionist who was from Denmark. I proceeded to talk her into coming to my room after she had got off work. We fucked all night because she really wanted to get it on and she did.

Don Preston, aka Dom De Wilde, had met this Malaysian girl while he was still on that Acid Trip and they went and laid out on the beach for most of the day where they fell asleep and he got roasted. He looked like a fucking lobster, Man! He forgot that we had a recording session that day and he came about four hours late and Frank was completely bent out of shape at him.

Houston & the Falling Elevator
The next day, we left for Houston, Texas and on the first day there we went and set the equipment up and did a sound check, even though we didn't have the gig until the next night. After the sound check, we went and did a radio interview with Pacifica Radio which was a progressive FM radio station. It was on the 28th floor of this big building.

After we finished with the interview, everyone was feeling good because it had been so successful and it really was one of the first interviews that Frank wanted all of us to do with him. They had put us up in the Houston Hilton. We all got in the elevator, there were fifteen of us in there and we started down. That was when the cable on the elevator slipped and we started free falling! Herb Cohen was right next to the stop button and he hit this button and the elevator suddenly stopped halfway  between the 17th and 18th floors. We couldn't open the door up because it was between the two floors so we took the panel out of the ceiling and Don Preston climbed up on top and pried the next floor's door open and crawled out. He had to come downstairs and prise the next set of doors open and we had to climb out. Man! I was shaking! My whole body felt like rubber! I am surprised that I didn't shit my pants. Art Tripp and I walked 17 flights down because there was no way I was even thinking about getting in one of those things for a while. I still feel funny when I get on an elevator.

By the way, the gig the next night at the Catacombs[34] was wonderful as usual. I remember going to a party after the gig with this beautiful Houston girl and someone had given us a big bag of Pot to take to the party. On the way, we passed a cop car going the other way and, as soon as they saw all the long hair in the car, they turned around to stop us. That bag of Pot went out the window. They tried to hassle us for a while but we weren't holding so they let us go. The lovely girl and I got it on after we left the party.

The day after that gig, we didn't have to leave until about 6 o'clock in the evening. My cousin came by and we went out and visited my uncle. They were living in Houston and it had been a while since I had seen either one of them, so we got a little fucked up drinking beer all day. My cousin took me to the airport in time to catch the plane to Rhode Island, where the next concert was happening.

 We got on the plane for Pawtucket, Rhode Island and the next evening we played at the Newport Jazz Festival.[35]

John Mayall was on before us and of course it was great to see him again. The last time we had seen him was in Copenhagen in 1967 on the first European tour. After we played a brilliant show, there was Miles Davis with his *Bitches Brew*[36] band with Chick Corea, Tony Williams, Wayne Shorter, Dave Holland and John McLaughlin.

That was the only time we ever played with Miles and he was cool. He told us that we did alright for white boys and I had to remind him that I wasn't exactly white but he just said, "You know what I mean, you ain't exactly black!"

Boston: Playing with BB King

We went back and played Boston again and this time we played at The Ark and there is the famous live recording (bootleg) of that show.

We went down to the club the night before and that's when Roy and I sat in with BB King. It was a real privilege to play 'The Thrill Is Gone' with the king of Blues. We had played on the same bill the year before at the Fillmore West in San Francisco and he remembered us. What a nice guy.

Philadelphia: Sly at The Spectrum

From there, we went to Philadelphia and played at The Spectrum,[37] which was a big basketball arena where the Philadelphia '76crs played. Eighteen to twenty thousand people fit in this place.

The Mothers were supposed to be the headliners and Sly and The Family Stone the opening band. But they didn't show up on time so the promoter came and said, "Look Man! You've gotta go on because somebody's gotta go on here!" So Frank said, "OK we'll play, we're ready."

We went on and played a hell of a show and then afterwards Sly was there and Frank says, "Man, you better play your ass off 'cause we know what you are up to!" I think that they did that on purpose because Sly thought, "Man, I'm a star now!" but you know he was so fucked up that night because he was heavy into Cocaine. They didn't top our show and they got bad reviews anyway for showing up late. That is what happens when you get too high and start thinking you are a big star when you're not!

At the Race Course

We went after that to the Laurel Race Course in Maryland for another open-air festival[38] and that was with Sly and The Family Stone again, the Jeff Beck Group, and Ten Years After.

I remember walking around backstage close to where the bear cage was (it was for the people who couldn't come backstage) and I heard somebody yellin' "Sonny, Sonny!"[39] I knew immediately that it had to be someone from Anthony. It was this girl Linda Eastwood and she was a lot younger than me. Her mother and father were best friends with my Mom and Dad. She was living there in Maryland and she'd just married some guy from there. I went and had a nice chat with her because it was always great to see somebody from back home.

At the Tyrone Guthrie

We got on the plane and flew to Minneapolis and played at the Tyrone Guthrie Theater.[40] Acoustically, it was the best sounding theater that we'd ever played in. It was built for music to be played in. After that gig, it was one of Frank's favorite places to play and I think he played there a few times after the old Mothers broke up.

Stage Telepathy

Nobody ever knew exactly what we were going to do during a show because Frank would make it up as we went along. At that time, we had hundreds of songs in our repertoire that he could call up at any time. We never had a set list because he didn't write anything out before the show. Everything was purely spontaneous and he'd play a phrase and we'd jump in with him. Sometimes he wouldn't even play a phrase, because we got to the point where we were almost telepathic with each other. We all knew what he was going to do before he did it. He would jump up in the air and come down and everybody would be right there with the song. Man! It used to blow him away! It blew us all away!

It was total concentration when I played and I wasn't looking out in the audience for girls. My eyes were glued to Frank and they never left Frank Zappa because you had to watch for the signals and for the things that were happening. I'd already been out by the girls' restroom, standing there before the concert happened. I already had the girl picked out that I wanted and we'd already discussed what was going to happen after the show. She was going to be backstage, because she would have a backstage pass I'd already arranged. She was just waiting for me to get off the bandstand.

But when it was show time, believe me it was show time, there could be no fuck-ups, because I didn't want those daggers thrown at me by Frank!

Sugarcane Harris
We went back into TTG and recorded 'Directly From My Heart To You' with Don "Sugarcane" Harris on violin.[41]

Sugercane never played live with us. I'm told he was always in and out of jail because apparently he was a big junkie. That was too bad because he was a one-of-a-kind musician.

Chicago at the Aragon
In Chicago, we did a show with Howlin' Wolf and Chuck Berry at the Aragon Ballroom.[42]

Me, Roy and Lowell backed Chuck because he never carried a band.[43] Chuck was kind of an arrogant guy but hey, he could be arrogant if he wanted 'cause he WAS Chuck Berry.

The Wolf was beautiful. He was the best part of that whole show and he was the opening act and I couldn't believe that. I'd been a huge fan of his for years but that was the only time I ever saw him perform live. I don't think he liked white people very much.

I remember Janis Joplin was in the audience that night as they[44] were in town to play the place the following night. I was always happy to see her as she was a very nice Texas girl and she liked to drink and party. If I remember right, she had her own band then and not Big Brother and the Holding Company. That is when she started to really tear it up.

Buddy Guy in Central Park
We went to New York City and played at the Schaefer Beer Festival in Central Park and it had a massive stage.[45]

Buddy Guy was playing there with us because he was the opening act. He gets up on the bandstand and he's wailing away. He had just gotten one of those cordless radio things for his guitar and it was probably one of the first ones that came out. He was running all over the stage, doing his thing and he was drunker than shit. He must have thought that the stage was about four or five feet[46] off the ground so he jumped off the fuckin' stage. It was about 15 feet high and he hit that concrete and broke his leg and needless to say, that was the end of his show.

Maryanne was there, the girl that I had met on the '68 tour of Europe - the Swedish girl that wouldn't let me fuck her but would let me eat her pussy. She got up on the stage and sang with us and she was a good singer. She was doing all these kind of operatic things that consisted of noises and nonsense.

She went back to the hotel with me again after the show and still wouldn't fuck me. I guess it just wasn't meant to happen.

Atlantic City Pop Festival
AUGUST 1·2·3
Atlantic City Race Track/Atlantic City, N.J.

After that show, we went to the Atlantic City Pop Festival in New Jersey.[47]

That was a big three-day affair with Jefferson Airplane, Buddy Miles, Joe Cocker playing on his first US tour, Janis Joplin with her new band (the Full Tilt Boogie Band[48]), Little Richard headlining, and also Canned Heat were there with Henry Vestine on guitar.

We hung with most of the bands that time. The backstage area was full of "groovy" people getting high and basically having a great time.

Janis Joplin

I had hung with Janis quite a few times but I couldn't keep up with her. We were both from Texas so we hit it off like a roof on fire! That night backstage at Atlantic City Pop, she had a Joint in her mouth with a fifth of Southern Comfort in one hand and a fifth of Tequila in the other.

Needless to say, the girl was getting fucked up and then she went on the stage and played a brilliant show. I couldn't believe that she could still sing and be that screwed up!

I knew the guys from Big Brother, but I didn't know these new session guys[49] she had touring with her.

The Prettiest Man in Showbiz

I remember the girl that Don Preston was with. She was young, probably 17 or 18 years old and we were all backstage when they announced Little Richard. They had a TV monitor back there and they said, "Introducing the Prettiest Man in Show Business, Little Richard!" The girl turned to Don and said, "Don, I think you're the prettiest man in show business!"

He still gets reminded about that one every once in a while and loves it.

Jerry Goodman

We played a lot around the Chicago area because we had a lot of fans there. There was the Playboy Club in Geneva, some place in Elgin, and a gig in Highland Park. It was a beautiful place that was built for classical music.[50]

After that gig, we went over to see Jerry Goodman because he lived near there with his parents in a big mansion. Jerry was a violin player that played with a band then called The Flock. He was an excellent player and a very nice guy.

Not at Woodstock

The last tour that we did was at the same time that Woodstock was happening.[51] Even though we were invited, Zappa didn't want anything to do with Woodstock. He thought that it wouldn't be a success. In retrospect, I think it was one of his biggest fuck-ups, because we were approached to do it. I wanted to do it because I had been living up there.

So, while all that was going on, we played up in Canada instead! We played in London, Ontario, in Ottawa for two days,[52] and then Montreal for three days.[53] Montreal was good because I saw my Uncle Cal. He was the pitching coach for the Montreal Expos baseball team. He brought half the team with him to the concerts.

Let Go Motor!

Where we played in London, Ontario was like a small Disneyland, an amusement theme park. It was called The Enchantment Park or something really dumb like that.[54] It's the place where Guy Lombardo used to play with his big band. Alice Cooper played that show with us and we played in a big tent. We had a couple of days off there and as it was on a lake, we decided to go water skiing. A few of us had done it before and knew how to ski. Of course, Motorhead said that he had done it a million times and was an expert at it. I think we all thought that he didn't have a clue as to what he was doing on those skis. We were right. When he finally got up on them, the guy driving the boat took off like Motor was the expert he had said he was and the first curve he was taken to came right past the docks. It was evident that he was going to ram the dock at about thirty miles an hour and probably kill himself, so we were screaming, "Let go of the fucking rope you fool, before you kill yourself." I guess he heard us or saw what was getting ready to happen to him, so he let go and saved himself. There was never a mention of how expert of a water skier he was again - not a peep out of him.

Frank Lets Go

About a week after we got home, I called Frank to talk to him about something. After a few minutes, he just said, "Oh by the way, I've decided to break the band up, your salaries have stopped as of last week." It was quite a shock! There hadn't been any signs while we were on the tour. Frank didn't seem any different than usual. I didn't feel like there was anything wrong, but sometimes it was really hard to tell with Frank.

 I was the first one to find out, so I immediately got on the phone to Roy. Frank also started to phone everybody but I beat him to the punch with Roy. Then we all started calling each other saying, "What the fuck is going on here?"

When I spoke to Ian, it seemed like he already knew something. I think Frank already had plans for Ian to stay around.[55]

The Meeting

So then we had a meeting, and Herb and Frank did sense that we were a little upset with what was going on with a lot of the business. They kept saying, "There's no money because we're losing all this money!"

I said, "Man, we're packing these places! How can we be losing money if we're packing these places? That's what I wanna know!" Frank said that he was tired of touring and losing money but I really don't know how he could have been losing all that money.

At that meeting is when I said, "Well, listen Frank, what about the publishing and stuff on 'If we were only living in California' and 'Hi boys and girls, I'm Jimmy Carl Black and I'm The Indian of the Group'. Why don't I get a writing credit for that?"

He said, "You know, there's the fucking door and it's gonna close pretty quick! I would advise you to get through it!"

So I said, "You mean you're throwing me out?" Then I said, "First of all. You won't throw me out because I'm getting the fuck outa here anyway, because I don't wanna be here! As far as YOU throwing me out of this house, you ain't big enough to do that! Let's see who throws who out of whose house!" Man! That really pissed me off! I just asked a simple question which actually was my right to ask, because he didn't write that stuff, Man! It was a band meeting, how can you write a band meeting? It was pretty cold, and everybody was pissed off.[56]

At the time, everybody thought that it might have been Herb Cohen who had caused all this crap but we found out later that he was just doing just what Frank told him to. Herb became the fall guy! It was decided to pay me and Roy an extra two weeks' salary because we'd been with the band the longest, so that was our little leaving present!

I called up this guy called Scooby Sorken, who was the Rock 'n' Roll Musicians' Union Rep. for Local 47. Frank "Scooby" Sorken was our friend and he was a cool guy. So we rang him to see if there was anything we could do about being sacked and if there was anything we could do about getting any of our performance royalties, because we still hadn't had any.

He actually got us some extra money because there was a fund for recording musicians. You know, for all the records that I'd played on, I think they gave me about $1000. Herb and Frank had been paying taxes on us, so we got unemployment benefits. I was getting $75 a week for about nine months. That was sure better than nothing!

by Geronimo Black

I just started to look around to see who was available to jam, and maybe form a band. Bunk was ready to try things out too. Scooby turned me on to Tom Leavey and Andy Cahan. Andy had just come off the road and had been playing with Dr. John. Tom was a bass player who'd just moved out to California from New York with a guy called Denny Walley who played guitar. Tjay Contrelli, who I knew from his days in Love, came and played sax along with Bunk. I used to go and watch Love play, after we moved back to California in 1968.

We started rehearsing in my garage in Woodland Hills at the end of September. I decided to call the band Geronimo Black.

So, when we started, we had me on drums, Tom on bass, Andy on keyboards, Bunk and Tjay on the two Saxes and an electric violin player named Greg Bloch. There was no guitar in the first band. We really wanted Denny to play with us but he was playing guitar with Rosy Greer, an ex-football player from the Los Angeles Rams. They were doing R&B stuff.

We only had about three rehearsals before we played our first gig, which was at a fairly progressive church in Pasadena, California.

Uncle T

I met up with a disc jockey called Tom Gomosh who I'd met in Boston and he went under the name of "Uncle T". The station he'd worked for was one of the first of the FM stations which was very underground at the time. FM stations were the only stations who would consider playing Mothers music or any music that had no commercial potential. The Mothers had done a couple of radio interviews with him in Boston and he was a big Mothers fan. He had just moved to California and that was when Uncle T became our manager.

Tjay had introduced me to Greg Bloch who was classically trained and his parents were both in the L.A. Symphony Orchestra. His uncle was this famous violin player from Russia. Unfortunately, Greg was a full-blown junkie, so he didn't last too long in the band. We got a young guitar player called Chris in for a while and he was a good little player. He had a band called Gorilla Balls, which amused Bunk and myself.

138

Topanga Canyon Corral

We started playing some gigs at the Topanga Corral, which soon turned into a residency. We ended up playing there four nights a week, for about six months. We were the house band and we played Thursday through Sunday. On the other nights they had some great bands playing. Monday nights were The Flying Burrito Brothers, with Chris Hillman & Gram Parsons and they were a real good band. Tuesday nights was Taj Mahal. He lived in the Canyon then and Jesse Ed Davis was playing guitar with him at the time. Wednesday was Canned Heat's night. The Corral was getting to be a pretty popular club in the L.A. area to play and the competition was getting heavy. Believe me, Geronimo Black was practicing quite a lot then so we could keep our gig!

Manson & Cupid

Manson used to come into the Topanga Corral all the time.[57] I know that he came and saw Geronimo Black there but I wasn't even remotely interested in that guy! I remember "the girls" coming in too; they were pretty nice looking. I can't remember what their names were, "Squeaky" and something else like that.

I knew that guy Bobby,[58] the one that killed Hinman. He used to hang around with the Mothers. I couldn't believe it when I found out that he had done that, because he was one of the nicest guys I had ever met. They used to call him Cupid - that was his nickname! He was a Flower Power guy, Man! I don't know what the fuck Manson did to him!

You know Sharon Tate lived very close to Frank's house, up on Woodrow Wilson. He was always really worried about his family when we were on the road.

Bob Hite

Bob "The Bear" Hite[59] lived in Topanga Canyon. I used to like to go over to his house because he was a nice guy to hang out with. Bob Hite had probably one of the finest and biggest blues collections of anybody in the world. He had old 78s and 45s because that was his Trip! Man! He was a collector and he had a whole room, with shelves all the way around completely full with thousands of records, and then a whole bunch more spread around the floor. It was some archive he had there.

Little Feat

Lowell and Roy started their new project - Little Feat - about the same time that I started Geronimo Black. I'm kind of responsible for that too and not only for giving them the name.

I met a producer named Gabriel Meckler in some bar in Hollywood and he had produced a lot of the Steppenwolf music. He was a really nice guy and a big Mothers fan. We were talking and he said, "I'd like you to play on a session for an LP we're doing for a black singer named Nolan Porter." He asked me if I could put some rhythm and blues musicians together.

I said, "Well, I can get Roy Estrada to play bass and Lowell George to play some guitar."

So we went into the studio. Lowell brought Bill Payne with him to play some piano and we started recording the tracks. I could only do half of the sessions because I had commitments with Geronimo Black and so for the other tracks they brought Richie Hayward in to play drums.

When we were in the M.O.I., I was always joking with Lowell about his little feet. They were like webs, so I started to call him "Little Feet"! After those sessions, those guys just carried on playing together and decided to take Lowell's new nickname, twist it a bit and use it as the name for their new band. So that's how Little Feat got started.

 The Nolan Porter album *No Apologies* was released on Lizard Records and it's very hard to find now. Nolan wanted me to stay with him and start touring, and I thought about it too because I really liked what he was doing and he was a great singer. I decided to stay with the Geronimo Black thing. As it turned out the tour didn't really happen because the album wasn't really a hit - it didn't do anything!

Chatsworth

Geronimo Black played for about three months but then Bunk, Andy and Tom left and went on tour with Tim Buckley[60] and so there I was, stuck with no band. I tried to keep the gig going by putting some "pick up" guys together but it didn't really work out.

SAN BERNADINO AUDITORIUM SWING
JOE COCKER
ZEPHYR
GERONIMO BLACK
SKIN

 Now I was finding it hard to make ends meet. I couldn't make the payments on the new car anymore, so we had to give the car up and get a cheaper one - and look for a cheaper house to rent!

I bought an old '59 Chevy for 200 dollars and we found a place about 10 miles north of Woodland Hills, in a place called Chatsworth. It wasn't nearly as nice as the last house because the area was a bit run down. It reminded me of an old western town.[61]

Photo above: Kim, Chatsworth, 2nd Grade; Dec. 5, 1970

No more free Diners
Right before that last Mothers' European tour, Diners Club had sent me a credit card in the mail. I never applied for that thing. So I signed it and started using it and we had some fun with that fuckin' credit card. I went out owing those guys about $3000 The band broke up and I said, "Fuck, I can't pay you guys, I've got no money and I'm on Unemployment."
They finally wrote it off after a while as I said, "Have you got an application form from me?" and they said, "No!"
So I said, "Well, if I didn't fill in an application, why did you send me a credit card?"

Notes to Chapter 8

[1] Jan. 24-25, 1969
[2] Took place on Jan. 31, 1969 at the War Memorial Auditorium. They may have finished after midnight and celebrated JCB's birthday as a consequence.
[3] MOI played twice in Miami in 1969: at Thee Image, Feb. 7-8, and the Jai Alai venue in June. [globalia.net/donlope/fz/chronology/1965-1969:] dates the Criteria visit to Feb., though it does not list 'Little House...' as being recorded at this time.
[4] They played 2 nights: Feb. 7-8, 1969 at Thee Image
[Ref: members.shaw.ca/fz-pomd/giglist/1969]
[5] Morrison performed this stunt on March 1, 1969.
[6] Feb. 11-12, 1969
[7] Feb 28 1969
[8] Woolsey Hall, Yale Uni, New Haven, on Feb. 13. Not mentioned by JCB are: Columbia Uni., Drew Uni. in Madison NJ and the Ballroom, Stratford CT, Feb. 14-16
[9] Feb. 21-22 1969; with Buddy Miles and Chicago. MOI went up to Toronto and played at the Rock Pile Feb. 23

[10] Mar. 31, 1969. Benefit concert for the LA Free Clinic

[11] "Also [on] were Canned Heat and Don Ellis" [Ref: Art Tripp, in correspondence]

[12] Power this, power that, power everything...

[13] The first two weeks of May, or until the middle of May

[14] Roger Stein or Bill Spooner (guitar) and Rick Anderson (bass)?

[15] May 17, 1969. Manuscript reads Chicago.

[16] May 19

[17] May 23, Lawrence University

[18] May 24, 1969. Also Played Feb. 23 [Ref: nashtheslash.com/history/00_artists]

[19] Roy's father once shoved $20 dollars into JCB's shirt pocket when he and Roy were going off on tour, asking JCB to look after Roy, which amused JCB [Ref: Moni Black]

[20] Birmingham Town Hall, May 30, 1969

[21] City Hall, May 31, 1969

[22] Palace Theater, June 1, 1969

[23] Colston Hall, June 3, 1969

[24] Guildhall, June 5, 1969

[25] MOI drove back the same night because they were playing the Royal Albert Hall the next evening, June 6, 1969. Jimmy is thinking of the 1968 gig at the Royal Festival Hall when they did have three or four days to prepare.

[26] Kansas J. Canzus (sic), a roadie who worked for FZ for a number of years.

[27] June 7, 1969

[28] 2 nights, 2 shows a night, June 13-14, 1969

[29] Thrice in 1969 [Ref: members.shaw.ca/fz-pomd/giglist/1969]

[30] June 27, 1969

[31] June 28, 1969. 'As I recall, Hugh Masekela headlined...' [Ref: Art Tripp, in correspondence]

[32] At the Jai Alai Fronton, Miami Jazz Festival, June 29, 1969

[33] "I had tricked Dick Barber into drinking the champagne. He didn't know it was laced with Acid." [Ref: Art Tripp, in correspondence]

[34] July 3 1968

[35] July 5, 1969. Art Tripp recalls that the Mothers were the first Rock band ever to play at the Newport Jazz Festival [Ref: Art Tripp, Prism Films]

[36] Recorded Aug. 1969 and Jan. 1970; released in April 1970

[37] July 11, 1969

[38] July 12, 1969

[39] JCB was always known in Anthony as Sonny. [See: Chapter 1]

[40] July 13, 1969

[41] TTG Studios, L.A. CA, between July 18 and 30, 1969

[42] Aug. 1-2, 1969.

[43] "He didn't even bring a guitar. He borrowed Frank's." [Ref: Art Tripp, in correspondence] Lowell George was no longer playing with the MOI, so it is of interest that he should be there.

[44] The Kosmic Blues Band? [See further: Note 48]

[45] Aug. 2, 1969

[46] About 1.5 m.

[47] Held at the Atlantic City Race Track, Aug.3 1969

[48] Is this an anachronism? Janis appears to have become disenchanted with the Kosmic Blues Band after the poor reviews of the album she released in Sept. of 1969. It is now Aug. 1969. [Ref: en.wikipedia.org/wiki/Full_Tilt_Boogie_Band]

[49] The Kosmic Blues Band did contain session guitarists. [See: previous Note and Reference].

[50] The Highland Park venue was at the Rivinia Outdoor Music Center, Aug. 6, 1969. Framingham and Warrensville Heights were the other two venues on this leg of the tour [Ref: members.shaw.ca/fz-pomd/giglist/1968.html]. The Playboy Club, at Lake Geneva, and Elgin may have been in 1968. JCB is recalling successful previous concerts in this region.

[51] Aug. 15-18, 1969

[52] Twice: Aug. 15 & Aug. 19, 1969

[53] Aug. 16-18, 1969

[54] The Festival at the Wonderland Gardens took place Aug. 13-14, 1969. MOI headlined on the 1st night [Ref: members.shaw.ca/fz-pomd/giglist/1969]

[55] "Frank had decided to start a 'power quartet' with Frank, Ian, Art Tripp, and Jeff Simmons on bass." [Ref: Art Tripp, in correspondence]

[56] The rest of the guys in the band were very pissed off as can be expected as we had just finished a very successful tour. I think that Frank should have made an announcement to the press about stopping the band and done a last farewell tour and then broke up the band. Anyway, that's the way I would have done it after all the loyalty we had given him through the years of starving for his music.[Ref: JCB interview with Steve Moore, 2003]

[57] Arrested around Oct 10/12th, 1969

[58] Bobby Beausoleil murdered Gary Hinman on July 25, 1969. [See further: Chapter 6, p. 76]

[59] Of Canned Heat fame

[60] History seems to record Bunk and Buzz Gardner playing with Tim Buckley from late 1970 [timbuckley.net/bios/timeline.shtml]

[61] The film *Panama Red*, in which JCB played a part, was produced in Chatsworth. It was probably shot around 1970 though it wasn't released until 1976. Jimmy seems to have made no recorded mention of this movie or his part in it.

Part Three:

A Mother's Lot

JIMMY
CARL
BLACK

Gillund 2004

Zubin Metha

Sometime in early 1970, I got a call from Frank and he told me he wanted to put the band back together for a gig he was planning with Zubin Metha and the Los Angeles Philharmonic Orchestra.[1] We went and had a meeting with him and Herbie, but there were still some very bitter feelings about the way the band broke up. It was not so much from me because I'd still kept in contact with Frank most of the time. The band asked if Herb was involved and when Frank told us yes, everyone just stood up and walked out.

I didn't want to do it because Frank wanted to go out on tour and at that time Geronimo Black was going pretty good. I think Don was the only one from the final Mothers line-up who went back and did it. So did Billy Mundi and Ray Collins but they hadn't been in the band for ages. I was surprised to hear about Billy doing it because nobody had heard from him in ages and we didn't know where he was.

Janis

Janis Joplin came into the Corral one night in 1970 and it was only a few weeks before she died. I remember she looked pretty tired and beat. Little did anyone know what state she was really in and what was going to happen. I asked her if she wanted to sing a song with the band [Geronimo Black][2] and she sang a blues song and sang it very well. To me, she still is the best blues singer around and always will be.

In December, I got a call from Frank. He was in England writing music and dialogs for a movie. He had finally found someone who was willing to collaborate on a film version of his *200 Motels* material. United Artists had agreed to finance the project. He told me that Ringo Starr was going to be in it, along with the latest line-up of Mothers with Flo and Eddie. Lucy and Pamela also had parts in it, along with Motorhead and Don Preston. He asked me if I would be willing to sing 'Lonesome Cowboy Burt'. "Just the one scene!" is what he told me. I asked him, "How much?" and he said, "500 dollars, plus expenses and you'll receive about 30 dollars a day per-diem!" I went straight down town to Herb's office and signed the contract.

My thinking then was maybe I could get some more acting parts in other films and spawn a new career that paid more than the one I had at the time.

I flew over to London in the second week of January '71 with Flo and Eddie, George Duke, Jeff Simmons, Motorhead and Don Preston. Most of the guys had their wives with them. George had just gotten married so that was actually his honeymoon. Aynsley Dunbar was already over there and so were the girls. We arrived at Heathrow in the morning and they took us to the hotel. We rested until about 7 pm - that was the time that we went to meet Frank and discuss the movie. We sat around and had a couple of drinks together and then he passed out the scripts and told us what was going to happen. I looked at my part and found that there were quite a few lines written for me. It was a pretty good-size script and a lot more than I'd originally been told about. It was certainly worth more than $500 as far as I was concerned. I knew from experience that asking Herb for any more money was a total waste of time, so I kept my mouth shut and did what I had to do.

So, we were all sitting around reading our parts when Jeff Simmons suddenly stood up and said, "I ain't playing this comedy music and I'm not gonna do this. I quit the comedy band!" They made the rest of that night very miserable on him and the next day they had him thrown out of the hotel. They told him he could pay his own ticket back and he'd brought his wife with him also! Luckily, he happened to have friends in London so they had a place to stay, while he sorted himself out. I thought it was very cool the way he stood up to Frank and Herb.

After the meeting, in the early hours, all the boys went to the Speakeasy Club including me. I met these two beautiful sisters from Copenhagen, Denmark who didn't have a place to stay that night. Fortunately, I had found myself in a bedroom with two beds in it and so I said, "Well, you're welcome to stay with me!" We were staying at Kensington Palace Hotel which is a very nice hotel. We got back there and one of the sisters got in one bed and the other sis got in the other bed which was more or less saying, "You've got your pick!" I liked that arrangement very much, as I had the both of them - which Bunk would have called a "ménage à trois"! After that I never saw them again because I had to get up at 6 o'clock in the morning to go to Pinewood Studios. We were starting the rehearsals for the movie.

On the first morning, I met Ringo Starr and Theodore Bikel. It was a great honor to meet Ringo. I told him that I really liked his playing and always had since the first time I heard it. I was surprised when he returned the compliment and told me that he thought that I was a good drummer!

On the very first day of rehearsals there were troubles. They had hired Tony Palmer to be the director and Gerry Goode from United Artists was the producer. Of course, Frank was already there telling him how he was going to direct the movie so Palmer said, "I was hired to direct this movie, so am I directing it or not?" So, the arrangement was, Zappa directed the dialog and Tony Palmer became the technical director.

Then it was the big search for who was going to play Jeff's part. They almost persuaded Marty Feldman to do it. That would have been great if he would have done it, because he is so hilarious, but he was committed to something else. Then they had Wilfred Bramble come down to try out and apparently he agreed to do it, but then it seems he freaked out after reading the script and wouldn't do it. They never really told us anything about what was going down. I guess it wasn't any of our business, like most things!

They were also still trying to find someone to play the part of the nun. They wanted Mick Jagger to do it because the part was really about Marianne Faithful. He wanted to do it but he was also busy, so they got Keith Moon to do it instead.

When I met "Moony", we hit it off big time and ended up hanging together most of the time. He wouldn't let me ride in the bus to the studio because he used to take me in his lavender Rolls Royce with Chalky, his cockney chauffeur. They used to pick me up first thing in the morning and on the way we would drink a little 50-year old Remy Martin because that was his drink. We became good mates during those weeks and I saw him quite a few times after that. Before we started filming the movie, he moved into the same hotel we were staying in, as he didn't want to miss out on all the fun we were having!

200 Motels
So, during the first week of rehearsals, they'd had a line of disasters and there was only one more week to go before shooting started. Then one morning, it was about 8 o'clock, Frank had just about had it with all the problems and he said, "The next guy who walks through that door is going to play Jeff!" Martin Lickert, who was Ringo's chauffeur, walked in and he was asked by Frank, "Do you want the part of Jeff?" and he just said, "Yeah, OK!"

After the first week, we moved out of the Kensington hotel and out to Windsor, because it was a lot nearer to the studios. That is when the real rehearsing got going. We worked twelve to fourteen hours a day to get everything right. The orchestra was also rehearsing there at the same time. We would work in our dressing rooms learning our parts because they were still building the sets up and also because the orchestra was too loud for good concentration.

My 33rd birthday was on the third day of shooting and Ringo brought me a big cake and two bottles of whisky. I shared the cake and whisky with the actors and some of the dancers. Luckily, that day was spent on shooting the orchestra sections, which took the whole day. We were on call but thankfully we weren't needed, which we were all glad about. Man! That could have been disastrous, as drunk we got!

We were finished by February 6th. The final day's party started on set and then continued at the hotel. We had had a lot of fun but I don't think anybody really knew what the whole thing was about. I am not sure that to this day anyone involved in the making of *200 Motels* knows what the whole thing is about. I know I don't! A lot of what we shot was eventually cut out of the final edit. I didn't get paid any extra for the other scenes, as I expected. Why should he pay me any extra? I was one of the original Mothers and those guys were used to getting screwed! Business as usual, I would have to say.

During the rehearsals, we were told there was a concert planned for the Royal Albert Hall where we would play all the music from the film. It was going to take place about a week after the end of shooting so we were to stay on and rehearse. The day after the end of shooting, we were told that the concert had been cancelled by the Albert Hall's committee. It was something to do with censorship so we were all sent home. Frank was very pissed off because the whole thing had been a very stressful time for him.

The 1971 Earthquake
Right after I got home, while I was still jet lagged, I experienced my first earthquake. I was drinking a cup of coffee at about 5.30 am[3] and the rest of my family were still in bed. It was just becoming dawn and the birds were singing. All of a sudden, I noticed that they had stopped singing and everything went very quiet. Then I heard a roar coming down Devonshire Boulevard and it sounded like a fleet of trucks. I looked out the window and saw that the street was buckling and waving up and down like the waves on a beach and then it hit! It shook the wood-framed house off the foundation about 4-6 inches[4] and all the family woke up startled. The kids were crying because it scared the shit out of all of us. For several months after that day, we experienced some heavy aftershocks that were more damaging than the actual earthquake.

The following day, I heard that my brother-in-law Philip (who was living with us) had stayed over with some friend in Northridge, which was nearer to the epicenter than we'd been. They'd gotten drunk the night before and Philip's friend had slept right through the whole thing. He woke up to find everything in the apartment was turned upside down. He turned to Phillip and said, "Boy, we must've had some fun last night!"

Santa Ana Winds
That wasn't the only scare we had at that house. A short while after the earthquake, we experienced some freak winds called Santa Ana winds. They were really heavy winds that were coming off the Santa Susana Mountains, which are in the northern part of the San Fernando Valley. A fire was started up in the hills and was heading towards the town of Chatsworth. People

started to evacuate their houses and I had my water hose out at the back of our house, ready for action. We lived right next door to a gas station and obviously, with everyone leaving, the guy there was doing good business and was pumping gas like crazy. The fire was coming down the gulch behind the buildings and he was still pumping away at the gas station. I got my whole family into the car and drove over to where Roy was living in Canoga Park. I was sure that place was going to blow, but somehow it didn't!

A Loan from Frank

So, after the earthquake and the fires, we had to leave that house because it was being condemned. I was earning some money, but not enough to be able to afford to move houses. I went up to Frank's house and asked him if I could borrow 500 dollars to help pay for it. That's the only time I ever went to him to ask to borrow money. I'm glad to say that he understood my position and gave it to me. I had agreed to pay it back in a few months time. We found a house not far away in Reseda, which is in the San Fernando Valley. The area around Reseda was still a little funky although there were no thieves or anything like that and it was safe enough for the kids. I had a nice little garden and grew some nice Pot there since it was off the road and surrounded in shrubbery. It was a perfect place to grow Pot, in the middle of "Valley" as it was called.

by Geronimo Black

A few months after I got home, I called the guys - Tom, Andy, Bunk and Tjay - to get Geronimo Black back together again. Most of the guys had been playing on a few tours with Tim Buckley but now they were all free to work again. Denny Walley was also free at that time so we decided to seriously put the band back together and they were all up for that. We set to work writing new music and getting a proper presentation together so we could start playing around, and also to get a proper recording contract. We started rehearsing about four times a week and it was at least for five to six hours at a time. I had written 'Low Ridin' Man', ''59 Chevy' and 'An American National Anthem' and we had a whole lot of other ideas.

I had met this woman Edwina Cruise who used to come and see us play at the Corral. Her son Brandon Cruise was staring in a TV comedy called *The Courtship of Eddie's Father* and, at that time, he was about 12 years old. She turned us on to a lot of her friends and one of them was a guy called Ray Dewey who had a studio called Devonshire Studios in North Hollywood. It was a 16-track studio with a 2-inch machine. He agreed to let us go in and cut a demo tape.

We went in there for about two weeks and cut five songs: 'Low Ridin' Man', 'Let Us Live', 'Thunder Buns Vs The Knumb Nut', 'Mayonnaise Mountain' and 'An American National Anthem'. At that time Ray Collins was in the band, so it was a seven-piece band. It was those recordings that got us the deal with MCA. Those recordings are on *Welcome Back, Geronimo Black*.

Pauley Pavilion
In August, Frank and the new band were touring the West Coast and they had a big show in Pauley Pavilion at UCLA.[5] As part of the show, they were going to premiere some sections of the *200 Motels* music and he asked me if I'd be interested in going and singing 'Lonesome Cowboy Burt' with them. After the show, he came over and said; "OK! That pays me back for the 500 you owed me!"

That was the best money I ever earned from anything I ever did with Frank.

200 Motels Premiere
In November, I went to see the opening of *200 Motels*. It was just before Frank left for a tour of Europe. That was the tour where all his equipment got burned up in Switzerland and, later, he got thrown into the orchestra pit in London.

The opening was in West Hollywood in a nice theater.[6] It was shown for two nights. Frank asked me if I would be there because it would be good PR. There was a big billboard on Sunset Boulevard with a big painted poster and it was beautiful. The first night, I took my wife and kids and they seemed to like it, especially the animated part. The second night, I went with all the guys from Geronimo Black.

Of course, there were very mixed reviews for the movie as some critics thought that it was total bullshit. It was the first movie that was shot on television cameras and then transferred to 35mm film. Some reviews made more of the technical process than the actual content.

It was even more interesting to find out what my mother and father's reaction was, because they went to the first night when it went to El Paso, at the Plaza Theater. After the first "Fuck!" that came out of my mouth, my dad left the theater, but my mother stayed through the whole thing. She said, "Son, I didn't understand the movie at all and your dad didn't understand it. What was it about? You should have your mouth washed out with soap!" I told her, "Mom, I only did what he told me to do!" "Well, why did you do that, you don't have to do everything that someone tells you to do!"

My dad went out and stood in the lobby, but he was telling everybody that it was his son up on the screen!

Getting the Deal

Uncle T decided to leave, but he turned us on to this other manager named Warren Duffy - so he started shopping our demo tape around. I think that the timing of the premiere of *200 Motels* may have clinched the deal with MCA for us because we got the best deal of 1971. They gave us $50,000 up front, all production rights and we got all the writing and publishing. In other words, we were allowed to produce the album ourselves, which in those days was unheard of, Man! It just didn't happen from a major company, so Duffy got a good deal for us.

The day that Geronimo Black signed our record contract with MCA, was the same day that Frank got dumped into the orchestra pit during a show at The Rainbow in London![7]

I'll never forget the day we got the money because it was just before Christmas. I had a party for all the band members and their families. We went to this place called the Captain's Table which was a very exclusive restaurant in Beverly Hills. I think we spent about $500 on this meal but it was a real celebration for us. I think we each got about $3000 front money and so we had a very good Christmas that year.

Notes to Chapter 9

[1] Took place on May 15, 1970 at UCLA's Pauley Pavilion

[2] Janis died Oct 4, 1970. We are left with the assumption that the period between the break-up of the original MOI (late Aug. 1969?) and the exit of Bunk from Geronimo Black is a good year. Especially if they were playing at the Topanga when Manson was likely to have seen them play. See: [Chapter 8, Manson & Cupid and Notes 57 and 60, same chapter]. JCB's "web-bio", written at a later date, questions this assumption: 'In 1970 Jimmy formed the band Geronimo Black (named after his youngest son) with Bunk Gardner and some very fine musicians. They played around LA for a couple of years before getting a record deal with MCA records. In the meantime in 1971 Jimmy went to England to make a movie called "200 Motels" with Frank Zappa...'

[3] Around 6 am, Feb 9, 1971

[4] 10-15 cm

[5] Aug 7, 1971

[6] Doheny Plaza Theater in Hollywood

[7] Dec. 10, 1971

Photo above: original photo by Albert Watson

1972

We went into the studio in January for five weeks to record the album. Just before we started in the studio, I slipped and pulled my hip out of its socket. I was forced into visiting a chiropractor and discovered the healing power of those guys. It was amazing to be in pain one minute and completely out of pain in a matter of minutes.

Photo: Bunk, Andy, Jimmy, Tom, TJ, Denny

At least I could play the drums again, since Tom Leavey and I were the most important two at the beginning of the recordings, the Rhythm Section! That was the beginning of one of the best albums I made.

Recording the *Geronimo Black* Album

The recording sessions were pretty interesting because we bought the studio for a 5-week block, which actually saved the studio from going under. Sound City Studios was a 24-track studio and it cost $15,000 including the engineer, whose name was Keith Olson. He was fairly young and had good ears. We liked what he was doing so much that we made him co-producer on the album. We paid him off with one ounce of Cocaine because that's what he wanted. I think we bought it for $500 because it was cheap back in those days. First of all, nobody knew what the fuck it was and I sure didn't have any idea what it was. I know one thing - we helped him snort it all up and enjoyed it mucho!

That was Keith's first co-production job so GB helped to start his career for him. He went on to produce Fleetwood Mac's *Rumours* album and made a ton of money off that. He produced all Pat Benetar's albums and tons of others. He was a lot of fun to work with and he became very good friends with the band. He did a hell of a good job on the album.

We had these two roadies named Larry and Billy and we called them the "Bumble Brothers". One day, we were all locked in the control room and they could see through the window we were all snorting Cocaine in there. They wanted some and they were begging for it! Denny Walley, being the clown that he is, gets out the Creamola, which is powdered coffee cream. He poured it out onto the table and cut it up into nice lines and then we let the boys in and they snorted this stuff. You should have seen them, Man! They were buzzin' 'round the studio like they were really high on "Coke".

The band got a good laugh out of that, but we never mentioned it to the boys because we needed them to haul the equipment.

We re-recorded the things we had demo'd plus a few new songs. In retrospect, I actually think that the demos were better than the album versions and I eventually released those versions on the *Welcome Back, Geronimo Black* album.[1] I think the first album was great but the demos were done with a lot of gusto because we were craving a record deal. Those demos got us one.

Powell's Liquor Store

In the five weeks that we were in the studio, our bill from the local liquor store was $700. All we'd bought were these six packs of Lucky Bock beer that cost 99 cent a pack. If you work it out, that's over 700 six packs of beer that were consumed. I put on pounds in that studio, as did everyone else.

During the fourth week in the studio, we took off two days to go shoot pictures for the album cover. The record company rented two big Cadillacs for us to travel into the Mojave Desert where the front and back covers were shot. We got to the Holiday Inn in Lancaster, CA about nine o'clock at night and proceeded to order every bottle of wine they had. I don't know if we got all of them but we sure did get a shit load of it. I really don't know how we took those pictures, because when we left the hotel at five o'clock in the morning we were stilled blitzed. That was a drinkin' band!

Inkanish Music

I started Inkanish Music in 1972.[2] Since the two songs that The Keys recorded back in 1962 had never been published, I decided to add those to the song list of mine. The writing royalties for the songs are still sitting in Austin because we couldn't find Larry Hurst.[3]

 So, the album *Geronimo Black* was released in May 1972 on UNI Records, which was a subsidiary label of MCA. Two weeks after, the president of UNI Records - Russ Regan - got fired! He had personally signed the band and really liked us. MCA had absolutely no idea what to do with our band because we had been Russ's pet project. If that guy would have stayed on as president, Geronimo Black may have done a lot more than they did.

Who knows, but as it was we were just left to try and promote the thing ourselves. Obviously we didn't have a budget for that. We had a tour lined up for England and we'd lined that up ourselves, but we needed $7,200 for air tickets and we couldn't get MCA to pay for them.

Downhill

So, after that, it was downhill all the way, although we managed to do one tour. We went up to Seattle, Washington for a two-week residency at a really nice club.[4] The band were instant hits there and we did a television show one afternoon. It turned out to be quite an experience because we got to meet and hang out with Jim Backus of *Mr. Magoo* and *Gilligan's Island* fame. We hit it off right from the beginning and later went to his hotel room with him and his manager. He told us some very funny stories of his career and we drank a gallon of Morgan David wine, which is super cheap. It's one of the preferred choices of Winos!

We were playing at the club that Trini Lopez owned in Hollywood. I remember I took some Speed that night and couldn't sleep, so I wrote a whole bunch of lyrics. Most of them were just a bunch of bullshit, typical Speed stuff, but two sets that I wrote came out real well and were the basis for 'Trail Of Tears' and 'Lady Queen Bee'.

'Trail Of Tears' was written about the recent siege on Wounded Knee. The Indians took over the Federal Agency of Indian Affairs building and, of course, that meant that the FBI had to get in there. We decided to record the new material and have it in the can, so 'Trail Of Tears', 'Lovesick Blues' and 'Teenage Credit' were recorded in April '73 just before I left to go back to El Paso. But they weren't released for years - not until I put out *Welcome Back, Geronimo Black*. More recently, they were put on the *Grandmothers Anthology* CD.

The last gigs that Geronimo Black played were in early '73. We went to play a gig in San Miguel, New Mexico - my old stompin' ground - and that's really when I decided to move back to Texas. I was really fed up with L.A. and the music scene out there, there wasn't that much happening with the band, and I wanted to move back home to the desert. It always was a great place to raise kids and I wanted them to have a chance to grow up where myself and Loretta had grown up.

The Front Money

My friends from my hometown of Anthony had wanted Geronimo Black to play there since the band had formed. The front money came in the form of an ounce of very good Cocaine. I received a call from my friends who were on their way out to California to bring it to me. Of course, we had to find someone to buy it - Coke wasn't very popular in L.A. at that time! A couple of years later it would have been a very different story. I knew some of the guys that played with The Association, a very popular rock band from the 1960s and '70s, so I gave them a call and they turned me on to their manager. I went over to his office and gave him a little sample. He bought the ounce from me and so we had the front money to go to the gig in New Mexico.

I had gone ahead to NM[5] with the friends that had come to California and about three days before the boys in the band arrived. I wanted to see my Mom and Dad and my brother and sister, who I hadn't seen in quite a while. I had a pleasant visit with all my old friends, and we really got stoned every night with them and planned the concert. By the time the guys arrived, everything was in place for a very good two-night concert in an old famous dance hall in the middle of San Miguel, NM.[6]

My friend Stanley Bartlett had made some peyote tea and the first day, before the concert, everyone in the band got wasted and introduced to the lifestyle of my home area. Bunk fell in love with that tea and drank it every day we were there.

We stayed there for one week and had a ball. The concerts went off beautifully as I thought they would, and the people that came totally enjoyed Geronimo Black - those concerts are still remembered there!

Back in Texas

I never regretted moving back to the El Paso area because we found a farmhouse about five miles from La Mesa, New Mexico. I needed to find a job and began working as a farm laborer for $1.40 an hour and it was on a big farm owned by an old friend of mine.[7] The guy's name was Jimmy Ulmer. I did that for about four or five months and I was doing everything that there is to be done on a farm. It was the hardest job I've ever had and for the worst pay! It was a terrible job and for wet back wages!

I got my leg caught in a hay loader and had to have 40 stitches put in it and so that was the end of that job, finally! After my leg had healed up, I found a job at the local cotton gin factory, ginning cotton, which was much better pay than I'd been getting on the farm.

The Donut Shop

When we'd lived in California, Loretta had worked for Dick Winchell, the son of Paul Winchell who was the owner of the Winchell's Donuts chain and Denny's restaurants. Sometimes Dick came out to El Paso and stayed with us. We were good friends with him and he was also a big fan of the Mothers. The guy who had ran the local Winchell's Donuts shop on North Mason Street had been fired because a lady had come in and said, "There's a fly in my donut". The guy said, "That's OK, Lady, we don't charge extra for the meat!" and that's when he was ousted from the donut shop.

So, we took over the shop and I went to work as the baker. Dick Winchell taught me how to make the donuts. It closed every night at 11.00 until 5.00 the next morning and that's when I went to work and worked all night long cutting those fuckin' donuts. I made at least 10,000 donuts a night!

I was on my own in that place all week long but on the weekends I had two helpers. One was called Gary Black and the other was called Darrell Black, and they were my two oldest sons.[8] The boys helped me out a lot.

I remember one time my niece Beverly got married and so, of course, we'd been to the wedding and the reception afterwards. I did a little drinking at the reception and I had a great time. Afterwards, me and the boys had to go and work at the donut shop. The boys

were really tired, so I let them sleep in the car. I told them that I'd come out and wake them up a little later. I got in there and made up two big 5-gallon things full of dough, which I then had to put up on the table to let it raise for about 30 minutes. I had to make three, so while they were rising I made another. While the third vat was mixing, I decided to lay [me] down and rest for a few minutes on a pile of flour sacks at the back of the shop.

I woke up about an hour later and found that the dough was climbing up and out of the fucking mixer and the other two lots had grown up so far that they had fallen off of the cutting board and onto the floor. It had plugged up the grease trap, so this greasy water was coming up everywhere and it covered the whole floor of the shop. The mixer was covered in dough and the two heaps of dough were lying in this greasy water.

So, I woke up to this mess which meant that everything was useless. I was still a little bit drunk when I ran out and woke the boys up. They had to clean the place up while I tried to mix some new stuff which meant we were about two hours behind schedule. That's when "The Boss" Loretta came in and started shouting and screaming. I just said, "Don't give me any shit right now or I'm walking and you can do it!" When she found out what had happened, she had a laugh out of it.

So after all that, I'm driving home and a cop stops me for having a taillight out on my car. He's writing out this ticket when he turns to me and says, "You know what, Man, you smell like a donut!"

Extra Dough

I had quite a nice little business going on the side. At 3.00 am in the morning, I would get a knock on the back door and it would be one of my friends. He'd hand me this bag of Weed and say, "We want two dozen blueberries today!" Nobody was around, so I'd mix up three dozen and I'd get to keep a dozen.

Photo above: Gary Black

You were never allowed to sell day-old doughnuts at Winchell's because it was their policy and so, at the end of the day, if there were any donuts left we were supposed to give them all to the orphanages or something. Sometimes, I would have 10 or 12 dozen donuts left over. I knew this Mexican guy who owned a little catering truck and used to drive around to all the construction sites in El Paso so he would buy a bunch of them off me. A bit of that money used to go to "Jimmy's Orphanage", so that was a little extra on the side and it was fine with my wife because she was getting her share.

 I used to close the blinds on the windows at night because I didn't want to be disturbed from my work. One night, I was cutting away and I heard this knock on the window. When I pulled the blind to see who was there, all I could see were three pressed hams against the window. It was three of my friends giving me moon shots! I never did find out who that was although I certainly had my suspicions.

I worked at the donut shop for over a year. I was putting in 70 hours a week and the only night I got off was at Christmas time. For seven months I never got to play any music because I worked there 10 hours a night, 7 nights a week.

Mesilla Valley Lo Boys
I told Loretta that I wanted to play music again, so we hired a Mexican baker called Gonzalo. That way I could at least have the weekends off. That's when I started the Mesilla Valley Lo Boys. That was the name of the valley that we lived in - it is where the Rio Grande River ran through. The "Lo Boys" were basically a blues band and I enjoyed playing with them very much. We had a lot of fun at that time and we were all drinking quite heavily.

You could say that we were a real blues band because we were a bunch of drunks!

The University of Texas at El Paso
While I was at the donut shop, I found out that anybody who had been in the military between 1958-72 was eligible for educational funding. When I'd got out of the military, we were what they called Cold War Vets and we didn't have any benefits, but since the Vietnam War they had included everybody. I was actually told about it by a guy I'd known for years that used to come into the shop. I knew he'd been in Service at the same time as I'd been and he explained it to me. I'd never been notified by the Veterans' Affairs Administration!

So, that meant that I was entitled to go back to school and I was entitled to four semesters. They would pay me $600 a month for 16 hours a week! Our rent was only $125 and as I had no other payments we could live off that pretty good. So I thought, "Fuck the donut shop! I'll go back to College."

I went and enrolled at the Texas Western College, which now was called The University of Texas at El Paso, or UTEP. I enrolled in the music courses. I took a bunch of different classes which only amounted to around 13 hours a week and played with the Lo Boys so I had it pretty easy and I was making good money. I did the college thing for 18 months, 4 semesters. We did music theory, sight singing and dictation, a bit of piano and would you believe that I also took up the guitar! I learnt a few chords and things but I never really could understand the string thing. I actually got good grades at school for the first time. Well, after all, I'd had seven[9] years of Music College with the Mothers!

Notes to Chapter 10

[1] Released in 1980

[2] Presumably to establish ownership of the songs he had been writing/co-writing

[3] The song's author

[4] 6 nights a week; John Denver was also there. [JCB notes]

[5] New Mexico

[6] Which is some 390 miles from Anthony, TX

[7] Asked in 2007, "Back to a day job in '72. How come?" JCB replied, "I had a wife and five kids by that time and they had a nasty habit of eating and wearing clothes. I had to work since the music business never paid me anything much. It was 1973…" [From: written answers that JCB gave to questions posed by Robyn Flans for *Modern Drummer*, Dec 31, 2007]

[8] Around 13 and 12 at the time

[9] JCB is including 1964 and 1970 in this calculation?

In the spring of '75, I was in school and the Mesilla Valley Lo Boys were rehearsing and playing a few gigs. Randy Russ was on guitar and he was drinking his balls off!

A Sad Accident

Loretta's brother, Phil, got drunk one night in a bar in La Mesa, NM and decided to walk home which was about five miles along the highway. It seems that he passed out and was lying in the road and some guy ran right over him. It was pretty obvious that the guy was going too fast and by the time he saw something laying in the road, it was way too late to stop. Phil's funeral was a closed coffin affair because that's how badly damaged he must have been.

By Philip Moreno

What a sweet guy Phil was, I missed him dearly. Phil used to work with Cal Schenkel at the Log Cabin in Laurel Canyon, after the Mothers moved back to L.A. in '68. He also did some baby-sitting for Frank and Gail, taking care of Moon. He was also quite an artist.

Bongo Fury

I was in school when Zappa and the band came through El Paso in May '75 during their *Bongo Fury* Tour. They'd just done the two gigs at The Armadillo World Headquarters in Austin, Texas where they had recorded for the live album *Bongo Fury*. Don Vliet (Captain Beefheart) was guest vocalist on that tour and Denny Walley was playing slide guitar in the band. He had called me to say they were coming to El Paso, so I went out and met them at the airport.

Frank and I had a nice time talking and he asked if I would sit in with them and sing a couple of blues songs. He was glad to hear that I was back at school and him and Loretta had a good time talking about old times together. Frank always liked Loretta because I think he remembered when we used to rehearse in her father's garage back in Santa Ana. All my kids came to the show[1] and we all had a meal backstage. I got my friend Chava Villagas in the concert and back stage as well.

That's where I first met Terry Bozzio, Tom and Bruce Fowler and Nappy [Napoleon] Brock. That is when I brought up the fatal question to Frank. I asked Frank, "Well, how's Don doing?" and he said, "That fucking guy's full of shit and not only that, he's driving me crazy!" That's all he said, so I left it at that. I didn't ask any more questions about that subject. Frank had just had it with him and apparently they hadn't been talking for weeks! Frank was tired of all the pictures that Don was drawing of him because most of them were of Frank as the devil, with horns, a tail and all that kind of shit, if you know what I mean!

All Don had with him on the tour was this brown paper shopping bag which was full of these books that he used to draw in. I don't think he took any clothes with him because Dick Barber said he wore the same things for the whole tour. I think everybody in the band was a little pissed about it, because he was starting to smell pretty ripe. I heard complaints from several members of the band about it.

Gauge

One of the first things that Beefheart asked me was, "Do you know where I can get some "Gauge"? I need Gauge for this tour because it's driving me crazy!" I had no idea what he meant by Gauge until he told me the story of when he was a shoe salesman back in Lancaster, CA during the sixties. Robert Mitchum came into the store to buy some shoes. He was out there in Lancaster shooting some film. Apparently they hit it off pretty good because I guess that Mitchum could see that this guy was out there in left field someplace. So Mitchum asked him if he could score some Gauge as that was his name for Pot.[2] Musicians and very hip people from the '30s through the '50s used to call Marijuana that name.

Mesilla Valley Madness

My friend Chava always had a nice stash of this good Mexican Weed we called "MVM". Bruce Fowler and Denny Walley spent the night at my house since it was a free night off and we had a nice time smoking and completely getting out of it, talking about fossils. Bruce was very interested in fossils and we told him the mountains around El Paso were full of them. We even took him up in the mountains the next morning before taking them to the sound check. He did collect some fossils to take back to California with him.

We got some Gauge for Don. I said, "You want Gauge? OK, we'll give you some Gauge, Man! This is called Mesilla Valley Madness!" I went to the concert the next day and sat in with Frank and the guys and sang 'You're So Fine' and 'Lonely, Lonely Nights'.

Don was supposed to come out to my house after the concert, but he was out of it because that Gauge put him down very hard. I think that it was probably the first time that he'd slept on that tour since it started.

Joining The Magic Band

The next day, Don came up to me and asked what the fuck it was that we'd given him. I told him it was just ordinary Mexican Weed and he started on about, "Oh no, Man! It had something else in it. It had some psychedelics in it!" I told him it was just normal Weed that we smoked all the time and he said, "How can you survive around here with THAT GAUGE!"

I spent some time talking with him and that's when he asked me if I would be interested in joining the Magic Band and going out to L.A. to do this tour with them in two months. I said, "Yeah, Man! I'll do that. I'd love to go out on the road with you." Little did I know what that was going to involve so I skipped one semester and went and did that tour.

Herb Cohen was also managing Beefheart at the time. He told me that the deal would be a seven-week contract, six weeks of rehearsals and one week of shows. I was to be paid a one-off fee of $2000.

The Magic Band & Rehearsals

So it was only about a week after they finished that tour that I went out to L.A. for six weeks of intense rehearsal. I skipped a session of summer school to go and do the rehearsals and the tour. I was back in L.A. again! I had driven my family out to Santa Ana, to my wife's father's house so they could visit him for a week. One of her brothers drove them back to New Mexico and visited with them for a couple of weeks.

I was staying with Denny Walley while I was in L.A. and we would go over and see Tom Leavey. Denny had told me that Tom was kind of off the rails a bit. So I actually stayed with Tom a few nights and he wasn't in great shape - L.A. was taking its toll on him - and he needed to get out of there. About three months later, I did arrange for him to move to New Mexico and start playing bass with me again. If you remember, Tom Leavey was the bass player in Geronimo Black.

We used the rehearsal room at Discreet Records, which was the company that Herb and Frank had set up. They called that rehearsal room the "Rubber" room. Frank was around the building most of the time so I saw him just about every day. He had some sort of studio there and was listening to all the road tapes from the *Bongo Fury* tour. We'd get there at 10.00 am in the morning and stay 'til 10.00 pm at night, seven days a week. Don and John French ("Drumbo") were living out in Lancaster and would drive in everyday.

At the start of rehearsals, there was Drumbo and me on drums, the "Winged Eel Fingerling" (Elliot Ingber) was on guitar and spaced out of his mind as usual at that time, and a guy named Greg Davidson on the second guitar. We still didn't have a bass player.

Drumbo was a great guy and he taught me everything about Beefheart's music that pertained to the tour. I had a lot of fun with him and he was one hell of a drummer.

It was good to see "Bro" again - that's what we called Elliot when he was with the Mothers, he was always tryin' to talk like a black man! - and it was really good to work with him again, the first time since the *Freak Out!* days for him and me.

Greg Davidson

I don't know where Beefheart had picked Greg Davidson up. He was from Chicago and at the time, as straight as an arrow. He seemed way too straight for this band (since I knew all the old Magic Band, personal) but it turned out that he was a big fan of the Captain and he could really play the hell out of that music.

Buell Neidlinger

We still needed a bass player so they were going to try out Tom Leavey. I still don't know what happened when he got to the first rehearsal, but he'd jammed his fingers in the car door getting his Bass-Amp out and completely fucked his fingers up. Needless to say, he was out of the picture.[3]

I knew this other guy (he had played with Geronimo Black briefly) who I thought could play this music. The guy's called Buell Neidlinger and he was a monster bass player. He'd done a lot of sessions and he'd played contra bass with the Boston Philharmonic.[4] He was also into the Blues and stuff and was a very good friend of mine and Elliot's.

Buell had also done some stuff with Frank in the past, but it seems that he and Frank had had a serious falling out. So, when Buell went to the rehearsal on the first day, Zappa came flying out of the office, pulled Beefheart off to the side and said, "That guy ain't playing in your band because he's not gonna rehearse on these premises and in fact, we want him outa here right now!"[5]

I guess Beefheart wasn't in any position to do anything about it because otherwise I know he would have told Frank to "Fuck Off!" Buell would have been a great player for Beefheart in my opinion.

It seems that back in '71, Buell had called the Musicians' Union and told them that Aynsley Dunbar was making all this money with Zappa and he wasn't in the Union and not only that, he wasn't even American. The Musicians' Union came down really hard on Herb and Frank. That is when Herb arranged for one of the girls in Herb's office to marry Aynsley, so that he could get a Green Card.

Bruce Fossil

Someone (I think it was Denny Walley) suggested Bruce Fowler. He said, "Put his trombone through an octave divider and let him play the bass!" So that was the beginning of the Bruce Fowler Air Bass! He'd had a pick-up on his trombone from the Mothers tour and had been experimenting so it was a logical step to try it out. He became Bruce "Fossil" in the Magic Band.[6]

So, we finally got everything lined up. John French[7] was the guy who was running the rehearsals, as he was the one that knew the material and had run the rehearsals for quite a few years before this tour. Man! Beefheart didn't even know his own stuff, which really surprised the shit out of me!

To be able to play that Beefheart stuff is not easy at all. Man! I had to learn to play the drums backwards! If it hadn't have been for Drumbo, I don't know what I would have done. He really helped me to understand the music. Most of the beats were a variation of a Bo Diddley beat. If it would have been left up to Beefheart, I wouldn't have known anything, Man!

So, Drumbo and I would rehearse and it would be just me and him together. Part of the time we would be playing exactly the same thing, and then he showed me some other stuff to play that would compliment what he was doing. By the time we went on tour we had quite a good thing going. At least the rhythm section was together since we also rehearsed with Bruce.

So, we did six weeks of rehearsals, but in reality there might have been 90 minutes of rehearsing done each day, because the rest of the time was spent listening to Don's bullshit, Man! We had to have all the light bulbs in the Rubber room changed because he said he couldn't work like that and wouldn't work until they were changed. He said, "They interfere with my brainwaves, Man!" and ran out of the room! But what an artist that guy was. I think he was the most avant-garde rock 'n' roller ever. I always thought that Frank was jealous of that, because he wanted to be as far out as Beefheart but he couldn't get that far out, because nobody could, Man! There is still nobody that is that "out", even today, although there are more and more bands doing things far out now because of Beefheart.

 We would spend four or five hours a day down at the Brown Derby Café, which was just down the street from Discreet Records. The Brown Derby is a famous place in Hollywood where all the stars used to go in the old days of Hollywood. It is located on Vine Street between Sunset and Hollywood Boulevard. We'd sit in that place drinking coffee and watching Beefheart drawing pictures of everybody that came into the fucking place. He filled up three of those books that he used to carry around with him during that rehearsal time!

One time, the whole band spent five days going around to every music and pawnshop in the Los Angeles area looking for the right guitar for Greg Davidson to play. He had a beautiful Gibson Les Paul of his own, but Beefheart didn't like the sound of that guitar because he wanted the sound of a Fender Stratocaster. So Greg had to try all these guitars out and, of course, all of us had to go with him. All the time Beefheart was saying, "No, that's not the one, that won't do!"

164

They finally found the shittiest looking guitar that there was. That fucking guitar didn't even have a finish on it, it was so shitty, but that was the guitar, and that's what this guy had to play whether he wanted to or not! By the way, he played the hell out of it on the tour.

Then Beefheart told Greg that he had to have a name for The Magic Band and so immediately his name became Greg "Ella Guru" Davidson. So I said, "Well, how about me?" and Beefheart said, "Well, you're Jimmy Carl Black!" and I said, "No, if I'm gonna be in The Magic Band, I want a name too!" So he just said, "OK, you're Indian Ink Con Safo!" and I said, "Perfect!"

The material that we played on that tour was all repertoires and there wasn't anything new. To me it was a real representation of all the Beefheart recordings up until that time.

England with The Magic Band
We only played four shows. The first was a TV show in Chicago called Sound Stage, then we went and played the Knebworth Pop Festival in England and it was the most people I ever played for in my career. There were over 250,000 people at that festival and it was scary. We finished with two nights at The Roxy, which were added later on.

Each member of the band got $2000 and all our expenses paid, for a total of seven weeks. Each band member was also supposed to get a painting from Don, but nothing ever came of that and I really would have liked to get one.

When we got to the rehearsal for the TV show in Chicago, Don couldn't remember one word to any of his songs. Herb was flipping out, Man! "God, what's with this guy?" He was screaming at him, "Don, they're your songs, you wrote 'em!" and Don says, "I know, but I can't remember the words to 'em!" I don't know what was wrong with him. I know he wasn't sleeping and I think he was driving his wife Jan crazy as well, because he is not the easiest guy in the world to live with. A person has only got to listen to the words to his songs to realize that!

So, Don's wife Jan sat up all night writing big cue cards with all the lyrics to all the songs. It took at least 15 sheets to do 'Orange Claw Hammer' because that thing's got so many words to it. She had to make them really big because he could hardly see. Those cards were gigantic and, of course, they had to go with us to England. I really have a huge admiration for Jan Vliet having to live with a genius like him.

Sometimes a Woman's Gotta Hit a Man
When we got out to the airport and checked everything in, Jan forgot to check in his black hat, his famous black hat which he kept in an old hat box.

He was raisin' shit about that, calling her everything, "You stupid fuckin' bitch, why didn't you check the fucking thing in? Now I have to carry it!" As if carrying the hatbox was a big deal. He was screaming and yelling, throwing a tantrum and jumping up and down like a little kid right in the middle of the Chicago O'Hare airport. Jan wasn't saying anything and she was being very cool about everything. But pretty soon I guess she'd had just about all she could handle, so she popped him one right in the chest. She really socked him hard right in the chest and knocked him down on the ground! I think she caught him off guard and he fell right down on the floor. The band sort of drifted away as if they didn't know who these people were. Bruce and I kind of stepped way back behind them. Everybody in the airport stopped and looked around to see what was going on. He has got this surprised look on his face and then he starts cracking up, Man, like it was the funniest thing that had ever happened to him! She helped him up off the ground and they walked off as if nothing had ever happened!

I'd heard that Don had a nasty streak in him, but he was never violent to me. Don and I have always been very good friends and always thought the world of the guy because he treated me very good when I played with him.

A Huge Road Accident
We were in London for three days before the festival and we stayed at The Kensington Palace Hotel on Hyde Park, which is a very nice hotel. The first thing Elliot asked me to do for him was score some Hash because he was having some sort of a freak-out. He said the only thing that would help would be to smoke something. He said also that he would need it if he was going to perform at the festival. Maybe the thought of over 200,000 people had something to do with that feeling. I told him that I would make a few phone calls and see what I could come up with. I called Ellen, the girl who had been the make-up artist on *200 Motels*, and asked her if she could do something for Elliot. She was very happy to hear from me, as it had been a few years since I had made the movie and she wanted to get together and visit. She came around that evening and we had a nice time talking about the movie and things in general. As it turned out, she took us everywhere and her and Drumbo hit it right off. They had a little scene happening and I was happy to see it since they are both great people. We all went to the Speakeasy and started having fun in London except Elliot, who by this time was completely blown out of his gourd. As long as he had Hashish he was OK.

I met a girl named Michelle that night and I thought she was very attractive although she couldn't have been more than 18 years old. At that time, I was 37 years old. As it turned out, I had an affair with her for three or four days although I really didn't get into it as much as with other girls. Maybe it was because she was so young. Anyway, nine months later I heard

166

that I had a new daughter and, being married to Loretta, that wasn't good at all.

Going back to when we were still in Chicago before leaving for England, Don wasn't with us much. He was with Jan and he was doing a lot of interviews. She was making out those big cue cards for him.

The last night in the hotel, actually it was six in the morning, I heard a knock on the door of my room and it was Don. He was nervous, couldn't get to sleep and wanted me to go down to the coffee shop and have breakfast with him. That was when he started drawing a picture of me and a jackrabbit out in the desert because he knew that I had grown up out in the desert just like him. He called that picture "Jack and Jim" and even wrote some lyrics to it.

The reason I mention this incident is because in 1993 I started touring with Eugene Chadbourne and, after telling him this story, we decided to call our duo "The Jack and Jim Show". I would've liked to have that drawing and the lyrics although I don't know what happened to it. It is probably in one of those books from that year around his house. Maybe it will be released someday. Anyway, back to the story...

KNEBWORTH PARK
CAPTAIN BEEFHEART
AND HIS MAGIC BAND
SATURDAY 5TH JULY

We left London and travelled up to Knebworth and I took Michelle with me. The bill was Pink Floyd, The Steve Miller Band, Captain Beefheart and his Magic Band, Family and Fairport Convention - I remember we used Pink Floyd's big quadraphonic PA system. There was a hell of a lot of people at that festival. You couldn't see the end of the people and the stage was really high up - about eight stories high! I remember thinking I'd never played to that many people before.[8] I heard from the promoters that there were more than 250,000 people there and I believe it.

The most beautiful part of it to me was when Don had finished with one of those cue cards, he would throw it out into the audience and it would seem to take ages floating down into the crowd.

We left the festival grounds right after we played because Beefheart was tired and didn't want to stay. I really wanted to stay and see the other bands, who were some of my all-time favorites. We had to get back to London because we were leaving the next day. That was my last time in England for a long time, the next time I went back was in 1993 with Eugene Chadbourne.

Leaving for LA

We got on the plane at Heathrow and got all settled in, when a couple of guys came up to me and said, "Are you Jimmy Carl Black?" I said, "Yeah, that's me." They said that they were in the band Black Sabbath and were on the way to L.A. to start a big tour over there. I said, "Isn't the guy that bites the head off of bats the lead singer?" and Ozzy said, "Yeah, that's me."[9] I had a great time rapping with those guys all the way to L.A. I'll never forget them as they were cool guys. I had never been a big fan of their music but as people go, I am.

 We played two more shows at The Roxy in Hollywood.[10] It was a separate thing that wasn't originally part of the deal. I had already gone back home to New Mexico, so they had to fly me back out to L.A. for those gigs and they even paid for a ticket for Loretta. My friend PeeWee Pairis flew out with us and we all stayed with his ex-wife.

One of those Roxy shows came out as a bootleg a few years later called *What's All This Booga Wooga Music?*

That was the last time I saw Beefheart. I would like to see him again before we leave this planet.[11]

Notes to Chapter 11

[1] May 23, 1975

[2] "Don told several variations of this story. The standard one was that Mitchum carried with him a shoe box full of pot." [Art Tripp, in correspondence]

[3] [John French, *Beefheart...*:] has it that Tom Leavey's playing was not to the band's liking anyway.

[4] "He'd played with Cecil Taylor, and also played bass on Zappa's Jean-Luc Ponty album, *King Kong*." [Art Tripp, in correspondence]

[5] [John French, *Beefheart...*:] has it that it was Herb Cohen who walked in, though maybe both he and Frank came in.

[6] "Fossil Man" [Art Tripp] or simply, Bruce "Fossil" Fowler [Internet]

[7] Aka Drumbo

[8] Is JCB revealing his own apprehensiveness about playing before so many people?

[9] Ozzy Osbourne bit a bat's head off on January 20, 1982 so this seems to be an anachronism.

[10] July 14 and 15

[11] Sadly, JCB did not, though Don Van Vliet lived another two years after JCB.

Back with the Lo Boys

So, I was back in New Mexico working with my little rhythm and blues band, which was called the Mesilla Valley Lo Boys.[1] We played with that line up[2] for about a year and a half and released one single.[3]

While I'd been away with Beefheart, the Lo Boys had been rehearsing quite a bit. Randy Russ had left the band and there was a new guitar player named Jeff Littlejohn. He was a black guy that had played a lot in England while serving in the Army. He was a kind of Hendrix-type player and was quite good.

So the Lo Boys were almost ready to start making some serious music. We only lacked a good bass player and I had a plan to remedy that problem.

Tom Leavey

Tom Leavey, the bass player from Geronimo Black, came to El Paso in 1976 to play with us when the bass player we had suddenly left the band, with our blessing.

Denny Walley had called me and told me that he was worried about Tom. L.A. was being a very bad influence on him and he was drinking heavily and popping lots of pills. I think he was pretty depressed from the break-up of his marriage and other things that were happening to him at the time.

My friend PeeWee Pairis worked for the Santa Fe Railroad and managed to get Tom a free ride to El Paso, Texas. Then they drove 125 miles in PeeWee's pickup truck to meet the band up in Ruidoso, New Mexico, where

we had a three-night gig at a place called The Buckaroo. They arrived about an hour before we were due on stage so, with no rehearsal, Tom became the new bass player in the Mesilla Valley Lo Boys. After about three months of playing around the bars in the area we recorded a single called 'Play Your Music' (written by Tom Leavey) and 'Funny Music' (written by Jeff Littlejohn).

Photo (top): The Lo Boys; 1976

169

A guy called Skank, real name Steve Brown, put it out but he never did anything with it. He's probably still got hundreds of them laying around in his garage somewhere in Austin, Texas.

Randy Russ

Eventually that band broke up. This Coke dealer had talked Jeff Littlejohn into leaving the band to form his own band and he would finance the whole project. Tom Leavey decided to go with Jeff and the other guys in the band decided to quit the music business. That left me, Chava the conga player and a few gigs to play that had been booked a few months before this all happened. Randy Russ was pretty sober at the time so we asked him if he was interested in playing. He agreed and we found this brother combination that played bass and guitar, and they both sang. We rehearsed a couple of days and started playing. The first gig was a total disaster. We all were set up and waiting for Randy to get to the gig so we could start playing. We needed him because he was the lead guitar player. Well, about fifteen minutes before we had to play, he came flying around the corner of the building across the street from the club, screeching to a stop. He literally rolled out of his car and couldn't even get up. He was completely drunk and so we carried him and his equipment into the club hoping he could at least play a little. The first song we played was a Chuck Berry song that he started playing about three keys from the rest of the band. After we finally stopped the song, he said it was time for a break. I said to him, "We just started the set" and he informed me that he was finished for the night. That was getting really close to the finish of the Mesilla Valley Lo Boys.

Panama Red's

The second gig we had was in Roswell, New Mexico and it was in a club called Panama Red's. We found out soon after arriving at the place why it was called that.[4] The first thing I saw when we walked in to set up the equipment was a bunch of people sitting around a table rolling "joints" and then lighting them up. The second thing I saw was some guy giving the bouncer a blast of "Shit". The guy then took a swing at the bouncer and knocked him on his ass. As the bouncer hit the floor, he reached down into his cowboy boot and brought out some kind of revolver, leveled it on the guy's chest and pulled the trigger.

The gun "dry-fired" - which means it didn't go off - and the guy just looked surprised as hell. I guess he thought he was a goner - so did I! Then they just looked at each other and both started laughing their asses off. The bouncer got up off the floor, put his arm around the guy's shoulder, took him to the bar and bought him a big beer. I guess that they were friends and had been for a few years, maybe since grade school! Then we did the gig and it was a wonderful gig.

We went back to that club at least ten or twelve times after that, as we had become big hits in Roswell. We smoked some really good Weed in that place because the police never went in there. I guess they were afraid to and I don't blame them.

Big Sonny and The Lo Boys

Randy started taking this program of medication to stop drinking. He called me to say that Big Sonny Farlow was back in town and looking to start a new band. Chava and I called Big Sonny Farlow and we started rehearsing out at my house, down in the cellar. We started Big Sonny and The Lo Boys that night and the band was together for about three years. We cut one album and one single in that time.

Chava

That guy's not a smoker but he's a midnight toker. I used to drive his van from the passenger side, steering it. He would be driving, but rolling a Joint, and I would be beside him steering the car all the way to Ruidoso to play a gig with Big Sonny. Chava was a terrible conga player but he had a "personality". In fact, we used to turn his mike off. Man! We had to do that! But, he owned the PA system and the truck that hauled everything and he was a personality in the band. Man! We used to get a lot of chicks coming to the gigs because of that little fart.

Leaving Loretta

I finally left Loretta in 1978 after 20 years. She was always pissed off at something and it was usually me. She was also a very violent woman, especially if she drank any booze. She liked to slug it out when she got a little high. She always took the first swing, especially if she started drinking. Fortunately it was very rare that she did. If she'd drank something, I'd just split right away because I knew something was going to happen and it usually did. I will say that she is a very good mother to my kids and she is also a good woman. I just don't think that our chemistry mixed well and that was the biggest problem with the marriage.

I lived with my friend PeeWee Pairis for a while. He worked for the railroad and he was gone a lot of the time, so I took care of his place while he was gone. After about three months with PeeWee, I actually moved back in with my Mom and Dad for a few months, although by then I was travelling back and forth between El Paso and Albuquerque, NM.

I met up with a woman named Husta, who I'd known since she was in the first grade and I was in the third. She was three years younger than me and we were just good friends. She lived out on a farm about five miles away from Anthony in a town called Berino, New Mexico, but she was a little too young for me at the time. I always thought she was the most beautiful girl in High School. I hadn't seen her for about 19 years or longer but every once in a while I would think of her, especially since I was taking a music class at the university with her brother, Mike.

I was playing a gig at the Kings X in El Paso with Big Sonny and The Lo Boys. I had been seeing a girl called Shirley, who was also a good friend from high school. She called Husta and told her that she was going to take her out and see somebody she hadn't seen in a long time.

So, Husta came to the gig and we talked for a little bit. I'd always had a heavy attraction for her and I think I fell in love with her immediately. She'd been married a couple of times and was getting ready to graduate from the University of Texas at El Paso with a degree in Special Education.

At that time, I was drinking pretty heavily and I got really smashed that night - terribly drunk! I still don't know how I got home that night because I was living about 30 miles from El Paso then, but I did, and woke up on the kitchen floor in the morning. I went outside and looked at my car to see if I had hit anything or anybody but found no signs of that happening.

I couldn't stop thinking about Husta. I knew that if I was drinking as much as I had been that I wouldn't stand a chance with her. She wasn't into alcohol at all, so I decided to quit drinking. I started working out with the barbells and getting myself in good shape. I hadn't been in good shape for quite a while and needed it.

I'd been on the wagon for about six months when I phoned Husta. I called her up one afternoon and she said to me, "Would you like me to give you Shirley's new phone number?" and I said, "No, I'm not even interested in talking to Shirley, it's YOU that I'd like to talk to!"

So she invited me over and we talked for hours and then we started smoochin' and all of a sudden we were in bed and that one kiss lasted for seventeen years![5] She was quite a girl!

Husta graduated from the University of Texas at El Paso with a B.A. Degree and went up to Albuquerque where she had gotten a teaching job and had a flat.[6] I was commuting up there at least once a week.

172

I knew my time in El Paso was coming to an end and I was really looking forward to that. So, in 1979 I filed for divorce. I had been thinking about it for a long time. It was time for that to happen, at least as far as I am concerned. A great mom for my kids but not a great wife for me; thank you very much! I was tired of all the fighting with Loretta and tired of the kids seeing it all.

The Banditos
Big Sonny and The Lo Boys were going strong as we'd cut the album[7] and were getting quite a bit of work around El Paso and in New Mexico, but Big Sonny became fascinated with the Banditos who were like the Hell's Angels, only worse. They were mostly in Texas, they were outlaw bikers and I really mean outlaws. Sonny wanted to hang with them and be the Banditos' band. Well, as soon as club owners found out that we were playing a lot of gigs for the Banditos, none of them would hire us in their clubs anymore.

They didn't want the Banditos coming into their places anymore because there was always trouble if they were there. What usually happened was there would be some smartass drunk that wanted to see how tough he was and kick the shit out of a Bandito and brother that's living dangerously, because if you try that you've got the whole pack to take on. I've seen many a guy go down for the count, from the Banditos.

Albuquerque Bound
So it was getting harder and harder to get gigs. Big Sonny lasted for about three years. I finished up with them on New Year's Eve 1979. After that, I moved up to Albuquerque and got as far away from that bullshit as I could.

173

My move up state to Albuquerque was a good move for me, in the sense that I was free from my marriage, but it was hard on me from the standpoint of my children. I know they couldn't figure out what was happening then. Maybe now that they are older they can - I sure hope so.

Loretta and I got divorced in 1980[8] and I quit drinking for five years that time.

Notes to Chapter 12

[1] [JCB:] "Actually we were called the Mesilla Valley Low Boys when we first started."

[2] JCB on drums and vocals, Jeff Littlejohn on lead guitar, Bob "Hopper" Shannon on primary drums, Mike Collins on rhythm guitar and Chava Villegas on congas and later, in early 1976, Tom Leavey on bass replaced the original bassist

[3] 'Play Your Music' b/w 'Funny Money', 1976, featuring Lo Boys: Tom Leavey (lead vocal, backing vocals, bass, harmonica); Jeff Littlejohn (guitar); William Randolph Russ III (guitar) and JCB on (drums).

[4] According to the Internet, Panama Red was a popular brand of "dope" during the Vietnam era.

[5] Which places meeting Husta again to 1978

[6] Husta spent three years in Albuquerque, during which time she also completed her MA

[7] In Heat was released in 1979, along with a single, Love Me Two Times b/w Love Potion 9

[8] JCB notes elsewhere that he got divorced in 1979, which was also the year he says he filed for divorce.

Moving to Albuquerque
I moved up to Albuquerque, New Mexico, right after New Year's Eve mainly because I was tired of all the travelling back and forward. The Lo Boys weren't doing much anymore and I wanted to be with Husta. I started to look around for someone to play with and found a few guys that were interested. I really needed to start working since I had no money and I didn't want Husta to have to support me. I was dealing a little Grass to keep going but I didn't think that was a cool thing to do, as I really didn't know the city very well and had hardly any contacts. That fact makes dealing very dangerous as you can imagine. I started putting up signs in music stores for anyone looking for a drummer or clerk in the stores. I found a part time job in a music store called Creative Music as a teacher and a clerk. I enjoyed my time at that place and met some really nice people.

Phil Applebaum
I got to know Phil Applebaum who was an engineer and worked in the little recording studio that was in the back of Creative Music. Phil turned out to be a huge Mothers fan and had followed my career since the beginning. He also happened to have dug the original Geronimo Black band. As Phil and I became good friends, we started to make plans to do some things there. Him and I compiled some of the old Geronimo Black tapes that I had brought back from California eight or nine years earlier and started making them into an album. Those tapes consisted of the original demo recordings we'd recorded in North Hollywood that had gotten the band the original deal with MCA. There were also some things we recorded just before we broke up and one live cut from one of the last gigs the band did, the San Miguel gig that we played in '73.[1]

Geronimo Comes to Live with Me
I had gone down to Anthony to visit my Mom and my kids when my ex-wife Loretta said she was having a lot of problems with my youngest son, Geronimo. He wasn't getting along with the kids in his class and he was always fighting and generally raising hell in school. It was partially due to me divorcing his Mom, or at least I think it was. Anyway, she asked me if I would take him up to Albuquerque to live with me for a while. I called Husta and asked her if it was okay and she said to bring him up, so I did. We got him enrolled in school and everything was going pretty good for him. That lasted for about two months and then he started to miss his mother and started the same shit up there. The school kicked him out and I had to take him back to Anthony!

Right after I got back from Anthony, I went to work for The Sound Warehouse which was a big chain of record stores from Oklahoma.

The Sound Warehouse
The store was an old Safeway Food Store and was huge. I started out working the cash register and stocking records for about a month and then an opening happened for me to move into the back of the store and receive all new stock coming in. I would put the price stickers on all the LPs, Cassettes, and Eight Track Cassettes from the record companies. It was a pretty fun job especially since I didn't have to wait on customers anymore. I did that work for over a year until I went to L.A. to play with the Grandmothers.

That's when I put out *Welcome Back, Geronimo Black* and *Clearly Classic*. I found a record company up in Santa Fe called Helios Records who were willing to release the *Welcome Back, Geronimo Black* album. I had met this man named Paul Mitchell who played guitar and was also a painter. I had an idea of the cover I wanted and explained it to him. About two weeks later, he called me up and said that he had finished it. I took it to the record company, they really liked it and paid the guy something like two hundred and fifty dollars for the use of [the painting on] the cover [but] he retained the original painting. I got a very good friend, Dee Lansbury, to do the back graphics on it. She used to be Tom Leavey's girl friend and was living in New Mexico then. The album was pressed in California and was distributed by some company that did a pretty good job of it because we sold a few thousand copies, although we never got any money for it! That seems to be the story of my life for some reason or another.

Harder Than Your Husband
One day in August,[2] I got a call from Denny Walley and he said that Frank had been trying to get hold of me and that I should call him. Frank had a country and western song that he'd been working on for a new LP called *You Are What You Is* and had decided that the only guy who could sing it was Jimmy Carl Black!

So I called him and he said, "I've got a song for you. I've been trying to sing it, but I figured that you would be better doing it!" He asked could I come over to L.A. in the next few days. I asked my boss for some time off so I could go record with Frank Zappa and he said, "By all means." I talked to Frank on that Monday and left for L.A. on Tuesday because he said they would have a ticket waiting at the airport on Tuesday morning.

The day I got to L.A., I didn't go into the studio. I checked into the Sunset Marquee Hotel in Hollywood. Thomas Nordegg, who was working for Frank at the time, gave me a tape of Frank singing the song 'Harder Than Your Husband' and a copy of just the backing - he also gave me a tape recorder - so I practiced in my hotel room on the first evening.

176

The next day, at six in the afternoon, Thomas came to pick me up in Frank's brand new Rolls Royce. He drove me up to the house, where Frank had just built a big new studio. We recorded the song that night and Frank loved it. I thought that that was it and I'd be flying out the next day but he said, "I want you to stay for another day or so because I've got some other songs that I'd like you to sing on."

The next night, I went back to the studio to check things out and watch what was going on. That's when I met Ike Willis and Ray White because they were doing some vocal overdubs. I thought they were cool guys. I liked them very much. They were snorting Coke in the studio there and I said, "Aren't you afraid that Frank's gonna get on your case?" They said, "Oh, forget it - what Frank doesn't know don't hurt him!"

One night, Denny Walley came by and so did Motorhead who brought his saxophone with him. We did a lot of recording that night for Frank. Denny put the slide guitar on 'Harder Than Your Husband' and I think that Motorhead did some freaking out on 'Mudd Club' or something. On the Friday, we recorded my parts on 'I Don't Wanna Get Drafted', 'Teenage Wind' and 'Goblin Girl'.

I was paid in very good cash for the sessions and, as I recall, they were double sessions and $40 per day for meals and stuff. He paid me real well, and I think it paid off for him because the album *You Are What You Is* was a great success musically.

I hung out there in his new studio with Frank quite a lot. One night, after we'd finished recording, he played me the video of *Baby Snakes*. It wasn't quite completed but he had a rough cut of it. It was mainly the animations, which I think are excellent. I thought that they were really inventive and very trippy and the best part of the movie - but I didn't tell him that. I did enjoy Roy's part where he's got the wig on. I thought that was hilarious, but then Roy[3] has always been funny whether he wanted to be or not.

I was working at the Sound Warehouse when I got a call from a very popular disc jockey in town - his call name was Mr. Bill. This was just before the presidential election between Jimmy Carter and Ronald Reagan.[4] Well, it seems that he didn't like either one of those guys and had started (as a joke) his own campaign for president. He had heard the show that I had done for the Heart Foundation[5] and was also a Mothers of Invention fan, so he asked me if I would write a campaign song for him that he could start playing on the radio. I wrote 'Thank You, Mr. Bill' and got some musicians that I had been jamming with to go into the studio with me and my old[6] friend, Phil Applebaum, to record it.

ALBUQUERQUE BOUND
Written by Dawayne Bailey
Produced by Jimmy Carl Black
Executive Producer, Larry Hillyer III

Jimmy Carl Black – Lead Vocal   Gary Patton – Bass, Background Vocals
Dave Tomar – Lead & Slide Guitar   Dave McKee – Drums
Gene Shields – Rhythm Guitar   Jimmy Blair – Background Vocals
Bob Reedy – Rhythm Guitar   Phil Appelbaum – Engineer

After recording it, I decided that I wanted to put it out as a single and I needed another tune for the B-side. I recorded 'Albuquerque Bound' which was written by my new song-writing "pardner", Dawayne Bailey.

One day at work, I got a call from Dawayne who was living in Wichita, Kansas. He had heard that I was working at the Sound Warehouse and told me he was a big Mothers fan. He was getting ready to pass through Albuquerque on his way to L.A. and very politely asked would it be possible to stop by and have his record collection signed.[7]

So, I had that single pressed at the same time we pressed *Welcome Back, Geronimo Black*, also on Helios Records. It is a silly little record that hardly sold anything, but it is a collector's item and is now going to be on a new CD of mine coming out around the end of the year. The CD is called *Can I Borrow A Couple Of Bucks 'Til The End Of The Week*.[8]

October 12th 1980 was Husta's 40th Birthday and that is when Frank and the band came to Albuquerque on their tour. It was the second gig of the *Crush All Boxes*[9] tour.

We went to the concert and Husta was backstage with me when Frank invited me up to sing 'Harder Than Your Husband' with them. The show was actually recorded and broadcast by the local television. I have a copy of that video tape. Before the show, Frank and I went to the local college radio station and did an interview with them. Frank explained why the new LP was going to be called *Crush All Boxes* instead of *Fred Zeppelin,* which is what he was originally going to call it. John Bonham had just died so he changed the name out of respect. Probably the only time Frank would do something like that.

At that time, I was on the wagon and wasn't drinking anything alcoholic at all. Frank offered to have a drink with me but I had to explain to him that I couldn't accept because it wouldn't work for me.

After the show, we were having a party for Husta at one of our friend's house and so we invited everybody back to the house. The band all came back but before anyone came in, John Smothers, who was Zappa's bodyguard, went in and said, "All Pot will be put out before Frank comes in!" Boy, that really pissed Dee off, the chick whose house it was, and she said, "I don't give a fuck whether he comes in the house or not, Man! This is my fuckin' house and if I wanna smoke Pot in it, I'm gonna!" So anyway, Frank came in and he stayed for about 30 or 40 minutes with his cup of coffee while the rest of us kept on smoking our Pot. Vinnie Colaiuta, Arthur Barrow, Ray [White] and Ike all came in the limo with him and, when he left, they stayed and smoked their fucking brains out with us. We really had a good time after Frank left. Sometimes Frank was so square, and didn't seem to want to have a good time. As far as I was concerned, that was his fucking problem!

The Grandmothers Anthology
Soon after that, I went back out to California for the second time that year. I got a call from Andy Cahan saying, "Hey Man! I'm putting together an album that Rhino Records want to put out called *Grandmothers* and they're willing to pay your air fare out to California so we can take some publicity photos for the album!" He said, "Oh by the way, Cal Schenkel is doing the album cover!" So I went out there for a few days and we had a great time. It was always great to see all the boys again. I stayed with Denny Walley, as I always did when I went out there.

We did the photos and I talked to Don and Bunk about trying to put together a touring band. Then we found out that there was an offer to go and do a tour of Scandinavia and Germany for the following year. That meeting was actually the beginning of The Grandmothers.[10]

I have talked to Elliot Ingber on the phone a lot of times since then but that was the last time I saw him!

At the start of 1981, I was asked to put together a kind of fifties rock show as a fundraising thing for the New Heart Foundation.[11] They gave me a budget of $1000 to organize a band. Phil Applebaum put me in contact with a band called the Jolly Rogers. We rehearsed for a week and did the show. The show was a total success and a lot of fun to do.

I knew a guy who sold specialty vinyl records by mail order and he suggested that we do a limited edition thing. We decided to record some of the music that we had performed at the fund-raiser. We went in the studio for three days and recorded and mixed it practically live. We put it out as *Clearly Classic*.[12] We had 500 copies made and each one was individually numbered. It has always been a topic with collectors to get one of those LPs since they were made out of clear plastic and were cut in a BLOB shape. If you happen to have one, it is definitely a collector's item.

Grandmothers on Tour

In April 1981, I went back to California to do rehearsals with the Grandmothers for the first upcoming tour. While I was there I called up Frank and asked how he was doing. He said, "Good. Listen! Come on by the house because I have a song that I want to give you!" So I went by his house and that's when he played me a song called 'Falling In Love Is A Stupid Habit'. He sat and played it on the piano and sang it onto a little cassette player. He handed me the words and the tape and just said, "Put a banjo on it and a violin."

I went over to Frank's house two or three times while we were rehearsing at Don Preston's house. Originally, Frank was not opposed to us starting the Grandmothers. He was well aware of what we were doing and didn't say a thing about it. I think he thought it was a good idea at that time.

So, the Grandmothers played six gigs[13] at the end of May, before we went to Europe. We played Vancouver, Seattle, Eugene, Eureka, two nights in San Francisco and then we finished with a show at The Roxy in Hollywood. Husta came out from where we lived in New Mexico, met me in Eugene, Ore., rode with me back to L.A. and spent a week with me before we left for Europe. We really had a nice time on that trip. It was through the redwood forest and down the coast of California. It was the first time for Husta in that part of the country.

When we got to San Francisco, we went to the concert hall where we were to play and saw "Wild Man" Fischer in front of the place waiting for us. I hadn't seen him in quite a few years and it was good to see him. Man! That is one crazy dude and he hadn't changed one iota! When we started the concert, Husta was sitting upstairs in the theater and saw this guy sitting next to her with something in his hand. It had a little red light on it so she said, "Are you recording this show". He said, "So what?" She said that Jimmy Carl Black, the drummer playing up on the stage, was her man and it was not allowed to record the show. So she said, "I'll take that tape." You know what? The guy gave it to her and said, "I'm really sorry, we didn't know we couldn't record this show." I was always proud of her for doing that. That guy could have kicked her ass and who would have stopped him.

I saw Vito at one of those shows as he was teaching dance and sculpture at a university up there. I went around to his studio and we had a nice chat. I invited him down to the show that night. Nobody ever knew how old he was. I think he must have been in his eighties[14] at that time because he sure looked like it, but he was still dancing like crazy, like a wild man! He was dancing right in front of the band (we were playing 'King Kong' or something like that) when he yanked down his pants - he had a big hard on. He used to love to do that. Man! When I'm his age I hope that I can have a fuckin' boner like that! He had a new wife at that time who was about eighteen years old, and a new little daughter!

Grandmothers at The Roxy

Motorhead turned up for The Roxy show. He was up on stage doing all sorts of wild shit. Don Preston had made this life-sized doll and put a drawing of Frank's face on it and he used to have it propped up by his amp. It was just sitting staring out at the crowd. Motorhead grabbed the doll and started abusing it. He was rubbing it in his crutch and stuff like that. Motorhead did more to the thing than anybody else and, in fact, he's the one who started it but he certainly didn't take the credit[15] for it. All the Mothers freaks were there and they were all laughing. Frank found out about the doll because I think he had sent someone down to check us out, and so somebody told him about it.

So, the call was made, by Frank, direct to Don: "I don't like what you're doing with that doll..." It was a picture of his face drawn on this stuffed doll, that's all it was, but that is all it took to really piss Frank off. You know, Frank used to do things like that with either Nixon's face or Reagan's face and that was alright, but don't do it to him! It was all in fun anyway, but he didn't see it that way. No sense of humor. Quote: "Does Humor belong in Music?"

Things changed drastically for us when he heard about the doll. I was going to record the new song he'd given me but I never got a chance to do it, because of all the trouble that had started! I doubt very seriously whether he would even have allowed me to do it. I know the Family Trust would not allow me to do that song now. I've heard reports that Frank denied he ever wrote the song. Unless I tried to record it! I am sure that they would change their tune if that happened. It has never been recorded.

Grandmothers in Scandinavia: 1981

So off we went on our first European tour in twelve years. A lot of really great things happened on that tour. First of all, it was a great band. We had three days rehearsal in Copenhagen before we started playing. The whole tour was promoted by a man named Jan Frieder. He had done several of the Mothers tours for Frank, and then the "Flo and Eddie" tour, and was also a good friend of Herb Cohen. We did a lot of travelling on that tour. Trains, buses, light aircraft, you name it and we did it. We started with a gig in the place that we'd been rehearsing in Copenhagen. The next day, we left for Lund, Sweden, then Gothenburg, Sweden and back to Copenhagen. Then we rented a little plane and flew out to Bergen in Norway for a few days. Bergen was where I met one of the most beautiful women I ever met. Her name was Mae. That is my mother's name and, as it turned out, she was born on the same day my mother was but of course, not the same year. I fell in love (more like lust) immediately with her. At the time, I was forty-three years old and she was twenty. Who gives a shit was what I thought. Man! I had her for two days!

The night of the concert, we finished at about two in the morning and her and I went outside of where we had played, and the sun was still shining! That was unbelievable to me. We were very high up near the North Pole in Bergen. I really hated to leave her and I will never forget her either. Then we flew to Oslo.

They drove us 30 miles or should I say 30 Swedish miles - it seems that one Swedish mile is 10 [US] miles[16] in Scandinavia. Anyway, we eventually got there and did a press conference. That is where I had my first and last reindeer steak which must have been rotten, because I really got ill from that steak. The next day, we drove back down to Oslo - I was still very sick - and then flew to Stockholm to play a show. After that, we had to go all the way up to Hamar to play a festival which was quite a nice one. Mike Oldfield was on the bill, playing his *Tubular Bells* thing. We had the same drive back to Oslo the next day, where we caught our little plane to Copenhagen. We played at an open-air festival on the beach called the Rattskeller Festival.[17] We had two days off of constant partying and fucking and then we travelled by train to Hamburg. That was the start of the German leg of the tour. Man! We were having fun by then - or at least I was!

Grandmothers in Germany
We were met at the main station by JoJo Productions: JoJo and Chris, who were great guys. The first gig we played was a jazz club called Uncle Pös,[18] which was a sort of warm-up promo show. They shot the whole thing on three video cameras and recorded it 24-track mobile. We played for two and a half hours. After that show, we had quite a party at JoJo's house. The next day we flew down to Stuttgart and played a great gig. We rented two cars and drove from Stuttgart on to Munich where we played another great show.

After we played in Dusseldorf and Hanover, our next show was in Berlin, which was still behind the Iron Curtain. It was our first time back there since that riot show back in 1968. We had a night off before we played and went to the Latin Quarter to see the Global Unity Orchestra, who had Hans Bennink on drums - a very interesting band. That was the venue where we were to play our show. We got a little smashed that night if I recall because we had [also] gone to the Quasimodo Club, which was one of the oldest jazz clubs in West Berlin. Bunk and I were holding each other up and singing all the way back to the hotel. I'm glad to say that this visit to Berlin was a little more relaxed than the last time we'd been there!

After the Berlin show, we went back to play the Hamburg show proper at the Market Hall. It was a great show, as we have always played good there. We had another party after the show but it seemed to me that the gas had run out of the promoters because a couple of the shows weren't that good, attendance-wise.

I still got laid by one of the girls that worked for JoJo Productions and she was wonderful. I have often wondered what happened to those guys. Oh, well, onward and upward to Holland.

Amsterdam at the Paradiso
We left the next morning for Amsterdam for the Dutch part of the tour. We got a chance to play three nights at the Paradiso and it was great.[19] We scored some Peruvian Blue Flake there that knocked our socks off. We enjoyed the coffee shops, which were just starting to happen and, of course, the red light district is always exciting.

The last night we were there, Chris from JoJo Productions showed up with his lovely girlfriend Maria and we started partying. She was running around the hotel with only her panties and a slinky t-shirt on. While the rest of the crew were snorting Coke, I couldn't help myself. I talked her into going to my room and we really got it on. We didn't need any help from anything to do what we did. Chris was a little pissed off because he couldn't find his girlfriend but she was well taken care of!

Back in Denmark
I remember we stayed in a hotel that was 500 years old. It was in a quite small town called Ribe.[20] It was fucking amazing, 1481 was when it was built, and it had gold fixtures in the bathrooms and everything! We played at the "Ring-Fin"[21] Festival with about 10,000 people, and I met a quite lovely lady there. By that time, the weather was really cooperating with us and it was actually warm enough for most of the girls at the festival to start taking all their little clothes off!

The next day we went to Odense to play at a jazz club. We did a live 24-track recording at that club that wound up on side one of *Looking Up Granny's Dress*. I only sang on four songs during that tour. Although I sang background on a lot of stuff, I was only out front for four songs and so we had this drum machine programmed for those four songs. Walt[22] was in charge of the drum machine. Right after the last show in Stockholm, someone stole the drum machine off the stage. Some guy just came up and grabbed it and ran. They also tried to get the doll too, but somehow we always stopped them from that. People were always tryin' to get that thing. They must have thought, "What a collector's item!" On a few of the gigs, a drummer named Gurt Ulibar sat in with us. He was really a great guy, a good drummer and a fan of the music.

New York, Here We Come

We went back to Copenhagen the next day and caught the flight to New York City. We had three gigs around there. The first one was in Long Island at a pretty famous club called Your Father's Place and the gig was really great. The Grandmothers had never played in New York City so it was like coming home to Don, Bunk, and me. We had a lot of fans from the old Mothers' days and we renewed some old friendships. The next gig was in New York City proper at some concert hall not too far from the Village. That gig was great also and we renewed more old friendships there. The last gig was in Trenton, New Jersey of all places, as the Mothers had never played there. The residents call Trenton the "Armpit of the USA" and I think they are proud of it. There was so much shit in the air down there that I can understand why the people called it what they did. That was the end of the tour and, as far as I was concerned, the tour was a huge success, and we had another European tour scheduled for about three months later!

Tom Fowler

When I went back to California to rehearse, I found out that Tony Duran had left the band, so Denny Walley was going to play with us. You can thank Tom Fowler for Tony leaving the band. Don Preston was musical director but Tom was the guy who thought he was running things, which is dangerous.

Let me tell you now that I don't like Tom Fowler and I never will, and not just because of that but a lot of things. I didn't really know him before. I'd only met him briefly when the *Bongo Fury* tour came through El Paso back in 1975.

His brother Walt is a great guy. He even thinks that Tom's an asshole sometimes. There are five Fowler brothers. When I was in L.A., I went to listen to their band, The Fowler Brothers Air Pocket Band and they were great. Ike Willis was singing with them, Chester Thompson was playing drums and Mike Miller was playing guitar.

Inkanish Records

I had the *Clearly Classic* album re-mastered and pressed while I was in L.A. It was the first release on my own Inkanish Records label. It would be quite a few years before I could get that label going again and when I finally did, it didn't last long. It is a hard business to try to do without any money.

Denny's Dad's Car!

So, I was in L.A. to do the rehearsals with the new line up and I was staying with Denny at the time. The day before the first rehearsal, we went out to the Mojave Desert, to Lancaster. Denny had to borrow his dad's car so we could get back and forth from the rehearsals. This car was a classic 1969 Nash Rambler - the company weren't even making them anymore and it was worth a lot of money.[23] This particular car was in absolutely immaculate shape. It was Denny Walley's father's pride and joy.

On the first day of rehearsals, we were at Don's house. He was living in Echo Park at the time and Denny had parked the car outside of Don's house. So, here is Tina Preston getting in their Mercedes that has no brakes and doesn't have a starter on it. They had to park it on the hill and then let it roll down that hill so they could get it started. She was all bent out of shape with Don about something, as usual, and so she got in the car and rolled it down the hill. That is when she ploughs right into the back of the Rambler, which flew up onto the sidewalk and hit a brick wall. The wall had an archway, which fell and crushed the top of the car good. We heard this noise and went outside. Denny just couldn't believe it and I thought he was going to have a heart attack! Of course Don said, "Well, no problem, don't worry, I'll pay for it." and I thought to myself, "Uh, with what, certainly not his good looks!" Don couldn't buy his way out of a paper bag!

So Denny put the car into the shop and it cost about $3000 to get the thing fixed. It was much more than the car was actually worth! He called his dad up and said, "Dad, guess what I'm doing? I like your car so much that I'm going to have it painted, so it's going to be a couple of weeks before you get it back!" His dad knows him so well that he says, "Yeah, sure, what the fuck have you done to the car?"

Warm-Up Tour

We did a few warm-up gigs before the tour to Europe was to begin. The band went up to San Francisco, Santa Cruz,[24] Monterey and Hayward. We were back at Frenchys again for the first time since the Mothers played there in 1966. Half way through that little tour, we got a call from Jan the promoter in Copenhagen saying that the European tour had been cancelled. Needless to say that everyone was completely down in the dumps over that news. However, Jan did say that the tour was going to happen in Feb. or March the next year. So there was no money generated for Don Preston to pay off Tina's accident and Denny was freaking out big time. He was forced into selling his beautiful Fender Stratocaster to pay for the car. He still, to this day, hates Don's guts and he'll never forget that car accident although actually Don didn't do it. That's Tina Preston for you.

Kludget Sound Studios

We decide that we would record the new Grandmothers' material during the time that we would have been in Europe. I had released *Welcome Back, Geronimo Black* on Helios Records out of Santa Fe, New Mexico and so I had a talk with those guys and they decided to do the 'new' Grandmothers' new record. The guys came to Kludget Sound Studios in Cerrillos, New Mexico to record the album.[25]

When the band got to the studio, I found out that Tom Fowler had managed to work Bunk out of the band. I was living in Albuquerque and I didn't know any of this shit was going on. Of course, Denny wasn't playing with us anymore because he was so pissed off with Preston over the car. Also, when I got there to the studio, I found out that I am off the drums and now I'm just the singer.

Tom Fowler brought Mike Miller in to play guitar and Tony Morales to play drums. Both of them had been playing with the Air Pocket Band at various times, usually when the other regular members of the band couldn't make it, and so that was the new line-up. The tour that had been cancelled was now going to happen in March the following year. The only thing about it was it was going to be a smaller tour of just two and a half weeks long.

Europe 1982

The 1982 European tour started in Stockholm, then we did Gothenburg, Lund and three gigs in little towns around Copenhagen that I can't remember the names of.[26] As it was [around] Easter time, they brewed up special beers that I swear were psychedelic. It was easy to recognize them because they had a little chicken on the label. They were some of the strongest beers I ever drank. That is one of the reasons I love Denmark so much.

In Gothenburg, Don and I were rooming together. He was still upstairs in the room when I went down to breakfast at the hotel. Tom got me over to the side and said, "Listen Man! How would you like to be the only Grandmother[27] in the band because we want to fire Don Preston!?" I said, "Fuck you, you son of a bitch, you're the one that needs to get fired. You got rid of Tony and Bunk and now it's Don. Am I gonna be next?"[28] So I told Don right away what was going on.

After that, we played in Copenhagen at a place called the Grey Hall in Christiana, which is a sort of free section of Copenhagen where it was legal to buy dope. Then we moved on to Germany. By then, Tom Fowler had managed to get Jan, the promoter, off the tour - that fucking guy was totally crazy and on a wild "Power Trip"!

We finished that tour although it was a slight disaster. It wasn't a happy tour at all and I was personally very happy when it was over. I was playing percussion and singing. I just had cowbells, tambourine, snare drum and little bits. I liked Tony Morales because he was a good drummer. He was a jazz-fusion type of drummer and we got on real well. It was Tom I couldn't stand to the point I even hated getting up in the morning, knowing that I'd have to look at him!

Grannies' Lost Album

After the European tour, Walt Fowler came back out to Santa Fe to mix the recordings, but by that time the band had disintegrated because nobody wanted to work with Tom Fowler anymore. He'd been such a troublemaker.

That Grandmothers' album was completed but never released as was intended. A lot of it has been released since - part of it was on Don Preston's album *Vile Foamy Ectoplasm* and part of it was on a Tom Fowler LP on Fossil Records.

When I re-started Inkanish Records in 2001, I released that material plus some live stuff from the first Grandmothers' tour in 1981. It was material from a live gig in Ribe, Denmark and sounds great. The CD is entitled *The Eternal Question* on Inkanish Records.

So that was the end of the Grandmothers right there, but I started the band again in Austin in 1988 when I was living there.

Buddy's Bus

Husta graduated with her master's degree in August 1982 and got a teaching job in Taos, New Mexico. The town is about 150 miles north of Albuquerque.

I had a band called Captain Glasspack and his Magic Mufflers in Santa Fe, N.M. It was the name that the Mothers had originally used back in California in 1965.[29] We were playing around a few places but not really enough to sustain a living. I started to look around for work and I took this job with a guy named Buddy Owen who was a singer and (so called) guitar player that had his "Blues Review".

I went and heard them when they played in Taos and they sounded pretty good - not great, but OK.

They needed a drummer and a bass player, so myself and a guy named Denny Young,[30] who was my bass player at the time, went to Austin to rehearse with them. It was my first time there and I really liked the city.

We played one gig in Austin and then we left for a tour in Florida. We actually left there kind of mysteriously, nobody in the band understanding why until later. I found out that Buddy had been "hanging paper" all over Austin. He was writing dud checks and that's what the police called it - "papering the city of Austin"! So we split in the middle of the night and went to Florida because that's where he was from. We were supposed to have all these fucking gigs lined up there!

So, we get out there and we're all living on this old tour bus. There were six of us, no gigs and for sure, no money coming in. That was the worst time I had experienced in a long time, if ever. I think I literally had one penny to my name. This went on for about three weeks. Buddy and his wife Annie would bring out food to us from his mom's house every day. We had tuna fish sandwiches for four days running. To this day, every time I eat a tuna fish sandwich I think of that crazy time.

Finally, we got this gig in Orlando at a very big club that was very popular with the people around that area. We started playing at 11.30 at night and there were about 700 people in the club. I would say that the place was packed out. Buddy was so bad that night that by 12 o'clock midnight he had managed to empty the place out.

There were about 75 people left in the club and most of them were friends of his. It literally took him thirty minutes to empty the place out because he was so terrible. I have to say that it wasn't the band's fault because we always sounded good. We were all professional except for him. We were supposed to play there two nights and at the end of that first night we got paid. He gave us each $150.

Because of Buddy, we went back the next day to rehearse. The owner told us to get out of his club. He said, "Pack up you gear and get the fuck out of here." Buddy was trying to tell the guy that it was our soundman who had fucked everything up and that we'd get a new one, but he wasn't having any of that shit. He just said, with gusto, "Get your shit off the stage and get out of here and never come back!" So we packed up and went down to Daytona Beach. Buddy said, "Come on, let's go down there and have some fun tonight!"

So, we went down there and had a couple of beers. It was April[31] by then and it was nice and warm, so we decided that we would spend the next day down there. We got in the bus and went to sleep, but that motherfucker got so out of it on JS whiskey he decided to take us back to his mom's house. He drove the bus. I don't know how because he was so out of it. He even stopped the bus once and beat the shit out of his wife Annie. None of us[32] knew what was happening because we were asleep, except for Denny, who saw everything that was taking place. He made Buddy pull the bus over, threatened to kill Buddy if he didn't stop and let him drive! He is the one who told the rest of us how Buddy had beat Annie up. It was only when I woke up that I found out that we were back at this guy's house where we had been parking.

Buddy and Annie had gone back to his mother's house early that morning and he was drunk. The rest of the band decided to drive back to the beach but Denny said, "I've got a better idea! Why don't we drive this fucking bus back to Austin?" So we stole the bus and drove back, the whole band. We just took off, as it was the best plan we'd heard since we got to Florida. We had all his clothes, all his books, the whole office, everything. We found that he was three months behind with the bus payments, so we rang up the garage where he had bought it and told them that we had the bus and were bringing it back to Austin. They were ecstatic about that. When we got back, they gave us a $400 reward and signed a paper that stated that it was OK for us to drive the bus back. That was to insure that we couldn't be arrested for stealing the bus.

Photo: Cabaret, Santa Fé; New Year 1982-3

Notes to Chapter 13

[1] See: [Chapter 10, p156]

[2] 1980

[3] Roy Estrada

[4] Nov. 1980

[5] JCB may be referring to an earlier gig he played for the Heart Foundation. See: [Note 11]

[6] Until he died, JCB remained in contact with Phil Applebaum, so the use of 'old' here is an appropriate anachronism.

[7] Dawayne Bailey recalls this time in an email to JCB

[8] Released 2008

[9] The album was never released

[10] "The three of us started the group, Don, Bunk and myself, in 1980. Actually you know, that's not when the Grandmothers first started. We did one recording session in 1970; right after The Mothers broke up. Herb Cohen got us together and said, 'How would you guys like to do an album as the Grandmothers?' And we said 'Fine'. Tom Wilson was the producer. After we did that first recording session, Herb said 'The title of the album is going to be Frank Zappa Presents The Grandmothers' and that's when everybody said 'No, it isn't gonna be like that.' Because we didn't want anything to do with Frank Zappa. 'Zappa's name will not be on it!' And then the deal fell through. But that was the beginning of the Grandmothers...The original Grandmothers was myself, Don Preston, Bunk Gardner, Art Tripp, Roy Estrada, Lowell George, Elliot Ingber and Motorhead." [JCB interviewed at Moers Festival, 19.5.91, by Axel Wünsch and Aad Hoogesteger, and printed in T'Mershi Duween, #24-25, March-June 1992]

[11] Feb. 20, 1981 at The Four Seasons Motor Inn [Ref: CD sleeve notes]

[12] Released in 1981

[13] 6 venues, 7 gigs

[14] About 67, according to the Internet

[15] JCB is being ironical here as by "take the credit" here he really means "take the can" or take the blame (and punishment!)

[16] By modern definition, a Swedish mile is 10 km, which would be around 6.2 US miles

[17] JCB may mean the Roskilde Festival, held since 1971 around 35 km from Copenhagen

[18] Onkel Pös Carnegie Hall, better known as Onkel Pö, was a music venue in Hamburg in the 1970s and the early 1980s.

[19] The Aug 8, 1981 gig was recorded

[20] July 10, 1981 [Ref: minidisc recording in JCB library]

[21] No history of a venue going by this name that I can find [Ed]

[22] Walt Fowler

[23] The 1969 Rambler was actually produced by AMC, successors to Nash and was the last year that a "Rambler" was manufactured

[24] Nov. 4, 1981

[25] With Baird Banner as engineer and mixer

[26] 4 gigs: Roskilde, Albertlund, Odense and Arhus [Ref: unitedmutations/comgrandmothers]

[27] JCB means "original" Grandmother here

[28] "They'd already gotten me off the drums. I was just singing." [JCB]

[29] JCB's manuscript reads 1964, but a cutting from a New Mexican newspaper interview JCB gave at the time says 1965! (1965 accords with the timeline that underlines JCB's account.) [Ed] The article lists the band members as guitarist David Gilliland, bassist Tony Young and keyboardist Sherman Rubin. "They used to play Club West" [Steve Terrell, in a 2007 Review]

[30] Tony Young's younger brother, I believe. [Ed]

[31] 1983

[32] The rest of us are...? Does anyone know? [Ed]

Moving To Austin

I stayed on in Austin for a few months and started a band called The Jimmy Carl Black Band. We started to play quite a lot because we had gotten an agent that was doing us right. Husta was still teaching in Taos but she wasn't that happy there and wanted to move. I found a band house that was huge and everyone had his own room. She moved down there on June 15th 1983, as soon as school was out.[1]

I found a job painting houses with a guy called Matt Fuller. I really couldn't make a real living playing in a city that had over six hundred bands and there were maybe one hundred places to play.

I was playing quite a lot and that is when I started the series of different bands that I played with in Austin. That's also when I met up with Arthur Brown again, the first time I'd seen him since that festival in  Miami back in 1968. Arthur had been in Austin for a couple of years and was already painting with Matt Fuller. Seems he'd had as much trouble trying to earn money from playing music as I had. Matt Fuller hired only musicians to work with him and I always thought that was a cool move. Arthur had done an album called *Speednotech* with an electronics guy - keyboards and drum-machine stuff - and they also did a very interesting video which got a little bit of play, but it still didn't pay the rent. Arthur was married and had a young son to support at that time so he needed as much work as he could get.

We hit it off right away and I only worked for Matt Fuller for about four months. We decided that we should start up on our own and bought one of Matt's old spray rigs from him. The name of our painting company was the "Gentlemen of Color"!

Arthur used to sing all the time he was painting and it started to drive me crazy! He'd sing lots of wild stuff, like 'Fly Me To The Moon' and things!

So, we would paint these houses and people would ask us to sign 'em! They were kind of like fans. Part of the reason that we got a lot of those jobs was because people had been fans of the Mothers and Arthur Brown. But we actually did some very good work; we were conscientious painters.

We actually started a band together for a while, at the same time we were painting. We rehearsed and rehearsed for months. Arthur would keep saying, "We're not ready yet!" So I gave up on that one! We were playing songs like 'We Gotta Get Outa This Place' and 'Unchain My Heart'. Fuck! What's there to rehearse, Man!? So anyway, that thing split up but of course we kept working, we still had our painting company. I was playing the occasional gigs here and there, usually standing in for people who couldn't make the gig. We had that company for a few years but then the "crunch" came.[2]

With the recession, it became very hard to earn any money in Austin. People were undercutting to get the jobs. You couldn't get anything for a paint job anymore. We couldn't keep both of us going so that's when we split up.

Starting the Lawsuit
In 1984, a friend of mine, Ed Moore, told me that Frank was planning on releasing all the old Mothers albums in box sets. So I called Don and Bunk and asked if they had heard anything about it and they said that they had heard rumors about it as well. So, we discussed things and decided that seeing as we'd not been paid anything royalties-wise from the first time they were released, what would be the chances of getting any royalties this time around?

Frank had also been saying pretty nasty things in the press about the Grandmothers. He was saying we were terrible players, that we were shitty players when we played in the Mothers. I didn't think Frank should be saying things like that because it wasn't true. If we were so shitty, how did he get to be so big? He sure wasn't playing all the instruments at the same time - not that I recall! If it hadn't have been for the original Mothers of Invention - us - nobody would know who Frank Zappa was. I know that's what got him where he was!

So we decided to get a lawyer. Originally, when the thing started, everybody was going to be in the lawsuit except for Roy and Motorhead. The reason for Roy possibly not being in the [law]suit was that we couldn't find Roy. Nobody knew where he was and Motorhead just didn't want to be part of it, probably due to his undying loyalty to Frank. We rallied some of the later guys too. Napoleon Murphy Brock wanted in on it, as well as Flo and Eddie. Ian Underwood couldn't have cared less mainly because he never needed the money.

We went straight to a lawyer, because we remembered the last time that we tried to talk to Frank about our royalties he just threw us out of his house! I always thought that he never cared about any of the guys that made him happen.

Filing the Lawsuit
I had had no contact with Frank since I did the LP *You Are What You Is.* So in 1985, we started that lawsuit against him even though we had done it before and got blown out of the water before it even started.[3] When we heard from the record stores that he was re-releasing all the old stuff and hadn't contacted any of us to tell us, we really got pissed off. We all thought that he owed us at least common courtesy to inform us all. After all, we still had our original contracts so we wanted to be sure that we would get some royalties from it this time around.

We were only after our artist royalties. It was not very much, but we were entitled to them.[4] We had talked to Herb and found out that when that Warner Bros. lawsuit went down, there was $200,000 that was supposed to go to the band as part of the settlement! That was for Artist Royalties and Frank never mentioned any of that. Herb agreed to turn over all the paperwork and stuff that he had, and there were boxes and boxes of that shit!

Herb and Frank had had their falling out a long time ago so Herb was on our side and Frank knew that and he didn't like it. Frank really hated Herbie. I really don't know why but when Frank got into a hate thing, he could really hate deep. I don't think he really won that lawsuit against Herbie although I'm not sure exactly what happened, but I heard that the whole thing started over $50 or something pretty stupid. Herb had done a lot for Frank's career and had allowed him to do the things he did musically. I think that Herb Cohen was a great manager.

SOAP CREEK SALOON About that time, I started playing with a black gospel group called Junior Franklin and The Golden Echoes. There's a bar in Austin, Texas that was owned by Willie Nelson and it was called the Soap Creek Saloon, on Congress.[5]

I'd been down there a few times and jammed with various blues bands, and I heard about this Gospel group who were playing there every Wednesday night. I thought that was kind of strange, because Gospel music usually means church and it seemed a very strange place for church music to be happening. So I went down there one night to listen to them and I thought they were great. I should have realized that the difference between Black Gospel music and White Gospel music is like the difference between night and day. Afterwards, I went up to Junior and told him I liked it and told him I was a drummer, but he had no idea who I was and had never heard of Zappa.

It seems that the band he had wasn't a permanent line-up and he was looking for a drummer and a guitarist. He found out that Dave Franklin, the guy who was working as the bouncer at the Soap Creek, was a guitar player and asked him if he would play the following week. Dave suggested that they call me, so Junior Franklin called me up and asked me if I would sit in with them. I said, "Why not, Man, it might be interesting!" We played without a rehearsal and it was great. I really hit it off with "Cool Breeze" the keyboard player. Afterwards, Junior asked me if I would remain the drummer and so I started playing with them there at the Soap Creek Saloon every Wednesday night.

On Sunday mornings, I had to go and play around the different churches in East Austin, the black area.

Junior Franklin and The Golden Echoes

The next week, there was a rehearsal over at Junior Franklin's little print shop. I went over there and knocked on the door, and this guy came to the door. He was kind of bald on top and had a grey ponytail. I asked him if Junior was there and he said, "Yeah! I'm Junior!" I'd only met him twice before and I'd thought that that hair looked funny! So that's how I found out that he wore a wig.

I finally said to him after a few months, "Junior, why don't you throw that wig away, Man, you don't need no fuckin' wig!" So he quit wearing the wig, and he looked a lot better.

They also needed a bass player and I knew this Mexican guy named Chuggy Hernandez, so I got him to play with us. They had this keyboard player called Alvin "Breezy" Hennington. Breeze had played with Lou Rawls for years and he was a very good player. He was what they called a high yellow because he was half black. Dave Franklin (No relation to Jr. Franklin, who was black) had just gotten out of prison because he'd been busted for trying to sell a kilo of Pot. While he was in jail, all he did was play his guitar and he'd gotten pretty good. It became quite a good band. We had up front the four singers: Junior Franklin and the three Bonner sisters, Claudia, Lisa, and Jackie who was the soprano. The Bonner family were nice - Daddy Bonner was one of the Deacons in the church. Junior Franklin's dad was a preacher at the biggest Baptist church in Austin.

We did a radio show for KUT Live, which put on a weekly radio show live out of the studio at the University of Texas campus. It was a beautiful 24-track recording studio with a huge room for live performances. I got an excellent recording of the band. I put it out on Inkanish Records for anyone who likes Gospel music. It was quite an experience to play with that band.

I played with that band for one year and I have to say that is the most I had been to church since I was a kid. Black churches are really cool.

In the first church that we played in, some old lady that was in the congregation flipped out and I thought, "What the hell happened to her?" I'd never seen anything like that before, or since then. It happened in every church that we played in, so I asked Junior what the deal was and he said, "Oh, the Holy Ghost goes into them." So I started to "document" this thing and it always happened in a song called 'Walk Around Heaven All Day'. There was a certain part in the song where Jackie Bonner hit this high note and that is what sent the Holy Ghost into somebody.

At one of the gigs at the Martin Luther King Street Baptist Church, five women flipped at the same time. They have these people who take them outside and calm them down. It's a strange Trip! to see it happen.

When I had been playing with them for about one year, Junior got all of us together one day and said, "I think that I've got to split the band because I have a little stay at the La Tuna Federal Penitentiary in Anthony, Texas." Naturally, we asked him why he had to go to prison. He had this printing company that was printing all the posters for all the gospel groups that were playing around the United States, but him and his friend had decided to print up $300,000 worth of counterfeit $20 bills. It seems that they were getting rid of them in Mississippi. These dudes were actually counterfeiters and so he got five years for that. He said, "It won't be so bad because the prison is in Jimmy Carl's Home Town.", whatever that means! Literally, it means that La Tuna Federal Prison is in my home town of Anthony, Texas.

You know, in the year that I played with that band I was paid $300, and I figured out that it had cost me about $600 for gas to play for them, and GOD! But one of the great experiences of my long career in the music business. I used to love to listen to those black preachers. They would shout a sentence out and the whole congregation would shout Hallelujah!

Arthur Brown used to love to come and listen to the gospel group. He even came to see us play in church a couple of Sundays. He got to experience one of those women that had the Holy Ghost come into them. I also remember one Sunday at the MLK First Baptist church, where the Holy Ghost came into Claudia (one of the Golden Echoes) and she had to be helped outside to calm her down - it was the strangest thing I ever saw!

One night, down at the Soap Creek Saloon, the band just finishing up for the night and who comes walking in but Stevie Ray Vaughan and Tommy Shannon from Double Trouble. Stevie had heard about the band and wanted to play with the group. They got up and played a few numbers with the girls and then we stayed up on the stage for about 45 minutes and jammed some blues stuff. It was a real treat to play with that guy because, to me, he was one of the all-time greats of the Blues. I knew Tommy from the 1960s when he played bass for Johnny Winter and it was good to see him again.

The Rhythm Rats

At that time,[6] I was also playing in an R&B band called The Rhythm Rats - Will Indian was the guitar player, Rusty Trapps was the drummer and Loose Reed was the bass player and horn player. I was just singing with them, I wasn't playing drums with that band.

Jimmy Carl Black & The Mannish Boys

I used to go jam with the Rhythm Rats at a club in Austin after playing the church circuit with Jr. Franklin on Sunday nights. One night when I was there, I heard a young harp player that completely blew me away. I introduced myself and so did he. His name was Gary Primich and he said he had just come to Austin from Bloomington, Indiana.

BLACK AND **BLUES**
THE
FEATURING
JIMMY CARL BLACK
THE **TAVERN**
IN CHRISTOVAL
AUGUST 16 TH
9:00 PM $ 3 00
♫ ♪♫ ☺ 🎵 ♪ ♫
DON'T MISS THIS HOT
AUSTIN BLUES BAND

I asked him if he was interested in starting a rockin' blues band and he said he was. He knew a guitar player named Gil Hartman and I said I knew a bass player named Leland Parks. That was the beginning of the Black and Blues but then we changed our name to the Mannish Boys.

We started rehearsing and getting our act together and I made a deal with a guy that had a studio. I had some Pot and so we traded time for smoke. We got our little demo together so we could start getting some work and we did. We started playing around town quite a bit which wasn't that easy to do in Austin. I was painting houses in the daytime with my partner, Arthur Brown, and playing at least three times a week. The money was not good but the music was. This went on for a year or so, until one day Leland called me up and said that he was leaving the band because he got an offer he couldn't refuse, to play in Houston with Alan Haynes and Uncle John Turner.

Well, we had to find a bass player to take his place and we got Frank Meyer to play. We did a lot more rehearsing out at my place, which was out in the country about 15 miles from town. I started talking to Jim Yanaway from Amazing Records about us doing an LP on his label. He had been coming to hear us play quite a few times and thought that Primich was indeed a great harp player, guitar player and a good singer. Gary and I did the vocals and he thought I was a good singer as well. We signed the deal but two weeks[7] before we cut the Mannish Boys album, we recorded the *Brown, Black & Blue* album, as I had recruited the "Boys" to be in the back-up band for the LP.

Arthur and I had been talking to Peter Butcher (an English guy who was living in Austin) for quite a while about him letting us go into his Europa Studios in Austin. I was put in charge of getting together the musicians that could do what Arthur wanted to do, which was some classic R&B and Blues songs. The core of the Mannish Boys band was together and had been for a few years[8] and Arthur was very familiar with the band. In fact, Arthur used to come down to wherever we were playing and say, "James, can I have a sing."

One night, a very good friend of mine, Bob Corbett, had just driven in from Madison, WI. He was getting ready to move back to Austin again.

I ask him if he wanted to play his sax on a couple of tunes and, of course, there was no money to pay him then but if we could sell the project there might be. He said he was willing to do that as all the musicians on the LP

196

were PLAYING FOR NO MONEY! That is a familiar song that all of us musicians have played before, lots of times!

I recruited Mike Francis, the sax player from Asleep At The Wheel, to play a solo on 'The Right Time'. We were playing at Antone's one night, one of the most famous blues clubs in the States, and he came up to me and said that he had heard about the recordings we were doing and wanted to be part of it.

That is also how I got Nick Conway to play Hammond organ. He was the premiere player in town at that time and was a fan of mine and Arthur's. I got Phil Fajardo to do percussion. He was the drummer for George Strait at the time. All the players on the LP are "Top Players". Arthur recruited the three girl singers: Ester Puger, Chevelle Hunter, and Demethea McVay. We got into the studio and put down the ten basic tracks in two nights as we had rehearsed the songs a couple of times before we went in. Arthur's got a great version of 'Smokestack Lightnin', Man! Different!

But we never even played a gig so that album took two years to sell and didn't come out until 1989.[9] Peter Butcher paid for the thing. I couldn't believe it when Arthur told me the guy dropped dead from a heart attack when he was only about 42 years old.[10] In 1991, a limited edition of 1000 copies was released on CD.

In 1991, Arthur played one gig with us in New York City - the Grandmothers backed him up. We played 'Fire' and a few other old things and a couple of tracks off that album.

We did all the backing tracks for [Arthur's] LP and then on the next Sunday night, the Mannish Boys played on KUT Live, a radio show which was very popular in Austin. We got a wonderful 1-hour show on tape that I used later to make the LP into a CD.

The next night, we started in the Austin Sound Recording Studio[11] to cut the LP.[12] I had gotten my friend Tony Young in as the engineer because he was the best and it proved that he was. We did the album in two weeks including the mixing. The band was hot.

It took quite a long time for the record to come out and I was getting a little bored with the politics of the band, so I quit and formed the Austin Grandmothers. The record finally came out and the guys continued to play for another two or three years after that but nothing much ever happened for them.

Gary Primich went on to form his own band. He passed away in Austin in September 2007 and it really made me sad. He was a good friend of mine even after we split up, as he had nothing to do with that. GARY PRIMICH R.I.P. my friend.

197

Highway Café of the Damned
The Austin Lounge Lizards LP was recorded about 1987.[13]

The Austin Grandmothers: 1988
I had always kept in contact with Don and Bunk so, when I formed the new Grandmothers, I called them and asked what they thought about it. I ask both of them would they be interested in being part of it. Bunk said he was, but Don at that time wasn't. So I formed the first version of the Austin Grandmothers with some musicians that I had met and played with in Austin.[14] I was on drums, Lyle Davis was on keyboards, Gerry "Eli" Smith was on woodwinds, Bro Betts was on bass, and Jeff Hogan was on percussion. I can't remember the guitar player's last name but his first name was Mike.

We rehearsed quite a bit but not really enough to really sound great. We started playing out at the Dam Café on Lake Travis and I got us on the KUT Live radio show that I had done with the Mannish Boys. We got a gig backing a dance company that was doing a few performances at a theater in Austin when I got very ill with a rectal abscess on the right cheek of my ass.

This thing got as big as a grapefruit before it broke and the smell was almost as bad as death. I finally had to go into the hospital and have an operation on it. They removed about a third of my right cheek that took almost a year to finally fill in. I was in the hospital for six days and, of course, I couldn't sit down to play the drums so I had to get another drummer to play the dance company show. I did the vocals laying down on a mattress back stage!

That is when the keyboard player, the bass player and the guitar player quit the band, so I basically had to start all over again. I formed a second version of the Austin Grandmothers with some of the best musicians I was able to find around town. I was playing with the Chris Holzhaus Blues Band[15] in 1988 and rehearsing the Grandmothers when Ener Bladezipper joined the band.[16]

The line-up for this Austin Grandmothers band was me on drums, Ener on bass, Gerry "Eli" Smith on sax, Mike Harris on guitar and keyboards and Jeff Hogan on percussion. Mike Harris was an excellent guitar player. He had a Master's degree in Music from North Texas State and he understood Frank's music real well. We were rehearsing three times a week at Jeff Hogan's rehearsal studio. We did that for at least six to eight months before we actually played our first gig.[17] I wanted the band to sound so tight with that music that nobody in Austin would believe us and that is exactly what happened.

We went out to El Paso to a studio in a little town called Tornillo (Screw), Texas that was built in the middle of a 2000-acre Pecan orchard. What a beautiful place to put a studio. There is nothing to do there but make music because El Paso was 50 miles away if you wanted to do something. We had plenty of refreshments there and we all had beds so we were set for action.

We recorded a new song that I had just written the words to called 'Waiting' and we also did 'The Great White Buffalo', 'Lonesome Cowboy Burt', 'Lady Queen Bee', and 'Freakout in Screw'. After we came back from the studio, we kept rehearsing and we also got the songs played on KUT radio. Now we had a demo tape, we could start getting a few jobs but the band wasn't complete yet. We still needed a keyboard player - even though Mike played keyboards, he couldn't play keys and guitar at the same time. That was the next problem to be resolved.

I was still playing gigs with other bands and one night, in late '88 or early '89, I was playing with the Rhythm Rats near my home in Oak Hill at a place called Trudy's. This guy came in with a little keyboard and asked me if he could sit in with us.

We were just doing some blues stuff, nothing fancy, and I didn't actually take that much notice of what he was doing because he was just playing along with the songs. We took a break and I walked outside to go smoke a Joint when I heard 'King Kong' being played. At first I thought it was a record or something, so I went back in and there was this guy playing away on 'King Kong' and doing it perfectly! So, I went up to him and said, "Can you play 'Peaches En Regalia'?" and he whipped that out also, so I immediately asked him if he wanted to join my band - the Grandmothers - and he said, "That's what I'm here for. I came down to audition for you!" His name was Roland St. Germain. Roland was a good musician, a great keyboard player and he also played guitar.

We almost had the complete line-up at that point. We were playing quite a few gigs after we got Roland broke in with the material, which didn't take too long since he knew all of it anyway. I have to mention that he was also a vocalist, as was Mike. They were great singing backup with me and also singing on their own. This was about 1989 and the band was really starting to smoke at that point.

Jeff Hogan was not very happy playing Zappa music, since he was really a Reggae kind of a guy, so he quit the band. We really didn't miss him that much because what we needed was another instrument that blended with what we were doing. Along comes Linda Harris, Mike's wife, who was also a graduate of North Texas State University in music and her instrument was violin. That was the cherry on top of the cake. She was also a great vocalist.[18]

AGMs on Tour

We played South by Southwest Festival in Austin that year again, and met a guy named John - I can't remember his last name! John wanted to be our manager so he booked us a small tour in Michigan, since that was where he was from. We played six gigs in different venues around the State and it went very well. The people really enjoyed the Zappa music that the band was playing.

After we got back, we were playing at least three or four times a month at the Dam Café. We were also playing at the Elephant Room, which was primarily a jazz club but our music fit in very well there. We did the KUT radio show again and I got a great recording out of it as usual.

Austin Pops

The Austin Pops was a one-off project which happened on Father's Day 1989.[19] This guy called Bill Abberback - a trumpet player - contacted myself and Rene,[20] who he'd known for some years. He told us, "It's a bunch of fathers getting together to record a session for Radio KUT." There were eventually four of us from the Grandmothers in the band. I'd never played a lot of that stuff before, like Miles Davis and John McLaughlin numbers!

On into the 90s

That year the Grandmothers played New Year's Eve at the Dam Café.[21] Mike [Harris] was with us until the 1990 tour, until he found his old lady and the sax player playing around on the road, on the same bus, so I can understand why he left the band. That was quite a little scene! Jimmy thought he was too old for all that, to be caught in the middle of all that crap. I couldn't believe that they did that, right in front of the band, and her kids! Mike and I have always kept in contact. He's a nice guy, a great player and an excellent singer.

So, I kept a Grandmothers band going right the way up until I moved to Italy in 1992.

We recorded some stuff in El Paso in 1988, which was pretty good. In fact, some of that stuff is due to be released soon.[22]

Photo: Jimmy, Gerry, Linda, Roland, Ener

Notes to Chapter 14

[1] JCB is remarkably exact about this date!

[2] JCB is referring to the "credit crunch" of the late 1980s when it became difficult to borrow money at low interest

[3] JCB makes no other reference to a previous lawsuit in his notes

[4] The plaintiffs sued for 16 million dollars in royalties [Ref: JCB interview with Ron Young, *Boogie Magazine*, St. Antonio Texas, Oct 1987]

[5] J. Franklin and the Golden Echoes began playing every Wed. in Sept. of 1984 at the Soap Creek; they were playing every other Wed. in Aug. of that year. They played every Wed. in Oct. too and then reverted to alternate Weds. until at least May 1985.

[6] The Rhythm Rats were also playing at the Soap Creek saloon by Aug. of 1984

[7] JCB also says two months in another note on this period but two weeks seems more probable.

[8] No more than three years with JCB, probably less

[9] Released 1988 on LP [Ref: unitedmutations.com]

[10] In 1992, aged 48; Butcher was aged about 42 when JCB worked with him

[11] Riverside Sound studios in Austin [Ref: unitedmutations.com]

[12] Recorded and released in 1987

[13] This statement is all that JCB makes in his manuscript or notes. He plays drums on three songs: 'Industrial Strength Tranquilizer', 'When Drunks Go Bad' and 'Get A Haircut, Dad'. [Ref: unitedmutations.com]

[14] Around Oct. of 1987, JCB was playing with a group called Jimmy Carl Black & the Bluz who were about to metamorphose into the (Austin) Grandmothers with the same members plus Jeff Hogan. [Ref: JCB interview with Ron Young, *Boogie Magazine*, St. Antonio Texas, Oct 1987]

[15] JCB released *I Just Got In From Texas* on Inkanish which is a live-recording of the band's last appearance, in San Antonio, Texas, Aug. 17 1988; "the band was together for about six months and played quite a lot of gigs around Texas" [JCB: Sleeve notes to June 2001 release by Inkanish Records]. Chris Holzhaus died some four months before JCB on July 11, 2008 of cancer.

[16] "I did a radio show in Austin with a guy who ... was from Amsterdam, name of Jan Donkers. He did an interview with me for Dutch radio, in about 1987... I met René (Ener) through him. [Jimmy Carl Black Interview: Moers Festival 19.5.91 By Axel Wünsch and Aad Hoogesteger printed in T'Mershi Duween, #24-25, March-June 1992]

[17] Less if the Austin Grandmothers played at SWSX in Mar of 1988 as JCB seems to suggest later

[18] Jeff Hogan and Linda Harris played together at least once [Ref: The Grandmothers at the Dam Cafe – 1989 at youtube.com/ (15/01/2012)]

[19] June 18 that year

[20] Ener Bladezipper

[21] It seems the Dam Café burnt down in the end

[22] 'Waiting' on *Where's the %#$& beer* and 'Lady Queen Bee' on *Can I Borrow* ... released in 2002, 2008 respectively, dating the writing of this part of JCB's Memoirs to before 2002.

On the Lawsuit

The whole lawsuit thing had started in 1985 but it didn't go to arbitration until 1990. Originally, the lawsuit was a Class Action Suit for $150,000. As the years went by, people started to drop out. I can't remember exactly how many of us there were at the beginning but at the end there was myself, Don, Bunk, Art Tripp, Ray Collins and Jim Fielder.

The lawyer that we got turned out to be not such a good deal. He was the only one we could find that would do it on a percentage, as we didn't have any money to pay anyone up front. At the start we felt like he could win the case, but it turned out that the guy was a Cokehead and made some fundamental errors during the process. Of course, I didn't know that at the time. It was three years before I even met him for the first time. I wasn't living in California. Anyway, he missed a filing date at the court and, officially, it shouldn't have gone to arbitration but somehow they managed to get it to go through.

That's actually the last time that I saw Frank. That's when I knew something was wrong with him because he didn't look good and he didn't sound good. He could barely talk. In fact, he had to change seats to get closer to the recorder because she[1] couldn't hear him. He was in there for four hours and we were sitting right across the table from him and he never looked at any of us one time. He wouldn't look anybody in the eye at all but Gail sure did - and with a shit-eating smile on her face!

The Arbitration

The arbitration lasted for three days but Frank was only there for one. If I remember right, Gail was there for all three days. It really was a crazy time for me, as I didn't feel bad toward Frank at all. It was strictly business, as far as I was concerned.

The first day, Jim Fielder testified. He was living in Austin at the time of the arbitration and we flew out to California together. I used to hang out with him in Austin after he moved there because he didn't know anybody there except me. He is a very cool guy. He only lived in Austin for a short period of time and was gone most of that time on the road with Neil Sedaka doing county fairs and such. I never did testify but Don and Bunk did and maybe Ray Collins.[2]

Frank's Bitch

I don't recall exactly all that was said but that doll incident[3] was one thing that was brought up against us among other things. I think that this is the time to explain that doll. When the original Grandmothers were rehearsing for our first tour of Europe, in 1981, we were also working on a good show that would give the fans a real taste of what the MOI's shows were like live. We did the hand signals and also did a simulated birth of FZ. Don made the stuffed head and painted Frank's face on it. When Frank got wind of our little skit, he flipped out and got word to us that we had to stop doing that. The skit we were doing was pretty tame compared to some of the stuff the MOI used to do on stage. Of course, we never stopped doing it for the rest of the tour.

Frank's Bill

The way Frank worked the budget out, he charged the old Mothers $400,000 to fix and re-master *We're Only In It For The Money* and *Ruben & The Jets.* That's what he said the bill was to fix[4] those two CDs in his new studio in his house!! He said that the tapes were damaged, that they had been stored badly, and that the bass and drum tracks for *We're Only In It For The Money* and *Ruben And The Jets* were not usable and had to be re-recorded.

So he turned around and said, "There is no money, in fact, you owe me money!" Now where have I heard that song before? He was always saying that to us, we always owed somebody money even though those CDs were selling pretty good. Frank charged the Mothers[5] five hundred thousand dollars for repackaging all that stuff![6]

Then Frank said that we wouldn't get any royalties prior to 1983 or something to that effect. That had to do with the statutes of limitations.

Mothers' Bitch

I know what it cost to record those albums. The original cost was $29,000 each, according to the contract from Verve. I was pissed off that he never contacted any of us and said that the bass and drum tracks were fucked up. I would have gone out to the studio to fix them because at that time we were getting along great. Instead of doing that, he hired those young guys to do it. I don't think he even put their names down on the cover for doing it.[7] We found out at the arbitration, those boys got $10,000 each for recordings that the fans hated! Nice move, Frank! We got paid, for two sessions, a grand total of $300 each - that was the union scale at the time!

My question now is - If he had to do that then, because the tapes were supposedly fucked up, how did Rykodisc re-release the original[8] in 1995? Where did those tapes come from? Somebody was telling a lie!

What I think Frank should have done if he didn't like the way the record sounded was to record it completely again with his new band of guys instead of messing around with two pieces of history.[9] I really think it was a waste of money because those CDs were not what the fans wanted in the first place. They wanted the real recordings, [like] the one they got from Rykodisc, even if it was enhanced from an old album. I still wish they would have released the real[10] recording of *Ruben & The Jets*.

The Settlement

So the settlement was made there and then, in November of 1990. That was the last contact that I had with Frank. I did try to contact him just before I left for Italy - by this time everybody knew that Frank was sick. I talked to Motorhead and asked if he would call Frank and find out if it was OK for me to call him. I wanted to tell Frank that the lawsuit thing was strictly business and that it wasn't personal, which it wasn't as far as I was concerned. When I called Motorhead back the next day, he told me that Gail had said that that it would be better if I didn't call. I still don't know whether that message got as far as Frank - I'll never know now!

That lawsuit cost Frank quite a bit of money but in the long run the ZFT did quite well out of the deal. Of course, Frank had died before all that business came into play. We had to pay our lawyers - they got $60,000. The new guy was Neil Goldstein - he was an expert negotiator at arbitration. He used to work for Frank's lawyers' law firm so he knew those guys very well. We didn't think that the first guy should have got paid anything, but we couldn't sue him because he didn't have malpractice insurance, which is what we wanted to sue him for! At one point during the arbitration, Goldstein had to tell him to shut up. He was really getting nasty with Frank's lawyers, but he didn't know what he was talking about. He was a dipshit! He just fucked it up all the way down the line and, for all we know, he may have been paid off to do that![11]

As it's turned out,[12] if we hadn't signed that piece of paper, with RykoDisc buying all the stuff, part of that money could have been ours, or at least we could have gotten royalties from them. They obviously thought that they could sell enough of Frank's catalogue for it to be worth the $44 million that they paid for the rights. I guess they figure that through the years he will always steadily sell, as he has done in the past.

Another thing that's kind of hard for me to figure is - I don't know why I don't get any publishing,[13] because I do get writing credit on one track on *Ahead Of Their Time*, for the first time! I'm surprised Frank did that, because he didn't give me writing credits for "Hi Boys and Girls, I'm Jimmy Carl Black and I'm The Indian Of The Group!" or "If Only We'd Been Living In California". Remember, I asked him about that right after the band broke up, and he told me real quick that there was the door and that he wanted me out of the house... I thought it was rather strange. "Why don't you want to talk about it, Frank?" What would have been the big deal, to give a little writing credit where it was due? He did it with Ray Collins on 'Deseri' and those things. And I don't know what the deal is with Roy, because he never signed anything, neither did Motorhead or Buzz Gardner, although Buzz did get paid $11,000, through the union, for *Beat The Boots,* for session. All of us were supposed to get that but I haven't seen any of mine. I've tried to get it, but that stupid Musicians' Union is a joke![14]

Notes to Chapter 15

[1] "she" is presumably the magistrate, and not Gail Zappa

[2] Art Tripp did not attend the case. [Ref: Art Tripp, in correspondence]

[3] Grandmothers at The Roxy, 1981

[4] create? - the original "albums" had been issued on vinyl

[5] The original MOI, as equal partners

[6] One of the original reasons for filing the lawsuit was the planned issue of a boxed set of the original Mothers releases. See: [Chapter 14: Starting the Lawsuit]

[7] They were: Chad Wackerman (drums), Arthur Barrow (bass) and Jay Anderson (string bass)

[8] The original *We're Only In It For The Money*

[9] [JCB's response to a question posed in a email June 2007:] "It was bullshit to do something like that. If he had wanted to re-record both of those LPs, he should [have] used all new musicians but it would never have sounded like the old Mothers because they aren't the old Mothers. That, to me, was the only band Frank ever had because we went through all the shit to make him happen. All the other musicians that played with Frank after the Mothers were hired guns. All great musicians but not The Mothers of Invention."

[10] JCB of course means 'original' here. Finally released in 2010, the original vinyl mix was (surprisingly?) released by the Zappa Family Trust as part of the CD *Greasy Love Songs*

[11] JCB was not the only plaintiff who "strongly suspected that the first attorney was paid off to sell us out." [Ref: Art Tripp, in correspondence]

[12] If we would've known... but we just went by the advice of our lawyers... if we'd not signed it, Gail Zappa couldn't sue us for anything, there's no way. [JCB]

[13] Royalties

[14] "As I recall, the original suit was for $1.2 million. We ended up not getting any royalties prior to 1981 (when all those albums sold well), and I believe we plaintiffs ended up with $250,000 to split up amongst us according to how many albums we'd each been on."

I got a phone call from Eugene Chadbourne in December 1990. It was totally out of the blue, because I had no clue who he was - he'd got my number from Evan Johns. He told me about this festival that he was doing in Germany and would I be interested in going. Well, I hadn't been there since 1982 - I was ready to go! He told me that it would be a 12-piece band so I said, "Well, are we going to rehearse?" and he said, "There is no rehearsal, it will be purely improvised music!" When he said purely improvised music he really meant it. The Mothers did a form of improvised music but it was always controlled to a certain extent. He asked me about Don Preston, so I gave him Don's telephone number.

Eugene sent me a couple of his records - *Country Music In The World Of Islam* and *Vermin Of The Blues* - so I had at least an idea of what he did and I thought, "Boy, this guy's out there!" I was happy that I had played with Beefheart. Eugene's music is even farther out than that was, if that is possible!

Eugene told me that we were going to be playing at the festival[1] with the Daffy Duck Dozen, which is what he called this band.[2] I was getting paid $1200 plus all our expenses for the four days so I bought Husta a plane ticket to come with me, which took a big chunk of the money. It was the first time she'd been to Europe and she fell in love with it. That's how we came to move over to Europe in 1992. She applied for a teaching job with the U.S. Government (The DOD school system) and she got the job so we moved over to Italy.[3]

Evan Johns was supposed to come with us to the Moers New Music Jazz Festival, but he rang the day before we left and said, "Man, I can't make it because I'm checking into the hospital!" He was a heavy drinker and he'd been on a binge and probably had a touch of alcohol poisoning in his system.

FESTIVAL MOERS PFINGSTEN 17.-20. MAI 91

The driver couldn't find the town of Moers so it took us about two hours to travel 120 km.[4] We finally arrived at the hotel and I took a little nap until about 5 o'clock in the afternoon when all the guys met downstairs. Don was there, and I was happy to see him since I hadn't seen him in about nine years.

I had never met any of the other guys and Don was the only person I knew there. That was the first time that I met Eugene. We sat around and talked and just generally got to know each other. I was a little concerned about what we were going to be doing and he told me that I could just play anything - it didn't matter!

There were several venues set up around the Music School at Moers, the festival site. There were three sets of drums, two in one big room and one in another building. We split up into two smaller groups and then started drifting between the stages and whoever we felt like playing with that day, from our group of eleven guys. We played lots of improvisations with bits of country music and bits of weirdness.

All of this was from 11 o'clock in the morning until 1 o'clock in the afternoon and went on for three days in a row. Then on the Sunday afternoon, we all played together as our final performance for the Symposium and then we played again all together over in the big tent at the Festival in the evening. The Symposium was held in the Music School but it was part of the Festival - the whole thing was a strange situation. On Monday, I think all of us but two guys[5] played a gig in a small pub and did all kinds of music that night. That was the end of the festival for us - this was all in May 1991.

Axel, the German guy, videotaped the whole thing and then he and Aad, the Dutch guy, interviewed Don and myself for *The Black Page*, which is a Dutch MOI fanzine.[6]

So after the whole thing, we went back to Amsterdam and Husta and I stayed for three extra days with Ener's folks. We just went around sightseeing, going to the museums and markets - Husta really enjoyed that.

Henry's New Album
Evan Johns called me and said, "I'm doing a CD with your old mate - Henry Vestine!" He knew we'd played together in the original Mothers. Henry was living in Eugene, Oregon at the time and he was only in Austin for about four or five days so I went down. It was the first time I'd seen him in 20 years. He did the album in two days and though I didn't play on all of it, I did play on five or six cuts. Mike Buck played on the other songs. Mike was the original drummer with The Fabulous Thunderbirds and he's a great drummer - a nice guy too! Evan Johns produced - he's a total madman!

Henry wasn't looking that good because his teeth were falling out and he was a total full-blown alcoholic junkie, but he could still play! I did one evening session that lasted about six hours and Henry drank a full bottle of Jack Daniels besides being fully junked out. He was quite a guy!

Some of the songs that we recorded were pretty good, mainly because Henry was still a good player. That CD isn't bad - I've signed a few of those things. It sold well in France because that is where New Rose Records were located![7]

The next night, I played a live gig with them at the Continental Club. It was so fucking loud I couldn't believe it. Henry and Evan got so drunk they didn't realize how fucking loud they were playing.

Photo: shows Henry crouching

207

Evan also played guitar. He's made a lot of records but he hasn't made it because he is such a lush. His band was called Evan Johns and The H Bombs and they played quite a lot around Austin, although he is from the Washington D.C. area.

KNITTING FACTORY In early 1992, I got another call from Eugene asking me to come to New York City to a famous club called the Knitting Factory and do a similar improvisation program with some of the same people - Tony Trischka again, on banjo, Lesley Ross was there too - and some different people. We had Lenny Kaye, who used to play with Patti Smith - he's a very good player! We had three drummers this time: myself, Murray Reams and a Japanese drummer. I can't pronounce his name but we called him the Kamikaze drummer because that is the way he played. He was the wildest drummer I ever saw play. He was a total Wildman! This one was over two nights and Eugene sent me my air ticket.

Ener decided that he was going to come along with me so he bought himself a ticket and jumped on. He ended up playing with us! That was a very interesting night of music and madness.

At the Continental
The next time that I saw Eugene was when he came through Austin on a little tour in June 1992, with his daughter, Molly.[8]

They had a gig at the Continental Club that night and I went and saw them play. Of course, Molly stole the show. She can still steal the show and does when she sits in with The Jack and Jim Show.[9]

I told him that Husta and I were getting ready to move to Italy. Husta was going on ahead because school was about to start and then I would follow a few months later. I had a few things to tie up like getting the house ready to sell and all that shit. The most important thing was to finish the new Grandmothers CD.[10]

So that's when Eugene said, "Listen, when you get over to Europe, let's do a duo, just drums, guitar and banjo." So I said, "Fine, but what about a bass player?" and he just said, "We don't need a bass player because they only get in my way. Besides that, I have to teach them everything!"

Billy James
In the fall of 1992, Billy James was introduced to me through Bunk and Don because they had done some musical things with him. He was living in California and had been doing some music copying for Frank. He asked me to record a talking tape that he could distribute in England through a fanzine there in Sheffield.[11] I didn't meet him until 1995, when I was in North Carolina with Eugene on The Jack and Jim Show's first USA tour.

Moving to Europe

So, I arrived in Italy in November 1992. I was only there a couple of weeks before I started making myself known. I called this guy Tono Roe in Milan - he booked a lot of American Blues players. He called back a few days later and told me he had a gig for me on New Year's Eve with a guy called Bill Thomas. I had seen Bill several times in Austin - he's a black guy, a good player. The gig was in Ortisei, a ski resort near Bolzano, 160 kilometers[12] from Venice.

Muffin Records

Then I made contact with the English Zappa Fanzine - *T'Mershi Duween* - and from that I got a call from Roddie of the Muffin Men. Roddie put me on to a guy called Reinhard Preuss who had just put a little label together called Muffin Records. I called him immediately and within a few days we'd made a deal for the *Dreams On Long Play* album.[13]

Notes to Chapter 16

[1] "Moers Festival Improvisation Project"

[2] With Brian Ritchie from the Violent Femmes on bass, Ashwin Batish on electric sitar, Chris Turner (an English guy who was living in the States) on harmonica and trumpet, Leslie Ross on electric bassoon, Jonathan Segel on violin and mandolin, Tony Trischka from Camper Van Beethoven on banjo, Don Preston from The Mothers of Invention on keyboards, Bob Wiseman from the Canadian band Blue Rodeo on keyboards, Murray Reams was the other drummer. Evan Johns (guitar) was the guy who didn't show.

[3] To Vicenza, in north central Italy ; DOD = US Department of Defense

[4] About 75 miles. JCB switches to kilometers now he's a "European"! 5 miles ≈ 8 km

[5] "On the fourth day, we played at a club which was owned by the director of the festival, but Don didn't play on that, he had to leave early." [JCB, elsewhere]

[6] [Ref: JCB Interview: Moers Festival 19.5.91 By Axel Wünsch and Aad Hoogesteger, and printed in T'Mershi Duween, #24-25, March-June 1992 (available on the Internet)] This Interview discusses the Austin Grandmothers and fills in a bit of what JCB has been getting up to musically at this time, for example "1987. I've had this band for four years, rehearsing not playing. We've had over three thousand hours of rehearsals."

[7] Recorded and mixed at Studio 1621, Austin TX, June 1991, the LP/CD was released on New Rose Records and entitled *Guitar Gangster*, not *Too drunk To Fuck* as JCB recalls in his notes. Dan McCann, bass guitar; Mark Kopi, guitar; Marcia Ball, piano, and Evan Johns, guitar, also played on the album.

[8] "...8 or 9 years old at the time" [JCB]

[9] The partnership between Eugene Chadbourne and JCB did not become The Jack and Jim Show until 1993

[10] *Dreams on Long Play*

[11] *With My Favorite "Mothers" and Other Bizarre Things*, Ant-Bee, 1992, on audio cassette

[12] 100 miles

[13] Released by Muffin Records in 1993

Photo by Reinhard Preuss

The Phone Call

I got a call from Eugene in January 1993 saying, "I've got a tour set up for April. It's for two and a half weeks and we could make some good money!" He was right - that first year we did four tours! Husta and I decided that we would move to Germany. I had lots of work coming up.

BLACK OLIVE

Jimmy Carl Black: Vocals, Drums, El.Percuss.
Sandro Oliva: Vocals, Guitar, Electronics

The Most Entertaining
Show
You Could
EVER
Book

For Italy: Supershow tel./fax 06/5880905

In March, I went to play at a little Zappa Day in Italy with a band called Ya Hozna[1] - that's where I first met Sandro Oliva.

The Coffee Shop Tour: April '93[2]

I was in contact with Reinhard almost every day. I went to Stuttgart for two days to meet him before I did the first tour with Eugene. So we hung out together and then he actually drove me to Holland to meet Eugene - he stayed with us for a day.

Eugene just flies to Europe with his guitar cases stuffed with merchandise. He has a guitar, a banjo and a trolley-bag. He brings a couple of T-shirts and wears the same pair of pants all tour that can stand up on their own at the end! So we did the whole tour by train. We would use whatever amps and drums that were at the venue - it didn't matter - that was all part of the deal. We travelled together - backpacking! We did all this shit together, like two hobos! We called it the Coffee Shop Tour: we played 9 gigs in Holland, one in Belgium, two in Germany and three in Switzerland.[3]

210

That's when I really got to know Eugene. Eugene told me that the Mothers made quite an impression on him during his high school days. I can understand why, as weird as he is now! He doesn't drink, but he has one shot of whisky at the end of every tour! He's released about 30 CDs, tons of tapes and albums. He's been playing around Europe for years.[4] He's got a lot of fans - it's surprising, you can always tell 'em - they'll be the weirdest people in the place!

I'll never forget that first gig in Rotterdam. I was actually nervous because I didn't know what the fuck we were going to do - we'd never rehearsed - and we still to this day have never rehearsed! We were playing stuff by Little Feat, Moby Grape, Spirit...there was a Dead Kennedys' song called 'Nazi Punks Fuck Off', some Shockabilly songs and Bluegrass stuff. We did Johnny Paycheck's 'Colorado Kool-Aid', one of my favorites, and 'Honky Tonk Angels' by Kitty Wells - some free jazz stuff like Thelonious Monk things and quite a few songs by Eugene. He got me up from behind the drums to sing 'Willie The Pimp' and I didn't even know the words to it, only the first verse. We did it with just banjo and voice. It went over very well - I was surprised! We went right through that show, we didn't have any problems - I listened very carefully to what he was doing and it was actually fairly easy to play with him.

We started doing a few of Beefheart's songs and quite a few Mothers' things too.

I was telling Eugene about my tour with Beefheart, he was very curious about it. He told me that the first time he brought *Trout Mask Replica* into the house his dad came into the room and said, "I don't understand you, why are you playing two records at the same time?"

Beefheart had written a poem called *The Jack and Jim* after he'd done a drawing of me, back in 1975. Eugene liked that story so much that he said, "Hey, maybe we should start calling our show The Jack and Jim Show!" So that's how we got our name.

From Rotterdam, we went to Arnhem, and then to Utrecht, Tilburg and Nijmegen. We played in nice little clubs or theaters, but in Nijmegen a Coffee Shop called the Sleeping Beauty! Then we played at the Democrazy in Gent.[5]

211

Who the fuck is Jim Black?

Next, we went to Enschede, which was a show at the Dutch Zappa Day. It was my first time at one of those things. It was quite interesting with all those little booths set up.[6] There was a guy there, and I had signed loads of his albums when this other guy came up to him and said, "Hey Man! Let me borrow your pen." The guy said, "Oh no, I couldn't let you use this pen, it's been touched by Jimmy Carl Black!" and the other guy just says, "Well, who the fuck is Jim Black?" I didn't hear it, but Eugene was standing near them and he heard all this. I told that story to Sandro Oliva and he went and called his album after that[7] - he gave us credit for it on the cover!

From there, we went to Haarlem and then a little place just outside of Amsterdam. From Holland, we went to Solothurn, Switzerland. The guy who was promoting our two German shows came to that gig and took us to Villingen-Schwenningen.[8]

We played Villingen the first night and Schwenningen the second night. He took us back to Switzerland to play our last three shows in Zurich, Bern and Thun.

While we were doing the tour, Eugene told me that there was going to be another one in June, this time it would be England, Scotland, Ireland and Wales!

Roman Holiday

During that tour I got real sick, I caught a bad cold. As soon as I got back home, Reinhard called me saying that I had to go up to Stuttgart to do six days of promotional stuff.[9] That's when I found out that we would be playing part of the tour with the Muffin Men. He gave me a copy of their first CD; I thought it was excellent!

Directly after that, I went to Rome with Husta and we spent a week with Sandro Oliva. He had invited us down there - it was nice little holiday! While we were there, I went into his studio and recorded versions of 'Willie The Pimp' and 'Take Your Clothes Off When You Dance'.

Grandmothers 1st Tour: May '93

While I was in England, Husta had finally moved to Germany.[10] She came to the airport with Reinhard[11] to meet me. All the guys had arrived from the States and were there too - they all came to meet me! Roland and Ener flew from Austin and Don and Bunk came from California. They were all staying in a little hotel near Stuttgart and had already started rehearsals for the tour.

When I arrived at the studio, there was a brand new set of drums that I'd never played before. We rehearsed for a few hours. Well, it wasn't really a rehearsal. Ener, Roland and I knew what each other was about but Don and Bunk hadn't

© Muffin Records Productions; courtesy R.Preuss

played any of that stuff for about 10 years. Bunk had just been doing the occasional little jazz gig. So, the next day, we went back into the studio to get the material together because the day after that we had to leave for our first gig in Arezzo, Italy at the New Wave Festival. I didn't think it went very well - nobody really knew what they were doing - but we made it through and people seemed to like it.

The next day, we went to Rome and played at an open-air Jazz festival, held at a big tennis court. We stayed at Sandro's villa for four days - every day we went into his studio and rehearsed for about five hours. We left Rome and played in Bern, Switzerland. By then, the band started sounding much better. We'd rehearsed and we knew what was going on - sort of!

the muffin men
play the music of frank zappa

We went back to Germany and played our first gig with the Muffin Men in Solingen. We played nine double shows with them during that tour.[12]

We had some fun times. The Muffins would open with a 90-minute set, then there'd be a short break and we would play a 2-hour show. I used to join the Muffins at the end of their set to sing 'Willie The Pimp' and then most of the Muffins would join us at the end of our show and do 'It Can't Happen Here' and 'Who Could Imagine'.

At the end of the tour, both bands went into the studio to record their new CDs. The Muffins completed a 72-minute CD - *Say Cheese And Thank You* - in about 12 days. I got to sing on some of the tracks on that album. It was

213

really too early for the Grannies to go into the studio, we weren't ready to make an album. We never did use any of the stuff from those sessions. There were a few conflicts going on between Roland and Don as to who was musical director. When we had been in Austin, Roland had the job, but it had always been Don's job before that so naturally there were differences! Roland spent eight days recording his overdubs before he went back to the States. It ended up a waste of time, he did 120 takes on one vocal track and it still never happened! After he'd gone home, they brought in another guy to try the vocal. He did it in two takes! When Roland heard about it, he hit the roof - he resigned from the band shortly after that.

Jack and Jim in the UK: June '93
On my way to England, I went back to see Reinhard in Stuttgart for two days. The *Dreams On Long Play* CD was released in June. I took 50 copies with me to England, I didn't have any other merchandise because all my stuff was still in storage in Italy.

That English tour was good fun. The first gig was on the south coast somewhere then we did three nights at the Bass Clef in London. From there we went [up] to Sheffield, Leeds, then up to Glasgow, came back and played in York, Newport, and The Swinging Sporran in Manchester, where I met Roddie[13] for the first time. Then we played in Hebden Bridge, Reading and Brighton.[14] We played the "electric rake" at Hebden Bridge. Eugene's done the electric rake for years - he's had the electric birdcage, the electric windscreen wiper and the electric toilet plunger! They had a rake in the back of the little place where we were staying so he asked if we could borrow it for the night. He hooked the pick-up to it and it was recorded - it's actually on *Locked In A Dutch Coffee Shop*. Fred Tomsett was at that show, he couldn't believe it. *T'Mershi Duween*[15] gave us a great review.

We flew from London to Belfast and played a gig there. When we flew back to London, we went directly to the BBC to do a 30-minute, live radio show. We did about six or seven songs. I didn't have drums - that was the first time that I played the telephone book with the brushes!

We did a radio thing in Manchester and also one in Glasgow. They paid us cash for those things, which was unexpected extra money!

At the last show in Brixton, London, BBC Television came out to interview me. They had just done a thing on Frank (on the *Late Show*) and they were going to add some new sections to it. So they asked me a bunch of stuff. Part of the interview was on Beefheart, they were preparing a special on him at the same time. They paid me £200 for that!

214

 On September 1st, I left for two weeks in Scandinavia, with Eugene again. I took the train and met him in Odense - we played in the Rhythm Room which was right next to the train station. We went to Copenhagen, played at the Café Rust and then did a radio show for Danish Radio - they paid us $200 each for that little session.

We went to ...[16] in Sweden, then two nights Gothenburg, then Oslo, back to Sweden in Karlstad, Gavle and Stockholm, the end of that tour. I got an overnight sleeper train back down to Stuttgart.

The Electric Umbrella

When we played in Denmark, these three brothers were at the gig and - it's really strange - all three big Eugene Chadbourne fans. One of the brothers went and bought six CDs from Eugene and do you think that those guys would share those CDs? The other two went and bought the identical ones - all three had to have separate sets of them! So that night, one of the brother's friends was there and he wanted to hear the "electric umbrella" he'd heard about.

Eugene said, "Yeah, but we don't have an umbrella." So the guy said, "Oh well, you can have my umbrella!"

Eugene said, "Well, there's nothing wrong with this umbrella." But the guy said, "Oh, please, just play it!"

So, we'd told him that it'd have to be skinned but he didn't understand what we were talking about. He must have thought that we were going to play this umbrella and then give it back to him! Well, we can't play the umbrella unless it's skinned so we skinned it on the stage. We hooked the pick up on it and then started ripping the cloth off it - the guy's eyes got fuckin' big! We skinned it with a fountain pen - the only sharp object that we could get to tear it - and it was wild sounding. As that thing was being skinned it was like - screaming! So we had the electric umbrella again. That one made it until we got to Karlstad.[17] We were playing it and holding it out of a window on the second floor of this club and pieces were falling off down onto the street - that was the end of that umbrella.

After the show we were hungry, so we asked was there any place we could get something to eat. The three brothers looked at each other and said, "Well, there's one place but we're not too sure that you'd want to go there!" They said that they should warn us about this place - it has quite a reputation - it's called the Ritter Bar. Apparently, one time not too long ago, there had been a big fight there between the bouncer and some guy. The guy had gone home and got his shotgun and came back and shot the bouncer in the stomach. The only thing was, the bouncer was wearing one of those moneybag things, it was full of those Danish Kroner coins and that's what saved his life. So we wrote a song called 'The Ritter Bar', and we tell the story of how those coins got the hole in the middle! Anyway, it was the worst food I've ever had!

Second Annual Coffee Shop Tour: Oct. '93

We were still living in the hotel,[18] but Husta had found us a place by then, she was just waiting for me to get back and show me the place. We went the next day and I said, "Shit, Man, let's take it!" So we signed the lease on it and moved in on October 1st.

We started moving the stuff over on September 30th, because on October 1st I left for yet another tour with Eugene. We met in Brussels - we didn't play in Brussels - it just so happened that I ran into him at the train station! We played in a town outside, in the French part of Belgium.

 After we left Brussels we went to Utrecht, to start the Second Annual Coffee Shop Tour.[19] ... first thing ... off the train, ... have to stop at ... "Coffee Shop" ... on the way ... a blend of incredible "Weed" ... Northern Lights, Orange Bud, Red Hair, The Haze brothers - Purple and Silver, Sheeba, and ... assorted mixtures of "Hash" ..., a big "doobie!", ... sit there and smoke ...until I've had coffee and stuff....

Eugene went into Amsterdam to send some money home. It's only 30 minutes from Utrecht so I waited at the hotel for him. When he came back, he had this white sweater on that he had found on the street and an umbrella with him - it was broken, it had been skinned. He'd decided that he was going to make an electric umbrella so now he put this contact mike on it. Man! It was beautiful - really ugly sounding! That umbrella made it almost all the way. We were making jokes like, "The umbrella's getting a little too popular, it's even starting to ask for its own room, wants special meals, thinks it's a star!" It finally fell apart completely in Zurich.

We did some interesting gigs. Three of them were with a band called Doo Rag, another duo, guitar and drums - except this drummer plays cardboard boxes and buckets! They were interesting fellas and they played interesting music - a very strange act! They're from Tucson, Arizona, Thermos is the drummer's name - they played with us in Venlo.

We played another gig in the Flemish part.[20] John, the promoter from England, came to that show. He had been in Holland working with some other band. He drove us to London and we played three nights there, one at the Bass Clef, the next night at The Swan[21] and on the third night back at the Bass Clef. He took us to Portsmouth where we took a ship over to Caen[22] in France and played a show there.

Eugene wrote 'I Got More Pussy Than Zappa' when we were in London.[23] I told him that I'd got more pussy than Zappa during the Mothers' time on the road, which is true. Eugene was always asking me questions about when we were on the road in the old days! "Making love on a Sunday - Was it Frank? No! Billy Mundi!" That's some of the lyric to it.

We went back to Brussels and played at the University Club there, then to Liege,[24] to Geneva in Switzerland, up to Wels, Salzburg and Vienna, in Austria. Then we travelled back to Switzerland. We stopped in Zurich to collect Husta. It was around her birthday so I took her on the road with me for five days! We went and played in Bern, then Grenoble in France, then two nights in Paris,[25] which she loved. Then back to Lucerne in Switzerland. We had two days off there after the gig.

We all went back to the new place at Bad Boll. Eugene stayed with us. Although there was no furniture in the house, we had a few little sleeping things scattered around. Don and Tina Preston were staying there, too! They'd arrived about three days after we'd moved in. A few days later,[26] me and Eugene left for Bochum to play at the old station, which is a great gig. From there, we went to Poitiers, France - a long fucking trip that day was![27] Then we played in St Etienne, then Montpellier. We left right after that show to catch a night train to Paris. We arrived there at about 6 or 7 in the morning and I caught a train to Stuttgart. It was a long tour. Eugene won't usually go for that long, but we made good money on that tour.

About four days after I arrived home, our furniture arrived from Italy so we set our beds up and all that stuff. About three days after that, the guys started arriving for the Grandmothers' Winter Tour.

 I'd been calling every few days to keep up with the news. We had Sandro in the band now! Originally, we were going to ask either Jumpy or Roddie from the Muffins to play with us, but Reinhard didn't want that, because that would've upset things a bit. It would've meant that only one of the bands could be out on the road at any one time, so we decided to ask Sandro to do it. Muffin Records were already negotiating to release his solo album anyway but the vocals had to be in English, they couldn't be in Italian. So Sandro had been in the studio changing all the lyrics into English. We asked him and he just said, "When do I be there?" His manager didn't want him to do it because it was going to stop the rest of the band[28] from working.

So Sandro had arrived. Don and I had to drive down to Munich to pick Bunk up from the airport.[29] Then Ener came. We had the whole band staying at my house. With all the fuckin' boxes, you could barely move, it was really not that organized. But Ener was there, and about five days later that place was organized. He's amazing! He set up the kitchen, putting up cabinets and building things. We'd walk back into the house of a night and Husta wouldn't even say hi to me before she was saying to Ener that she had something for him to do![30]

We started rehearsing at the studio; we did two full weeks. Sandro learned all his parts. Regina was having a little thing with Roland on the first tour. She had designed a band T-shirt that had our pictures on it and she'd had 100 of them printed before she heard that Roland had left the band - they'd cost her 18DM each! As soon as we went to rehearsal, all of a sudden, we'd be wondering where Sandro was. So we knocked on Regina's studio door, and there was Sandro; he'd took Roland's place! They had quite a hot love affair going for a long time, until she found out that he'd gotten this girl pregnant in Rome! She was married, so was Sandro and so was Roland! Her and her husband have a strange relationship!

Grannies' 2nd Tour: Nov. '93

The first gig was in Umea, Sweden. We flew up there, six of us, the band and Reinhard. We got there a day early and did a big press conference. After that, we flew down to Stockholm and played there, then onto Copenhagen, played there and flew back to Stuttgart. We had one day there, back at the house. The next day, the "Magic Bus" arrived. We left at about midnight and drove to Vienna.

We met Jörg from Beat The Street there - the tour promoter.[31] That was the beginning of the bus tour. We played Vienna, Munich and Fulda, and then we went to Weimar, Dresden and Cottbus. We had four days off then so we drove to Amsterdam, because Ener had gotten a gig for us there.[32] We stayed at his mom's house and did a radio show. From there we went all the way back down to Lindau, to the Club Vaudeville. We spend the night once again at my house in Bad Boll and the next day we left for Mainz. After that, we went back to Amsterdam.

The Grandmothers

Hi Boys and Girls....
Your Grandmothers are coming to your NEIGHBORHOOD club with lots of rockin' teen fun, weird sounds and unnatural behaviour. The current band this week is: Jimmy Carl Black, Don Preston, Bunk Gardner, Ener Bladezipper and Sandro Oliva. Here is the schedual of the last tour in 1993.

Date	Venue	City
23/11/93	Rockhaus	Wien
24/11/93	Panzerhalle	Munchen
25/11/93		Fulda
26/11/93	Weimarhalle	Weimar
27/11/93	Scheune	Dresden
28/11/93	Glad House	Cottbus
3/12/93	Club Vauderville	Lindau
5/12/93	Kuz	Mainz
6/12/93	Parker's	Amsterdam
7/12/93	Knaack Club	Berlin
8/12/93	Sumpfblume	Hamlin
9/12/93		Bamberg
10/12/93	Live Station	Dortmund
11/12/93	Raider's cafe	Lübeck
12/12/93	Markthalle	Hamburg
14/12/93	Borse	Wuppertal
15/12/93	Villa	Kirchheim/T
16/12/93	Kulturgelande	Salzburg
17/12/93	Theater & Music	Zug
19/12/93	Democrazy Club	Gent
20/12/93	K F Z	Marburg
21/12/93	Klimperkasten	Aschaffenburg
22/12/93	Festival Hall	London

Support your Grandmothers. Tell your friends - Tell your grandmother - Tell total strangers.

We sincerly hope to see you at one of these concerts.

Tour List above: courtesy Reinhard Preuss

'Bye Frank

We got to Amsterdam at about 10 in the morning. Ener went into the little shop next to the club and bought a paper and there it was, front page: "Zappa Dies!"

Phew! Weird day, Man! Strange, strange day! We did at least 15 interviews, the television from France came, everybody! Well, we did that show and then we left for Berlin, [and the] Knaack.[33] After we played in Hameln, we had a day off but we'd been invited to Köln to do interviews for the television, for the special program they were making.

We sent a letter of condolence, by fax. "She"[34] sent a very nasty fax back saying, "I haven't forgotten about the lawsuit and don't you ever try to contact me or any member of the Zappa Family again!" That upset us very much, we meant it - all three of us cried the day Frank died.

From there we went to Dortmund,[35] Lubeck, the Market Hall in Hamburg, Bamberg, Wuppertal, Kirchheim for a live recording, Salzburg, Zug[36] in Switzerland, Gent Democrazy, Marburg KFZ and Ashafensburg - that was the end of the tour. It was two days before Christmas. That was a long tour as well, Man, from November 18th to 23rd December!

Zappa Tribute Concert: 1994

The Grandmothers were asked to play as part of a special Zappa Tribute Concert which was being arranged as part of the Jazz Open Festival in Stuttgart. We were told that we'd be playing with some other special guests who had played with Frank over the years. Ike Willis and the Muffin Men were also lined up to play and other ex-band members [of the Mothers] were asked to participate.

The original idea was for each special guest to perform several numbers each, donating their services for free. Lufthansa, Marriot Hotels and various other sponsors would provide all travel, food and accommodation. With these factors catered for, the actual amount of cash budget was minimal.

After a few weeks, we started getting news of who had been approached to perform, who had agreed and - a bit later - the conditions that various individuals had begun to negotiate. It soon became clear that a bunch of the L.A. based guys had started discussing their plans for serious rehearsals in both the States and Germany. That's fine - nothing like dedication to the cause - only problem was they wanted paying for all this stuff, at top session rates! The budget limit was reached - and surpassed - within days of their plan starting.

We also learnt that they had demanded (and got) an advance. At least one of the guys, who agreed to perform and was sent his advance, didn't show up for rehearsal let alone the shows!

We were then told that because of the budget overrun, the Grandmothers wouldn't be playing as a band but me, Don and Bunk would be performing, probably with the Muffins. All the press releases and the posters were printed up - listing many of the featured artists, including Don, Bunk and me.

About six weeks before the show, we were told that, unfortunately, there was now no budget left. We and the Muffins would not be able to attend. All the flights, hotels and money had been used up! We were very pissed off at the way it had all been handled. The finger could be pointed in many directions, but let's not go into it.[37]

Two weeks before the gig, we got news that a bunch of the guys who had been in the 1988 band[38] were putting an evening's worth of material together and calling themselves the Band From Utopia. We were then asked to attend again! The promoters had realized that they now had one big band that were going to play a long set. Fine, but not what you could call a varied evening of events! The Muffins were asked to put together a 45-minute opening set. I refused to attend.

Before the show, I decided to go down to the rehearsal just to say hello to all the guys. I knew a lot of them - they weren't totally to blame for what had happened. I only lived 45 minutes from Stuttgart, it would be nice to see them all again.

The show was on 1st July, in the Liederhalle - a classical concert venue. I walked into the hall while they were all on the stage doing a sound-check. I said hello to Ike and a bunch of the guys. When I saw Tom Fowler, the first thing he said to me was, "What are you doing here?" and I said, "I live here, what the fuck are you doing here!?" God, I don't like him. I don't like saying that I hate anybody but, if I was going to hate anybody, he'd be the number one candidate for the job!

Trouble on Tour

[The Grandmothers] had four dates in Holland. I knew something was starting to happen, that thing was coming back on my arse.[39] We played in Utrecht and Tilburg.[40] It was OK, but we got to Amsterdam and something was happening, so I decided to go to the doctor when we played in Rotterdam. He said, "It's not ripe enough, I can't do anything but I can give you some antibiotics." So I stopped drinking and tried to take care of myself, it was hurting a bit.

We travelled down to Rennes. By the time we got there, I was in pretty bad shape, it was starting to get pretty infected and swell up. The promoter from Paris was at that gig. He got on the phone and arranged for his doctor to meet us when we arrived there the next day.

So, I got to the hotel and in walked this beautiful woman, a real fox. She turned me over, took a look at me and said, "I want you to take a deep breath and then let it out!" Just when I started letting it out, she came flying at me with this knife and started squeezing.

 I almost came unglued, Man! Jörg was in the next room and he swears that the whole hotel must have heard me - I was cussing up a storm! She didn't look quite so attractive after that! I was OK after that, it was draining and it wasn't hurting anymore.[41]

Trouble Backstage

We got to the gig, everything was nice backstage - there was good food and everything. It was a good gig. It was sold out, 1500 people, and they charged a lot to get in. They paid us $10,000 for the gig. I don't know exactly what happened. Half the money was paid to Beat The Street and we were having problems getting our money from those guys. Natalie was there and almost got killed by the promoter. She and Jörg were arguing about the money, she was trying to keep half of it. Jörg had booked most of the tour, although some of it was booked by Beat The Street.[42] Jörg said that the band would not go on unless we got all the money!

It was about 15 minutes before show time and the promoter was going ape-shit. Natalie was saying that she didn't have the authorization to give it to us, so now they were arguing.

Natalie was no small woman and she can get very pushy sometimes, but this time she had pushed the wrong guy. This guy was massive - his hands were twice the size of mine. So now it's about 30 minutes after the time we should have been on, and the crowd is getting restless. We heard all this crashing and banging and the next thing he was strangling her, he had her by the throat, she was begging for him to stop! Finally, she got her credit card out, signed [for] $4500 and gave it to Jörg. So we went on stage 45 minutes late - it was a great show!

Polygram

We had to leave right after the show because we had to be at the ferry at five or six in the morning, to get to Manchester. It took us three hours to get across the channel, it was really rough and everyone was sick. We got there at about 7.30 at night, and the show was supposed to start at 9.00, so we didn't get a sound-check - we just had to go straight on. From there we went to Leeds and then on to London to play three nights at Dingwalls.

In Paris, they had advertised us as the Grandmothers of Invention, there were posters everywhere, and they did the same in London. Polygram came to Dingwalls[43] to hear us - they were going to sign us. The booking agents, LPO came and they did sign us!

On the second day, Bunk, Ener and I went down to the music stores down in Soho. We had to buy a few things - sticks and stuff. We walked around, we had a Chinese meal, we walked by a wine store and Bunk can't resist going in so we walked into the store. I had my beret and my sunglasses on. The guy behind the counter snapped to attention and saluted me. We thought that he was crazy or something.

We were walking around looking at the wines and he followed us. Every time I turned around to him, he saluted me so I asked him what the deal was. He called me general or something and told me that I had liberated Crete and was his hero. I tried to tell him that I wasn't the general, and he told me that he understood that I must be in disguise and that he wouldn't tell a soul that he had seen me!

The Italian Job

We had seven dates booked for Italy...[44] When we played the second day in Genova,[45] we found out that the five remaining days of the tour had been cancelled by the promoter. I have no idea for what reason but he said that he was going to pay us off anyway. The guarantee for that section of the tour was $25,000. The Agency in London had been given half of the money so there was about $9000 owed. The guy arranged to meet us in Vicenza the next day. We got to the place where we were supposed to meet him and waited all day for the guy to show up. He didn't show; it was late, so we decided, "Fuck this shit, let's go to Venice, to the guy's house and collect our money!" We drove to Mestre, the little town next to Venice - you can't drive into Venice.

We called the guy up and he said, "Yeah, OK, sorry, I went to the wrong place in Vicenza and you guys weren't there." He arranged to meet us in Mestre the next morning at 10 o'clock so we spent the night there. 10 o'clock came and he called and said that he couldn't get there until four!

We all started thinking about it - it was Friday and by 4 o'clock the banks would be closed. So five of the guys took a bus to Venice and, with a city map, went to the guy's house. They were ringing the bell and knocking on the door - finally, the guy came out. They dragged him to the bank and demanded that he draw out all the American dollars that the bank had -

$7500 - which wasn't enough. He agreed to give us a check for the rest of it from his bank in Monte Carlo, so he got on the phone to his bank manager to arrange for him to be there on the Saturday at 2 o'clock in the afternoon, to give us the rest of the money. He wrote the check and the guys were really happy - we hadn't been paid for a while. They'd got $7500 in cash and we would get the rest when we arrived in Monte Carlo, which was on the way to our next gig - a 2-3 day drive across Italy, France and Spain, all the way over in Portugal.

So we left that night and drove across to Monte Carlo to the bank. When the manager saw the check, he said, "I can't cash this, there's no signature on it!" Jörg went completely bananas. The bank manager was saying, "Don't scream at me, it's not my fault!" Ener and I finally calmed Jörg down enough to get him out of there and we left for Portugal.

The next morning, Jörg went downstairs and borrowed a typewriter and typed a letter - which was supposedly from the [Italian] promoter - to the Agency in London. The letter said that the promoter had cancelled those five dates of the tour but had agreed to pay the band, so it was alright to release the other half of the money to them. We still had the original contracts that the guy had signed for those gigs, so * - the master forger - copied his signature from the contract and put it on the letter. While he was at it, he went ahead and signed the $2500 check from Monte Carlo as well! Well, five days later Jörg came in and said that the money was there from the Agency, so they went down to the bank and put it in. We actually got everything from that Italian gig, but it was quite a James Bond escapade to get it!

Rehearsals at the Treibhaus
We went to Innsbruck and rehearsed for six days at the Treibhaus. We played a gig there at the end of the rehearsal. They paid for our hotel and food. It was a very nice hotel - we all had our own room. There were 600 people at the gig, a nice place to play.

Critics Sell Out
We went to Bresna, Italy and, from there, went to the Olympic Theater in Rome. It was sold out. Sandro had invited all these guys to come and sit in with us, all these other musicians. The show was about three and a half hours long, way too long. The "Critics" put Sandro down, not so much the band, just Sandro, for getting all these guys to join us on stage.

223

Street Life

We went to Bern, Switzerland to play a very strange show. The club wasn't even in town; it was way out someplace. This was the beginning of us finding out what Beat The Street were doing. They were making the posters they were selling to the clubs. Well, this club in Bern never ever got their posters and they were really pissed off, they'd paid for them. So at the end of the show, when we got paid, they took out the money for the posters. Beat The Street were getting half the money from each show, up front, so we got right on the phone to them!

We left for Hamburg to play at Grosse Freiheit. Somehow, our roadie Michael[46] had left one of Sandro's guitars in Saarbrucken - his spare one - and of course Sandro was going fucking berserk! He was always breaking strings; every night he would break a string during 'Lonely, Lonely Nights'. (He was using a guitar synth. on that tour.) So, when we got to Hamburg, he had to go and buy another guitar. He found a nice Guild guitar up there, a semi-acoustic thing. Three days later, in Keil, the guitar turned up - they'd mailed it up from Saarbrucken, so now he had three guitars.

After the concert, we went around to the forbidden street (for women!) in the Reeperbahn. We went window-shopping. I had a baseball hat on and one of those whores wanted the hat, so I said, "What'll you give me for it?" She said, "Well, I'll take a hundred Marks off the price!" so I asked her what her price was. She told me it was 500 Marks,[47] so I said, "You can stick the other 400 Marks up your arse and I'll keep the hat!"

We got back to the hotel and Ener and I were staying in the next room to where Sandro was. We heard the door open very quietly, and tiptoes down the corridor, so we had a peep out of the door and there he was disappearing around the corner.

We went to Millstadt, which is right up by Flensburg on the Danish border. The owner was a really nice guy. He had this really crazy wife, especially when she started "tilting".[48] By the end of the show, she had gone around smooching with all the guys in the band, and she had decided that she was going to go with us on the rest of the tour! We had to go all the way down to Brussels. It took us about 30 minutes to get her off the bus - she had been drinking tequila all night and she was blasted!

I remember that I changed the drumhead on my snare drum. The guys from the merchandising got me to sign it – then they sold it for 50 marks!

You Can't Do That On Stage!

We were almost ready to sign a deal with Polygram in 1994. They wanted to release the CD as the Grandmothers of Invention but "she" stopped that deal. We had a big agency in London – the LPO Agency. She threatened to sue them if they didn't drop us.

She just threatened to do all these things but finally, at the end of 1994, she actually did sue the three of us - not all the Grandmothers, just the three of us.

She sued us because some of the promoters had been billing us as the Grandmothers OF INVENTION. The lawsuit she filed said that we had violated the terms of that agreement[49] and we hadn't done anything, everything that we... all our contracts read "The Grandmothers", period. Nothing "... of Invention" was ever there, it was the promoters did that. We had no control over what they did.

We were on stage in London. It was December 21st 1994 - Frank's birthday! We'd played the first part of the show. I went up to the dressing room and there was a girl there with an envelope. It was dark, she had this manila envelope, and I thought she was a fan and wanted me to sign something. She handed it to me and I said, "Have you got a pen?" She said, "You don't need a pen for this!"

So that's how they served it to me. They can't make you take it but I had already touched it! Bunk didn't take his, he threw his hands up, it didn't touch him and it fell on the floor. Don Preston was hiding - I went down and told him. He took off as soon as the show was over and ditched her.

They didn't get him until the next day. The next night, when we were on stage, we said, "Don Preston's not here tonight, so Biff Debris is sitting in for him, on the keyboards!"

We called him Biff all night, but it didn't do him any good because they served him on the stage, they just went up and placed it on his piano.[50]

In my part of it, it says Jimmy Carl Black living somewhere in Texas. Well that's not true, so that part is wrong, technically. But I think that it may have all been a scare tactic. After all, I haven't got any money and "she" knows it!

I responded back, it said that I must respond within 30 days. I was on tour with Eugene. It was the week before Husta died. He helped me write the letter explaining all the stuff that had happened; that the promoters had done all that stuff and that we didn't have any control over any of what they did.

I paid 30 Marks to have it registered and sent to the court. You know, I got it back about a month and a half later with a letter saying that it was illegal[51] and that they were not accepting it. I didn't have a lawyer so they wouldn't even read it!

So, when Don and Bunk got back to California they got straight on to Neil Goldstein - she knew where those guys were! The last time I spoke to Don, he told me that he had received notice from Gail's lawyers claiming that she wants to make some sort of agreement with us, a letter of apology from us and four or five other points...

...They can't stop us saying, "Jimmy Carl Black, former member of the Mothers of Invention", but now she says that those letters have to be very small, she's even got the size down that she wants!

...Tommy Mars was telling me that there are three songs that are not allowed to be played, by anybody: 'Zoot Allures', 'Black Napkins' and 'Watermelon In Easter Hay'.

Notes to Chapter 17

[1] For the record, Ya Hozna moved from Italy to Germany in 1998 [Ref: ARF Dossier Vol. #15]

[2] "Starts The Jack and Jim Show with Jimmy Carl Black, performing more than 100 concerts in Europe." [Ref: eugenechadbourne.com]

[3] But JCB lists 8 Dutch and 4 Swiss venues

[4] JCB actually says 15 years here so this suggest this chapter dates to around 1994

[5] In Belgium

[6] But see above, The Phone Call, March '93, when JCB says he was at a "...little Zappa Day in Italy..." JCB probably means it was the 1st time he'd played at a modern music festival where the sideshows and stalls are almost as important as the music.

[7] *Who the fuck is Sandro Oliva?* (1994)

[8] Two towns that merged in 1972

[9] Including a Radio Ohr (Offenbach, Germany) live promo interview

[10] Husta has spent barely nine months living in Italy and JCB much less

[11] According to Sandro Oliva, it was Reinhard Preuss who was instrumental in getting the Grandmothers playing in Europe

[12] Solingen; Modernes, Bremen; The Cult, Arnsberg; Cascade, Münster; Live Music Hall, Köln; Subway, Karlsruhe; Zappatag, Stuttgart/Ruit; Jazzhouse, Freiburg; ZuckerFabric, Kirchheim

[13] Roddie Gilliard of the Muffin Men; they had spoken on the phone

[14] Brighton was possibly the 1st gig, "on the south coast"

[15] 'Fanzine' edited by Fred Tomsett that ran until April 2000

[16] JCB writes "Lemshurpen", which seems to be nowhere?

[17] In Sweden

[18] In Stuttgart; they were there for three months or more

[19] 6 months after the 1st one!

[20] JCB's recollection of part of this tour is confused. There is no time to play in all the places he mentions here and be in Caen, France for Oct 6

[21] JCB's manuscript reads "Swamp". The Swan is much more likely if Ben Watson's recollection in ARF #59 is correct! Andrew Greenaway concurs with Ben!

[22] Univ. Of Caen, on Oct 6, 1993

[23] "...the second time, on the October tour." [Ref: JCB, elsewhere]

[24] In Belgium

[25] "Instant Chavires à Montreuil"

[26] two days only

[27] Around 550 miles or 900 km!

[28] Sandro's band, The Blue Pampurios

[29] 500 km / 300 miles there and back

[30] "Husta loved Bad Boll and was learning to speak German. I was always on the road with the Grandmothers and Jack & Jim [1993-1995] so I didn't care where I lived." [Ref: JCB in conversation with Georg Stock (of the band Behind The Mirror) & Marcus Pfeffinger of the band Capt. Ahab, Sept 8/9, 1997]

[31] Jörg Philipp of "Beat The Street Touring Service Company", from their Austrian office

[32] "We'd wanted to play there but they [the Promoters] hadn't been able to get a gig for us." [Ref: JCB elsewhere]

[33] The Knaack Club in Berlin

[34] Gail Zappa

[35] VHS tape in JCB Library

[36] K7 live recording in JCB Library

[37] The finger points in only one direction. See: [this Chapter: You Can't Do That on Stage]

[38] Zappa's band

[39] The rectal abscess that JCB went into hospital for back in 1988

[40] Tilburg Live - on CD

[41] "We got to Paris and I had to have an operation again, at the hotel, she split me wide open, drained me - milked me!" [Ref: JCB, elsewhere]

[42] Earlier, JCB says that Jörg is from Beat The Street. Did Jörg do some bookings as an independent agent?

[43] At the beginning of April, 1994

[44] "... in October." This seems wrong [Ref: sandroliva.com]

[45] Genoa, Italy

[46] Michael Prackwieser, noted as the Monitors/Equipment technician in the promo tour brochure.

[47] A large amount of money!

[48] drinking

[49] 1990 settlement

[50] "At the last gig of the tour, in London on December 22 1994, we got given a lawsuit on the band-stand - they came up and handed it to us." [Ref: JCB, elsewhere]. Which was when Bunk was also got, presumably? [Ed.]

[51] Because it wasn't from a lawyer?

Part Four:

A Mother's Rest!

[JCB only completed Chapters 1-17. He wrote extensively about some tours and events after this time but from this point onwards his "recollections" are also drawn from other writings, mainly the autobiographical digest he wrote for his website, which he wrote in the 3rd person. This has been edited to the 1st person where appropriate.]

Richard Ray Farrell[1]

I first met Richard in February 1995. We talked about the blues and I played him some of the music that I had recorded in Austin before moving to Europe in 1992. As my wife had just died, I had a lot of time on my hands. I liked Rick very much from the beginning and we discussed putting a real

blues band together. I had two tours to do before we could start.[2] When I got back in June we started gigging...To me, Rick is one of the best guitar players that I have ever played with. Then I found out that he's just as talented as a singer and harp player...

Tommy Mars in Sardinia[3]

...I got a call from Sandro Oliva saying that this promoter was interested in doing a night of Zappa music and would me and Ener Bladezipper be interested in playing with Sandro and Tommy Mars. I had met Tommy on a number of occasions through Denny Walley and Frank. I asked Ener, who was living in Amsterdam [now], if he wanted to do it and he said OK. The money was great so we did it. As it turned out, we had only two hours to rehearse and one of the songs we pulled off was 'Brown Shoes Don't Make It', the *Tinseltown*[4] version because Tommy knew that way. All in all, it was a great concert[5] and a great time in Sardinia.

About Gabby

Gabby...my youngest daughter...Michelle, Knebworth, 1975.[6] Gabby...15th March 1976. I found out about three years ago.[7] She had a stepfather who got killed in a car wreck when she was about 16, when she was living in L.A. She already knew who her real father was, so when she met Herb Cohen at a party she told him the story. Herb got my phone number from Don Preston and called to tell me. So right after that, Gabby's mother called me and asked if it was OK for Gabby to ring me.

Of course I said, "Sure, I'd love to talk to her!"

I got a call from Gabby in Boll[8] - she asked if we could get together. She was out in California. So I first met her when I went back [with] Chadbourne.[9] She came and stayed with me for about nine days, so we got to know each other.

Then she went off to introduce herself to the rest of my family. Loretta and I got divorced in 1979; she told Gabby when she met her to call her Aunt Loretta. (She's a nice lady - we're better friends now that we're divorced. She never remarried.) So now she calls herself Gabby Black and is living close to my son Garry. She had a little baby but unfortunately it died. She is now the manager of a strip bar in Phoenix.[10]

Jack and Jim in the States: 1995

Eugene's a great inventor of noisemakers. It's very easy to record with him but you wouldn't believe the equipment he has! In the States this last year, we had the electric windshield wiper and the electric plunger. We had a battery on the motor of the wiper - it whirls and makes the strangest fuckin' sounds, especially through a pick-up, and then the plunger is making this funny noise. They were all in the same unit on a board.

His home studio is like a junk shop. He's got this set of drums, a strange percussion set. He has this 4-track machine - an Ampeg - it's a dinosaur. We recorded two albums on it this last summer,[11] one is called *Pachuco Cadaver*[12] and the other is called *Jessie Helms - Busted With Pornography*.[13] We've never played the same show twice - I never have any idea what we're going to do when we get up there. Some of the stuff on that *Pachuco Cadaver* was recorded when we played three nights at the Lunar Cabaret[14] in Chicago, a real intimate little place. They had a very good PA and DAT machine there, so we recorded all the shows.

Most of the stuff was done in his studio.[15] 'The Dust Blows Forward and the Dust Blows Back' was done outside in the back yard. I played a cardboard box with the brushes and he played the banjo. I think it sounded pretty good.

That album took about five days. I'd be up at 7 and drink coffee 'til about 9 and then we'd start recording until the afternoon.

[16]...the Cedar Cultural Center in Minneapolis...was the 6th show that The Jack and Jim Show did on the first ...American Tour in 1995. The tour started in Greensboro, North Carolina and from there covered at least 20 states and a stint in Canada. Our road manager on this tour was Jenny Chadbourne. We had just finished our 2nd Coffee Shop Tour in Holland and were ready to bring our music and craziness to the States; ...We did two shows at the Cedar that night to a very receptive audience and lovers of creative music. Jack starts off on the banjo on the first five songs and then switches to the guitar. We covered some Zappa, Beefheart, Kitty Wells, Phil Ochs and some great tunes from Eugene Chadbourne. We didn't have time to talk to the fans after the show because we had to pack up and move over to another club for a third show of the night!

Jack and Jim in Europe: 1995[17]
We featured the great Italian guitarist, Sandro Oliva, for some crazy fun on the stage in Florence, Italy.

This was the last major tour of the millennium and we took a 6-year break.

When Do We Get Paid? (1996)
...released a CD of old unreleased material in 1996 on Cargo Records.[18]

Tom Shaka
In April [1997], I went into the studio with Tom Shaka to record *Blues Magic* with Lars-Luis Linek.[19]

Power Trio
Jim, Sandro and Ener toured Germany in the summer of 1997 as "The Grandmothers Power Trio".

COCKROACH ALBERT

**BEHIND THE MIRROR
& JIMMY CARL BLACK**
LIVE AT THE documentaX AND ELSEWHERE

A band called Behind The Mirror, who are big Mothers fans, got in touch with me and asked me if I would play a few shows with them.

They recorded the shows and later they came over to my house in Bad Boll and recorded a bunch of other stuff.[20]

They compiled an album from all the tapes; it was released on a CD called *Cockroach Albert*.[21]

- I think, a really good album, they're very funny guys!

Photo by C. Vafeidis

Sculpting: 1997
Sylvia said that she wanted to do this little exhibition. By now I'd probably about 75 pieces - it was time! I made a bunch of candleholders - mainly soapstone and alabaster.[22]

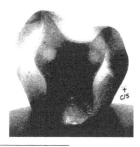

Photo: Georg Stock, Jimmy, Steffen Moddrow; 1997

Tired of Touring: Winter 1997

I'm getting tired of Touring; it's been pretty tough for me. I've just arrived from Belgium, eight hours on the train, having on Thursday played with the Muffins in Koln, on Friday morning went to Belgium for two gigs with my Blues Band and now come on Sunday back to here in Heidelberg to perform with Muffins and continue playing the tour.[23]

On Bended Knee: 1997
"3 days off from Muffin tour to get married on Dec 5/6"[24]

photo by Tom Kastermans

Grandmothers Tour Again: 1998[25]

Farrell & Black
The Farrell & Black Band have been playing together for almost five years [now] and have two CDs.[26]

The first one released in 1996 is called *Cataract Jump* on Fritz Records. The new CD is called *Black Limousine* on Stormy Monday Records.[27]

Muffin Men

Roddie Gilliard, the leader of the Muffins, has been a big fan of the MOI since *Freak Out!* came out and in 1993, [the Muffins] opened up quite a few gigs for the Grandmothers first tour in Europe. I got to know them and used to sit in on the last song of their set. I sang 'Willie The Pimp' and then recorded it on the *Say Cheese and Thank You* CD in 1993. When my second wife died in 1995, I was in pretty bad shape over that and the Muffin Men really saved me. They asked me to go on a tour of Germany with them as a guest vocalist and second drummer. I've done every tour with them since then and will always be with them as long as they're together.

I have done six tours [now] with this band as lead singer. They are very dear friends of mine and I really have fun on

the road with those English WANKERS.... There are a lot of Mothers' fans in England so touring over there is great with the audiences. The money is shit but - what the hell - you can't have all the cake and expect to eat it, too![28]

I'm on three CDs of the Muffins [now], the first is called *Say Cheese And Thank You*; the second is called *Frankincense* and the third called *MufFinZ* and they are all on Muffin Records Productions. Those records are over a four-year period of time. There is a new one coming out.[29]

236

Notes to Chapter 18

[1] From sleeve notes to *Cataract Jump*, written by JCB

[2] With The Jack & Jim Show and with the Muffin Men

[3] [From: JCB interview with Andrew Greenaway, for idiotbastard.com, Aug 7, 2008]

[4] *Tinseltown Rebellion*, Frank Zappa, 1981

[5] Feb 14, 1995

[6] See: [Chapter 11, A Huge Road Accident]

[7] Exactly when JCB means by "... three years ago" is not clear. 1994 is the most likely year.

[8] Bad Boll in Germany, where Jimmy has been living since Oct. 1993

[9] In 1995

[10] At that time; JCB is relating this situation around 1997

[11] Summer of 1995, so this passage was written late '95 - early '96

[12] Released in 1995

[13] Released in 1996 by Fireant. JCB writes, "[Helms] is such a Redneck. I think he's head of the Armed Forces; it's like a joke. He's so against pornography, any nudity or art. But actually he was caught with a hooker in Washington. His wife's name is Dorothy, so Eugene does this parody about him and Dorothy smokin' "Crack". That's pretty funny, but he doesn't do it much in Europe because people don't really understand." Re-released on Inkanish in 2006 as *The Perfect C&W Duo's Tribute To Jesse Helms*

[14] Closed sometime after 1995

[15] "Part(s) of 'Veterans Day Poppy' is live. The background to 'I'm Gonna Booglarise You Baby' is something that he recorded a while ago with Lesley Ross and some other people." [Ref: JCB]

[16] From the sleeve notes to the Inkanish release of the *Live Cedar Cultural Center* CD

[17] From the sleeve notes to the 2002 Inkanish release: *Taste of The Leftovers*

[18] Divine Records? JCB commissioned Ant-Bee to write the sleeve notes for him. In 1995, Billy James wrote... "Jimmy Carl Black is a legend" and notes the variety of JCB's output as well as his versatility.

[19] [Ref: Sleeve Notes]

[20] [Ref: Georg Stock of BTM:] "Those recordings in Boll were mainly narrations and 'narrative improvisations' by Jimmy. BTM released another CD with the contribution of Jimmy, called *The Secrets Of Crater 6*. (In 1999)

[21] In 1998

[22] JCB says elsewhere that he had several exhibitions of his work. He would sell pieces at gigs and to private customers and give or sell to friends: "I did sell a bunch of them about four or five years ago but I haven't pursued it much." [Ref: JCB interview with Steve Moore, 2003]

[23] [In Nov. 30 '97 JCB interview with Stefan Kleiber, printed in *Trust* magazine, Issue 69, '98]

[24] [Ref: JCB in conversation with Georg Stock (BTM) & Marcus Pfeffinger of the band Capt. Ahab, Sept 8/9, 1997]. But this didn't happen. JCB and Moni had to wait until Dec 22nd to get married. Moni Black says JCB presented her with a single rose on bended knee when he asked her to marry him!
[From www.sandroliva.com/98old1:] "December '97: Jimmy Carl Black got married with the wonderful Monika in Germany. Just a few days off from his successful winter tour with the Muffin Men. Many congratulations to both!!"

[25] The band now included Steve B. Roney on drums and Mauro Andreoni [front] on keyboards.

[26] The Farrell & Black [Blues] Band played all over Germany, often three or four times a week. Husta had died so Jimmy was by himself in a little apartment that cost four hundred marks a month, until he met Moni and moved down to SE Bavaria [Ref: Jon Larsen, *The JCB Story* (audio); available on CD].

[27] It was Rick Farrell who wrote 'The Indian Of The Group' for Jimmy. It was on *God Shave The Queen*, the Muffin Men CD released in 1999.

[28] Extract from JCB interview with Steve Moore, 2000 (both paragraphs)

[29] This dates the writing of this section to around 1999.

News Letter

The new century was really great for Jimmy as he got more into the computer. He was learning about music production and [has] the dream of forming his own record company for the release of rare material he's been toting around for many years.[1]

Jimmy is in the process of finishing a new R. & B. CD with a great band from Salzburg, Austria.[2] He also has plans to record a CD of American Indian music that he has been wanting to do for a long time.[3] Two dear friends of his are helping with the music. Essra Mohawk is writing the music to a song called 'For the Little People' and Dawayne Bailey is writing the music to a song called 'Chief Old Fox'. He is providing the lyrics.

The year 2000 was the year Jimmy did the most touring he has ever done in his career. He did over 150[4] dates in Europe and the United States. In the States, the Grandmothers played 58 shows in 66 days[5] and travelled 17,200 miles and were in 42[6] States. They were promoting the new CD, *Eating The Astoria*. He did two tours with The Muffin Men and two tours with The Farrell & Black Band.

At Home

I got married again about three years ago to a wonderful German woman.

 Her name is Monika and she is beautiful.[7]

She is one of the biggest women Zappa fans I have ever met in my life. She has all the albums of Frank's and when we first met, she had been looking at my picture on LPs for 25 years. She says she's been in love with my picture for that long. AMAZING!

My home is my castle and there is a lot of stuff around to remind me of the old days - thanks to Ms Monika. Every morning I go into my living room and the first thing I look at is the picture of Frank sitting on the toilet!

I am also a sculptor of soapstone for relaxation and have had exhibitions of my artwork. I have sold quite a few pieces. I really don't have a theme when I start a sculpture. The rock guides me to the final sculpture. I think that is true for many creative sculpture artists. I have done over three hundred sculptures, over the last five years.[8]

The Tumor

The new century started out pretty slow for me, as I had only two gigs between January and April. However, I had a small operation on my shinbone. I had gone to see Pete York[9] on my 62nd birthday and got a little drunk at the affair. When my wife Moni got to our house, I got out of the car and slipped on the ice by the car door. I really hit my knee hard and thought I had done some terrible damage to it. The next day, Moni took me to the doctor for an X-ray of the knee. The Doc said your knee is OK but you have a tumor inside your shinbone!

I went for a series of tests and it was decided that I go into the hospital and have a biopsy on the tumor. I was in for three days and was limping around the house for a couple of weeks after.

I played a gig with Behind The Mirror, a German avant-garde duo, in Bregenz, Austria in the first week of April.[10]

Muffin Tour 2000

On the 12th of April, I left for Liverpool and the first spring tour I had done with the boys. It was the first tour with the new drummer and, as it has turned out, a very talented one. Tilo Pirnbaum was just finishing his studies at the LIPA School, also known as The Paul McCartney School.

We played the first gig at the LIPA School but the next day was the official beginning of the tour.

It was at the Hanover Hotel in Liverpool. What a great gig it was as most of the old Muffins were in attendance. **HOTEL HANOVER**

That night, after we finished the gig, we got in the van and drove all night [down] to the far reaches of England, to Penzance and Land's **THE FIRST AND LAST INN** *Free House* End. It was a wonderful gig as the local girls showed the lads from Liverpool what line dancing is all about. It is a lovely little theater there and the weather was beautiful, the only good weather of the whole tour.

The next day we were off to Southampton and a venue called The Brook. It is a nice little gig as I have played there a few times before and knew a few people. After **The BROoK** the gig, we split back to Liverpool as Roddie was still working at LIPA during the day.

On the 18th, we went to Croydon, which is basically south London, to a place called The Cartoon and it is![11]
Of course, we drove back to Liverpool that night again. I have to say that the "band-van" was slower than a fucking turtle and it took forever to get to Liverpool.

Anyway, the next night was a little closer in Stourbridge at the Rock Café 2000. It was a good gig except the sound in the place sucked big-time. We must love it because we seem to play there every time we tour in England [and] - you guessed it - we drove back to Liverpool that night after the gig.

On the 20th, we went to Sheffield and The Boardwalk.[12] That is a GREAT GIG and we had a hotel that night. Carl[13] and I were sharing a room. The hotel was kind of spooky and I had a strange experience there. I don't know if it was a dream or not, but I felt myself being lifted out of my bed and completely turned around and put on the floor. I got up[14] and went to the toilet and then got back in bed but didn't sleep worth a shit for the rest of the night. If it was a dream, it's the wildest one I've ever had and if it was a ghost then it was even weirder.
I'll never know, but Carl said that he felt weird in that room also.

Anyway, the next night was about 20 miles away in Matlock (the English people have weird names for their towns) at a place called The Fishpond and, as usual on this particular tour, we drove back to Liverpool after the gig.

The next day, it was off to London again to play at a historic club called The Torrington.[15] Almost everyone has played that venue. It's the size of a large living room and I still don't know how they get 250 people in there. It was a great gig as the London audiences were starting to appreciate the talents of the Liverpool lads.
Of course, it was back to Liverpool after the gig!

On the 23rd, we started the last week of the tour in Stockport at our home away from home, The Thatched House.[16] This is a special little gig as we always play it. Every tour I have done in England with the lads, we've played there. We have some very big fans and very good friends [there].
Since Stockport is only 30 miles from Liverpool, it stands to reason that we would go back after the gig!

The next night was also close to Liverpool in Chester **ALEXANDERS** at Alexander's. I had played there two years before with the Grandmothers[17] and always have a good time. Some of the original Muffins were at the gig again. Nice Time!

The next day it was off to London for the third time of the tour and we played in Worcester Park. We had played there before and it was a good gig and, of course, the drive back to Liverpool. This was beginning to get old!

The next night was in Bristol at a place called Fiddlers *Fiddlers* and as it turned out, it was a great gig. One of the most important parts of the gig was we didn't have to drive back to Liverpool. A real treat! The lads had friends there and they put us up for the night.

Zak's in Milton Keynes was next and it was a tiny little *ZAK's* place. We hardly had room to set up the gear. All in all, it wasn't a bad gig. The people were nice to us and enjoyed the music MUCHO! Back to Liverpool, but I didn't mind since the next gig was the last one of this tour.

We left for Whitley Bay, which is right next to Newcastle, and a place called the Dome.[18] It looked like a tiny Albert Hall and sounded like it also. That was one of the worst sounds of the whole tour, for such a beautiful building! We left after the gig for Manchester and the airport to drop me off for my flight back to Germany. I was ready to go home after driving 3500 miles in two weeks. I thought England was a small country. Hell, 3500 miles is like driving across the USA. I should say that the tour was an experience I'll never forget as long as I live. Anyway, this tour was just the beginning of a long and hectic year. I'm getting too old for this shit!!!

The Farrell & Black Band

I left Manchester at about 7:30 in the morning and flew to Amsterdam, where I had a layover of about five hours. I had bought my new computer just before leaving for England so I was reading all about MS Windows and how to do some of the things that I wanted to do with it. The airlines never made a gate change announcement so I almost missed my plane to Munich. I made it though, and my sweet little wife Moni was waiting for me. We got in the car and headed for Goppingen, which is about 200 km[19] from Munich where I had to play with the Farrell & Black Band.

That started a three-week tour with them in Germany. That band featured Richard Ray Farrell on guitar and vocals, Uwe Jesdinsky on bass, Klaus Brosowski on keyboards and me on drums and vocals. We have two CDs out, *Cataract Jump* and *Black Limousine*, so we had something to promote on tour.

I had gotten an eye infection before I left England and it was pretty bad that night.[20] There was a doctor, a fan of the band, at the gig that night. He went to his house and got some eye drops for me and it helped. We played a street gig the next day and Moni and I drove about 250 km[21] to our house in Siegsdorf after the gig. I hadn't been home in three weeks and believe me it was wonderful to sleep in my bed again with my wife. I had one day off and went to the doctor and he gave me some very strong eye-drops and told me to come back after the tour.

The next day was the real beginning of the tour and we played all over Germany and had a great tour. I really enjoyed playing with that band because I got to play drums all the time. I only had to sing on a few songs so I could really concentrate on the drums, which is my instrument.

I had a week off with my computer to catch up on correspondence for my [new] website, and to answer e-mails that I received from my fans while I was gone. Then I caught the train to Rome for a five-day rehearsal with the Grandmothers.

We started a three-week tour of Austria and Germany in Greifenburg, Austria and then about 30 km from where I live at the Kleinekunstbühne in Obing, Germany. They were both great gigs and it was good to be back out on the road with the boys.[22]

We had a couple of days off at my house and enjoyed Moni's cooking, and then drove to Berlin, [to] Rostock for the ARF Society (a Zappa organization), then down to Marburg and then to Würzburg, and then the Feierwerk EV in Munich.

We took another couple of days off again at Moni's kitchen and then left for Köln and the MTC Club, for a great concert in one of the most beautiful cities in Germany. From there, we went back up north to The Fabrik in wonderful Hamburg. In Köln, we had picked up a new passenger.

Photo by Helmut King

Rose - Ener's wife now - had come over to Germany from Austin, Texas for the finish of our little tour.

We went from Hamburg to a little town somewhere on the way south and spent the night before going on to Mannheim. That was a great gig because, once again, Moni joined our little troupe of wanderers. The last two gigs were in Bregenz, Austria and Jena, which is about the middle of Germany.

Ener left our little troupe and went back to Amsterdam while the rest of us went to my house in Siegsdorf. They spent the night and left for Rome the next morning.

It was, all in all, a great tour and a great way to start the millennium.

The Grandmothers' Tour of the USA:

On August 1, 2000, the Grandmothers started their marathon tour of the USA. We all arrived in Nashville, Tenn. to start a week's worth of intense rehearsals for a tour that would take in 60 cities and 17,200 miles (27,680 km) in two and a half months in a 35-foot Winnebago with a trailer on the back for the equipment. Sandro Oliva, Steve B. Roney and myself arrived in Atlanta, GA and immediately had a three-hour layover because of severe weather. That was the first time Sandro wanted to get back on the plane and go back to Rome. We talked him out of that, explaining that nobody has any control over the weather.

Sound Advice

Anyway, we arrived in Nashville and Essra Mohawk picked us up at the airport. The rest of the guys arrived the next day and we moved into our little apartment and started the rehearsals. The first day of rehearsals we discovered that we had two musical directors in Don Preston and Sandro Oliva. Compromises had to be made immediately in the direction the band would go musically. It's hard enough with one, much less two directors but we managed to put together a pretty good show.

The tour officially took off at the Exit/In on Aug. 9th and at the sound check Don immediately pissed off the **EXIT/IN** sound-man, so we didn't get a good sound the first night. The next gig was in the Barrelhouse[23] in Cincinnati, Ohio. That gig went pretty well after us telling Preston to keep his mouth shut about the sound and the soundman.

After that, we left for Peoria, Ill. and the Zappening 2000 Festival, where we had a nice three-day stay in a very nice hotel.

We went out to the staging area that [first] night and watched Project Object with Ike Willis performing. I got up on stage and sang 'Lonesome Cowboy Burt' with them and it was a lot of fun.

The next day, we were out there in the early afternoon to set up our merchandise stand and saw Ray White play with his band. They were great! We took the stage after Essra Mohawk played and we did two hours of great music. The audience loved the Grannies.

On one of the songs, about one hour and fifteen minutes into the set, a beautiful girl with BIG TITS came on to the stage and started doing a striptease. To me, that was the highlight of the show.

The next day, which was the end of the festival, we saw Banned from Utopia play and Ike got up and sang a few songs with them. It was great!

Mothers' Territory

We travelled the next days to Omaha[24], NE and then to Kansas City, MO to a club called the Grand Emporium[25] and had a great gig there. It was a blues club and at first we didn't think anyone would show, but it did get packed and there really are a lot of old Mothers fans there. From there, we headed north to the Turf Club in St Paul, MN and that was real Mothers' territory. We met a lot of nice people up there and had a wonderful time. From there, it was back down south to a hotel called the Ft. Des Moines in Des Moines, IA and then on to the Canopy in Champaign, IL. That is the place where I married my first wife Loretta, when I was in the Air Force - there were some strange memories for me!

Saving Grace

Onward and Upward to Detroit, MI and a place called The Magic Stick, which was a gigantic pool hall that had concerts once in a while. As it turned out, it was great. Sandro "fell into lust" there with an American-Italian woman that was right up his alley.

From there to Bunk's hometown of Cleveland and the Beachland Ballroom. It was a pretty strange place and the saving grace of that gig was Bunk's sister came to the gig.

It was good to see Mitzy again and she followed us **3IST STREET PUB** to the next gig in Pittsburg, PA at a place called the 31st Street Pub. A wild biker bar and we had a few of them there.

We left Mitzy and went on up to Buffalo, NY. A kind of strange thing happened there, as everyone wanted to see Niagara Falls. We got into the wrong lane of traffic and wound up on the Canadian side of the border. Well, here we are with two Italians that had no work permits in the States and I had a bag of Weed and we had to go back across to the American side. The driver told the Border Patrol that everyone was an American and luckily they didn't pursue the inspection. We might have ended the tour right there.

Anyway, we got to the venue, the Laffayette Tap **LAFAYETTE** Room,[26] and that's where Sandro quit the band again. **★ TAP ROOM ★** Radio signals were coming into his amp and he flipped out. He said to us if you will give me 2000 dollars, I will go home and not bother you anymore. Now that was a tempting offer, except we were all doing this tour on a shoestring anyway so we said to him, "You give us 2000 dollars and you can go home with our blessings." Needless to say, he didn't go home.

Saving Money

From there, it was up to Massachusetts and a place called the Iron Horse[27] in Northampton where they wanted 25 percent of all sales of merchandise that was sold in the place. We sold our merchandise out on the sidewalk by the Winnebago - so much for that fucking place!

Next was Boston at Johnny D's. Now that was a great gig except that, after the concert, Bunk forgot to put the radio mike for his horn in the RV and we drove off without it.

We met a lot of nice people there in Boston and did a great radio show. While on the show, we got a phone call from Dale Bozzio,[28] who lives there. We invited her to the show but she didn't come.

From there, we were at The Met in Providence, RI and an enthusiastic crowd of Zappa lovers.

THE MET

The next day, it was off to the Wetlands[29] in New York City and an early show there. It was great to play in NYC but we were only there for 10 hours in total. That is the quickest visit to the city I have ever done.

Wetlands

Saving Bunk

Next, it was the Pontiac[30] in Philly and there is where we saw Cal Schenkel at the show. It was great to see

Pontiac Grille

him again as it had been at least 25 years since I had seen him. After the show, some people were helping us to load the equipment and Bunk lost his flute. That was the last straw for him and he said that the next gig, which was in Washington DC, would be his last one on the tour. He quit the band.

When we got to Iota's to play, Sandro looked in the back of his amp and, lo and behold, there was Bunk's

IOTA Club & Cafe

flute. Somebody had stuck it there when we were loading the night before and we didn't see it. So, Bunk was back on the tour again!

Heading South

The next gig was in Carborro, NC at the Cat's Cradle. It wasn't a very good gig since hardly anyone came.

CAT'S CRADLE

That is a gig that Preston will never forget and that's all I will say about that![31]

AUG 30 2000
GEORGIA
THEATRE
Presents

We were heading south and the next gig was in Athens, GA at the Georgia Theater. This was one of the best gigs of the whole tour. What a beautiful old theater and a very great crowd of people.

**G R A N D
M O T H E R S**

The next gig was the last gig of Aug. at Potbellies in Tallahassee, FL. It was on the campus and wasn't that great a gig since the kids mostly didn't even know who

Potbelly's

Frank Zappa was much less the Grannies. I was glad to see that gig over with.

On Sept. 1st, we were in Jacksonville, Florida and played at a club called Jack Rabbits. It was quite a

Jack Rabbits

dump, if I remember right. The PA sucked and the soundman didn't have a clue what we were doing. The fans that came out to the gig were very enthusiastic though, so it turned out to be a pretty good gig.

Bogus Pomp

From there we went to Tampa Bay and a place called Skipper's Smokehouse. Here is where Sandro quit the **SKIPPER'S** band again because the club didn't provide helpers to haul the gear in. You have to know that, by this time, the band had been on the road without a day off and about 5000 miles. Tempers were quite short. I told him, "Fuck it, I'll carry your fucking equipment in myself." The gig was a great success as we met some very nice people. A couple of the guys that I had been in contact with by e-mail showed up, as did the lead guitarist from the Zappa tribute band, Bogus Pomp. His name is Jerry Outlaw and the other guys are Dave Black and Ed Hunt. Dave videoed the concert and I had a great time rapping with them.

Alligator Alley On the 3rd of Sept., we went to Miami to a big club[32] that was not even on the itinerary and played a great show. Don Preston's sister came to the gig and we had a nice visit with her. I hadn't seen her since the 60s in Detroit. Don stayed with her that night and she drove him to the next gig in Key West.

It was probably one of the best gigs of the tour. The venue was called the Green Parrot. Key West is the farthest point south in the U.S.A., at the end of the Keys. **Green Parrot**

It is a smuggler's paradise and I know there must be pirates lurking about. We met a guy who called himself Skippy but whose real name was Scott. He said he came to the Keys 28 years before, while on the run. I really didn't want to know who he was on the run from but I'm sure he wasn't the only one there in the same boat. It was so much fun that night and the audience was wonderful. We met people from all over the world that night. The next day was our first day off since the beginning of the tour and believe me we needed it. There was a guy from Philly that had an eating establishment that kept inviting us to eat as much as we wanted. I think we had three meals in all - it didn't cost us a penny!

That evening, Skippy invited the band for a twilight tour of the Gulf of Mexico. We went out on a gigantic schooner for about three hours of sailing. It was memorable!

The next day we were in Ft. Meyers, and I don't even know the name of the club. We should have stayed in the Keys. There were about five people at the gig and we were playing for the door! At least we got a free meal. Forget that place!

On Sept. 7th, we were in Orlando in the Sapphire Club[33] and that was a good gig. One of the ex **SAPPHIRE SUPPER CLUB** members of the Austin Grandmothers, Lyle Davis, was at the gig. Boy, some things never change and he's one of them. Completely out to lunch! It was great to see him again, though - I needed a good laugh by then!

After that, on the 8th, we were in Sarasota at the 5:00 O'Clock Club. Dave Black and Ed Hunt were there again, and Fred Hemmer, and Dave videoed us again. It was an interesting place. We started playing at 5 o'clock and played until 8 o'clock. There were tons of very beautiful girls there because there's tons of money in that town. A lot of Mercedes and Bentleys and of course, Rolls Royce cars parked outside of the club. I think most of those girls were 500-dollar hookers.

Bamboo Willie's in Pensacola was a dud.

Howlin' Wolfs
Finally out of Florida, we were in New Orleans at The Howling Wolf. I had played there a few years before with The Jack and Jim Show so I had a bunch of fans that came to see us play. Before the show, at the sound-check, Don and Sandro got into a screaming musical director's disagreement that almost went to blows. If you don't know what it's like to have two musical directors in a band, you don't want to experience it, believe me! They tried to pull me into the conflict, but I wouldn't have any of it. Ener and I went and ate alligator meat instead. It was a great show, despite everything. We had a couple of days off and headed for Austin, Texas. Finally in God's Country, I started to relax a bit.

God's Country
On the 13th of Sept., we were at the Satellite Lounge Club[34] in Houston, Texas and played a great show. It was a pretty good turnout for a Wednesday.

After that, on the 14th, we were in Club DaDa in Dallas and really had a great turnout of fans there. My cousin Cal McLish came down from Oklahoma City and brought another batch of T-Shirts. We were selling a lot of them and we had to keep ordering them as we went along. We had a nice time in "Big D".

We drove back to Austin after the gig because we had a radio show in the morning promoting the two shows in Austin.

Both shows were outside affairs and, since I had lived in Austin for 10 years, as Ener did, we had a great turnout for the concerts. Those two shows were promoted by Ener Bladezipper and were total successes.

The next day, I flew to El Paso because my sweet little wife had come over from Germany to be with my family and of course, me. We had a day off there so it worked out well.

The rest of the band arrived the next day and we played at La Tuya Cantina in El Paso. We had another day off so  I got to see my whole family, but more importantly, my wife Moni.

the Rhythm Room   **KNITTING FACTORY**   **LAS VEGAS LEGENDS**

We left the morning of the 21st and drove to Phoenix, Arizona and the Rhythm Room. My oldest son Gary and youngest daughter Gabby were at the gig since they lived there. It was a great gig as it was also Don's birthday. Don and Bunk stayed with my son that night and he took them to the airport the next morning to fly to L.A.

We played that evening in Hollywood at the Knitting Factory.[35] What a great gig that was. All the old fans from L.A. were there. After the gig, we had a big party at Bunk's house and I got to visit with all my old friends. We had a great time.

Photo: Gary Black, Hopper, Chava, Jimmy

The next day we left for Legends in Las Vegas. We did a little sightseeing of the casinos and my son Gary was there again to see us play. It was a great gig in a very famous city for entertainment.

On the way back to L.A., Barb,[36] our bus driver, and I got into a little conflict and so she quit the tour! I apologized and she was back on board. We couldn't afford to lose her. As you can imagine, the tour was taking its toll on everybody.

Reunions

The next day, we were in San Juan Capistrano at the Coach House and it was memorable because Roy Estrada was waiting for us when we got there that afternoon.

I hadn't seen Roy in about 20 years and I almost cried - it was so much fun to be with him again.

Roy couldn't stay for the gig because he had to take his son's car back. Too bad, since we wanted him to sing with us on 'Love Of My Life'. It would have been great for us and for the fans.

All of my ex-wife's brothers were there and it was great to see them again.

The next day was just as good because we went to Fresno and, low and behold, there waiting for us when we arrived was Motorhead. Another great reunion! **Club Fred** During the show, I announced to the audience that he was there at the gig, and after he got to sign autographs along with the rest of us.

The next night was in San Francisco at a club called the Paradise.[37] We did a radio show in the afternoon before the show and the place was sold out. We always did have a lot of fans in Frisco. As  the night before, Motorhead was in attendance. This time, I asked him to sit in on tambourine on one number, as we couldn't get rid of him. He played the whole night with us! He was in seventh heaven. He hadn't played that music since the Mothers last played. After the show, he got on his motorcycle and rode off into the sunset. Goodbye Motor!

Two gigs got cancelled in northern California, so we headed for Lake Oroville and stayed with Billy Mundi - another memorable visit with another ex-member of the famed Mothers of Invention. He really lives in a lovely place and we completely enjoyed our short visit with him.

Cooking The Blues

Oct. 1st was in Portland, Oregon at a place called Berbati's Pan with Ike Willis's band opening up for us. It was a great night for the fans and for us. Both bands were cooking that night.

The next day, on our way to Seattle Washington, the RV blew up so we had to have them bring us another one. It was just like the old one except it worked. By the time we changed all the gear and hooked up the trailer, we were already pretty late.

We called the Club I-Spy[38] and told them we might be a little late. They had people waiting to help us get everything in. We did a quick sound-check and got something to eat and it was time for the show. In the audience for the show was another ex member of Zappa's... Jeff Simmons was in attendance and it was great to see him again. It was a very good show that night.

We had to leave right after because we had a power drive to Boise, Idaho. We played in a place **Bouquet Blues** called the Blues Bouquet[39] and it was a great gig. I didn't know there were that many fans in Idaho.

Don Sweaters

The next day, we were in a club (I can't remember the name[40]) in Salt Lake City. Before loading in, Don tried to move the RV and hit some guy's van - that's what we get for letting him drive! It turned out to be a great gig, though.

The next night, 5th of Oct., we played a beautiful theater in Boulder, Colo. called the Boulder Theater. We were now in Barb's territory and some of her friends were at the gig. It was wonderful. It also was snowing for the first time of the tour. Before that, most of the time we wore shorts while travelling. Now we pulled out the sweaters and jackets.

Saving Steve B Roney

The next gig was in another club in Steamboat Springs that I don't remember the name of. The ones I don't remember are not on the tour list.[41] This is the gig that Steve B. Roney (drums) quit. Sandro pissed him off big time so he said, "I'm going home after the Denver show." By this time, almost everyone in the band had quit at least one time and some more than once.

Anyway, the next night was at the Gothic Theater in *Gothic* Denver, a very beautiful old theater that had been renovated. Another ex-member of the Austin Grandmothers, [Gerry] "Eli" Smith, was there and sat in on 'The Great White Buffalo' playing the wood flutes like he did on the original '*Dreams On Long Play*' CD. I really enjoyed that concert.

The next day was off and it was in a multi-million [dollar] house in Santa Fe, New Mexico. The promoter of the Albuquerque show the following day arranged for us to have a relaxing day off in the country. We sure did have a relaxing time that day and night. What a place, what a nice lady that owned the house.

The next day, my sister June and her friend Linda came up **SONNY'S** from El Paso to see us play again. Also in attendance was my old friend Vic Mortenson, the original drummer with **BAR & GRILLE** Capt. Beefheart. I used to live in Albuquerque in the early 80s and so a lot of my old friends were there at the gig. It was a very good gig despite the PA that sucked a big banana.

Steve and I scored some magic mushrooms and ate them that night on the power drive to Ponca City, Oklahoma and a place called the VZD.

Good Timing

The old roadie from the original Grandmothers in the early 80s was there, and his lovely wife. His name is Jerry Ford. We had another nice visit with them. My cousin Cal and his wife Cathy were also there again. Good Times!

The next day we were in Clinton territory, in Little Rock, Arkansas at Juanita's. It is also a great Mexican **JUANITAS** restaurant and so we ate well and had a good show. By this time we knew the material so well that it was impossible to play bad even if we tried - and sometimes we did!

The next day, we were off to the next to last show of a monster tour. We played in Memphis, TN. Bonnie, Bunk's wife, was there waiting for us and so we had a great time. It was an out-door gig because we were back down south and it was still hot, even in the middle of Oct. I was extremely happy because we only had two more days and I was going home.

Sound Sense

We left for Nashville on the morning of the 14th and checked into the hotel, then down to the club to set up - one of the first hotels we had on the whole tour. We saw Denny Walley at the gig that night and I was very happy to see him. It had been a while since I'd seen him, so another great reunion. The gig went well despite the soundman that was still pissed off at Preston.

The next day Sandro, Steve, and I flew to Atlanta and that's where we parted. I flew to Munich and they flew to Rome. All in all, it was an experience that I'll never forget and never do again - not even for a million dollars![42]

Notes to Chapter 19
[1] JCB had previous formed Inkanish Music in 1972, and the Inkanish Records label in 1980 to put out *Clearly Classic*
[2] X-Tra Combo
[3] Not completed?
[4] Take away weekends and this schedule means JCB is playing 3 of every 5 days in at least 8 diff. countries and 2 continents. JCB was 62 years old.

[5] 52 gigs in 67 days [Ref: sandroliva.com/2000UStour]. [unitedmutations.com:] differs, but it lists the tentative tour venues!

[6] I make it at least 49 State Lines but around 38 States [Ed]

[7] "She is the 'Love of My Life'." [Ref: JCB Interview [#]3 with Steve Moore, 2003]

[8] The major pieces remaining in JCB's collection amount to less than 20

[9] Former drummer with the Spencer Davis Group

[10] Helmut King presented his homage to Jimmy at this concert. [Ref: Robert Riedt]

[11] The Cartoon had a famous wall-length cartoon; closed since the end of 2006

[12] Has been closed since Nov. 2010

[13] Carl Bowry, lead guitar

[14] From the floor or the bed?

[15] The Torrington Arms closed its doors in 2004, after 37 years as a music venue

[16] Closed sometime since 2010

[17] The 1998 Tour

[18] Closed 2005 as part of a 5-year regeneration scheme

[19] 125 miles

[20] This infection was in fact the 1st symptom of JCB's leukemia which was diagnosed in Oct. 2000 when he got back from touring with the Grandmothers

[21] Around 150 miles

[22] The boys: Sandro Oliva on guitar and vocals, Ener Bladezipper on bass and vocals, Steve B. Roney on drums, Mauro Andreoni on keyboards and me on lead vocals and percussion. [Ref: JCB]

[23] Has closed

[24] The Music Box

[25] Has closed

[26] Closed March 2010

[27] Iron Horse Music Hall

[28] Wife of Terry Bozzio, the drummer

[29] Closed Sept. 2001

[30] The Pontiac Grille, closed

[31] Intriguing!

[32] The Alligator Alley

[33] Now known as the "Social"

[34] Closed Nov. 2002

[35] This venue closed its doors in 2009

[36] Barb Dyer was the band's road manager!

[37] The Paradise Lounge Club has been closed since 2009, if this is the venue JCB records here

[38] Closed Dec. 31 2002

[39] Has closed

[40] Just outside Salt Lake City in Ogden at Brewski's [Ref: sandroliva.com/2000UStour]

[41] The Tugboat

[42] [Jon Larsen, *The JCB Story* (audio), 2007:] JCB reminds us that he was 62, Bunk Gardner 67 and Don Preston 68 at the time of this marathon tour, 60 gigs in 66 days and over 27,000 km of travelling.
"We did 42 states in a Winnebago with seven people on board: Six musicians and a woman driver that also did our merchandising. Everyone except Don quit the band at least once along the way and some quit more than once. We saw Cal Schenkel in Philly; Adrian Belew in Nashville; Denny Walley in Nashville; Ike Willis and Project Object and Banned From Utopia in Ill.; Roy Estrada and Tom Leavey in L.A.; Motorhead Sherwood in SF; Billy Mundi in northern California, and Jeff Simmons in Seattle. We did meet a lot of old and made a lot of new FANS along the way. It was a very successful tour, except financially, with all the fans. There were a lot of best shows and hardly any worst shows."
[Ref: JCB Interview [#]3 with Steve Moore, 2003]

2001 was…a busy time as…I released several CDs in CDR format on my new label, Inkanish Records.

In Oct. 2001, I joined forces with my new "pardner" Robert O'Haire, and the official beginning of Inkanish Records was solidified.[1]

I did quite a bit of touring, but not as heavy as the year before as I was told by my doctor in October [2000] that I had a weak case of Leukemia!

Also a new CD from The Muffin Men called *More Songs From The Campfire.*

…I did get together with Eugene Chadbourne…and The Jack and Jim Show was in business again. Two CDs resulted from the two small tours we did: *2001: A Spaced Odyssey*[2] and *Reflections and Experiences of Jimi Hendrix.*[3]

2001: A Spaced Odyssey

The Jack and Jim Show saddled up again, after a six-year period of inactivity, to start the new millennium with a bang. The tour started off in Paris and ended in Tilburg on the 10th of September... Not only are the boys six years older but six years better. Jack's banjo work is brilliant, as his guitar work, and Jim's drumming puts the beat where it belongs, and the vocals are very funny as expected from this DYNAMIC DUO...THE JACK AND JIM SHOW is back in business with more great music to offer in the future to one and ALL.

Reflections & Experiences of Jimi Hendrix[4]

26 October 2001, Theatro Cavallerizza, Regio Emelia: It was a very beautiful theater in a very beautiful city in northern Italy. We were there for four days of which three were rehearsing and then in the morning of the performance, we played a mini-concert for a girl's high school in which about 200 beautiful girls attended. The evening performance was one that will go in my book as one of the best gigs I have ever performed.

The X-Tra Combo Project: *Mercedes Benz*

[X-Tra Combo] is a very good R&B horn band from Salzburg, Austria that Jimmy sings with. This band can really groove. There's a bunch of classics on this one such as 'Mercedes Benz' with a Bo Diddley beat; a couple Zappa classics, 'Big Leg Emma' and 'Road Ladies'; Lowell George's 'I'm Willin'' and some original songs by Jimmy like the classic 'Low Ridin' Man' and 'Lady Queen Bee'. All in all, this one SMOKES.[5]

The first gig[s] performed with Jimmy Carl was at the Rockhouse in Salzburg in Feb. 1997...and at the Arge Nonntal. Two weeks later, we met at Apple Studio and recorded nine tracks. We only played a few gigs [the] next four years and finally decided it was time to finish the project. We met in April 2001 and finished the CD. This has got to be one of the best R&B horn bands that Jimmy has had the pleasure of performing and recording with in his long career as a musician.[6]

Touring 2002

It looks like an interesting year...touring-wise for Jimmy coming up: April-May-June will be with The Muffins in Europe, England, Scotland, and Ireland.

In Sept-Oct., there is a tour with the "EU Grandmothers" featuring Candy Zappa on vocals, that is going to be great - *but unfortunately that didn't happen*.[7]

I did the winter tour with the Muffins again.[8]

In March of this year, the first two [CD] releases from Inkanish Records: Jimmy Carl Black and The X-Tra Combo released *Mercedes Benz* and The Grandmothers, *The Eternal Question*.[9]

There's going to be two more releases before the end of the year.[10]

The third official release on Inkanish Records was...*Hamburger Midnight*.

This is the first recording with Jimmy's old "pardner", Roy Estrada, from the Mothers of Invention years. This great rhythm section hadn't played together in 32 years!

Mick Pini is on guitar for this recording. [11]He's one of the premier "white" contemporary blues players around. He is also a very soulful composer of both music and lyrics.

When Jimmy told him that Roy was coming to visit, Mick said, "Why don't we go into the studio...cut some songs and see what happens?" They did some of Mick's songs and some they wrote together. They did a Freddy King, a couple of Howlin' Wolf and two songs from the first Little Feat LP - a song that Roy and Lowell George wrote together called 'Hamburger Midnight'. Mick says, "HIT IT!"

Photo above: Roy, Mick, Jimmy and Peter Bruder

2003 was more touring with the Muffins and with Mick Pini. It is also the year that Jimmy started to receive his Social Security check from the Bush government because he turned 65 that Feb. 1st.

WHERE'S THE $%&$#@' BEER?

JIMMY CARL BLACK

...released late last year...is a 30 Year Anthology of Jimmy's singing. There are some songs from Geronimo Black, The Muffin Men, and some from the Austin Grandmothers. There are four songs that have never been released in this format such as 'Lady Queen Bee', 'Waiting', 'The Great White Buffalo' (first recording) and 'Thank You, Come Again' (never heard before). This is a CD that I have been wanting to put out for a long time and it was worth the wait. It BURNS!!!

Drummin' The Blues

This was also released late last year and is a collection of blues songs that Jimmy recorded over the last 23 years with five different Blues and R&B bands which include the Legendary Arthur Brown, J.C.B. and The Mannish Boys, Holzhaus, Black, and Teresas Band, The Farrell/Black Band, and Big Sonny and The Lo Boys.

There are 17 songs of Jimmy just playing the drums including songs like 'Fever', 'Summertime Blues Medley', 'Stand By Me', 'C.C. Rider', 'Hound Dog', 'I Feel Good' and many more like that.

If you like Rockin' Texas Blues, this is the TICKET!!!!

Singin' The Blues

This one was released this year and features Jimmy Carl singin' 19 songs from his legendary career with some of the bands he has played with over the years. If you like the way Jimmy sings you will love this CD. On most songs he is just singing but on some of them he is also playing the drums as well. I hope you will enjoy this little collection of great songs. THANKS MUCHO for being a fan...[12]

We'll Be Together Again

Did a tour of Holland and Scandinavia with The Jack and Jim and Pat Show and put out a double CD called *We'll Be Together Again*[13] that was recorded on that tour.

ZAPPANALE 14

About three weeks later, The Jack and Jim Show, without Pat, went to northern Germany to do the Zappanale 14 and we put out a wonderful CD from that show called *Live at the ZAPPANALE 14*.[14]

On the same festival, I also played with the Muffin Men and the whole festival was great.

A few months later…finished out the year with the annual winter tour of Germany with the Muffins. I had to go into the hospital during that Muffins tour because I contracted Pleurisy. That was actually a blessing because I finally quit smoking cigarettes after smoking for 45 years. HURRAH!!!!!!

Leg-end

…now that I've been in this business for 46[15] years…I'm what they consider a "leg-end". I'm in all the Rock 'n' Roll books and all that stuff.

So it's like the old black guys. They couldn't make a dime when they were young. But after they all hit about 60 or 65 years old, now they all can play until they die. All these festivals, they'll hire these old black guys to come and play. And they'll do the same for an old Indian.[16]

Jimmy zaps to fame wall

2004 The year that I started my 25 treatments of Chemotherapy. Fortunately, it was a fairly weak one, meaning that I didn't lose my hair or get sick at my stomach, although it did have some bad side effects on me. Nothing I couldn't cope with.

Inkanish Records
I did the annual spring tour with the Muffins - that went well.

When I came back from that tour, I found out that the distributing company for Inkanish Records had gone bankrupt and we not only lost a bunch of money but also all the CDs we had in stock.

All in all, about 15.000 Euros and that bankrupted Inkanish Records and put us out of business. My biggest regret from that experience is for my "pardner", Robert O'Haire, who had put the money up originally.[17]

The music business SUCKS...but I don't know anything else. So it is onward and upward and maybe when I die my products will start to sell!

Ella Guru & *The First Album*[18]
Those guys are big fans of the Muffin Men and always came to our gigs in Liverpool. I met John at the Cavern when we played there and he asked me if I would be willing to sing on two tracks of their new CD. I said, "Sure!" and I did. It is a very nice CD, although I wasn't expecting that type of recordings with the name Ella Guru. I thought that they played more like Captain Beefheart, but that wasn't the case.

[19]As the 15th year anniversary of Boogie Stuff approaches, the band has just completed this new CD titled *Have Mercy*. It has been my pleasure to play with the group and also record some songs for this album.

I have been singing with them on the road and it really has been a lot of fun for me to tour and perform with musicians like Fred, Andy & Horst. In these days of one hit wonders and casting shows it's so good to see a band like Boogie Stuff stickin' together for such a long time and keeping that boogie-rock alive and kickin'... I hope the guys will have mucho success with this CD and I thank them for allowing me to play with them.[20]

2005 was a good year touring - playing with the Muffins[21]

...and Mick Pini-

...and making more CDs that don't sell that good but were fun to do:

Hearing is Believing[22]

We started out in Dresden, Germany and that was the first gig. My wife Moni drove me up there and we played a great gig. Got good dough for 45 minutes of madness, especially with "The Artist Formally Known As"[23] on keyboards.

We left there the next day and went to my house until the next gig which was in Slovenia. It was a "free-jazz" festival which was wild to me, being a good ol' boy from Texas. Had a lot of fun with my buddies Jack and Pat. Pat played a wonderful solo concert on Saturday afternoon and I especially enjoyed 'God Shave The Queen' by him.

Back to my house where we went to the movies in my living room one day and night and watched all three of The Lord of the Rings in the extended versions, taking time out only for some dinner. Man! That was a 14-hour marathon! I will never do that again in one sitting no matter what Pat Thomas does to me!

We went to Freiburg and recorded this masterpiece of a CD in Schroeder's nice little studio in two days - GREAT CD! It sure brought a smile to my face... Chadbourne is a pretty "trippy" guy and I ought to know since I have been playing with him since 1991. We had been playing some of the songs on the tour and the rest of the songs we put together in the studio. That is the way we usually do things anyway, so it was no problem.[24] The CD sounds GREAT. It is the best of all The Jack and Jim Show CDs. ...There are some really classic tunes on this jewel. 'Chenny's Huntin' Ducks' is a Chadbourne classic about the V.P. of the U.S.A. There's a drinking song called 'It's 5:00 Somewhere'. There is some classic Beatles and a Hendrix song on there. If you like The J&J Show then this one is right up your alley...[25]

From there, they went to play a "free-jazz" festival in Nancy, France, then to Amsterdam and finishing up in Brussels.

2006 started with the recording of the newest CD called *How Blue Can You Get?* This CD was recorded in February 2006 in Ulm, Germany and it was a lot of fun recording it.

It features Mick Pini on guitar and vocals; Roddie Gilliard on bass and vocals. I am singing and playing drums. It is a collection of songs that we all have wanted to do for a long time. Some very classic Dylan stuff, a BAND classic, and a Lou Reed classic plus much more for your listening pleasure. The band did all cover tunes this time around just because they could!

How Blue Can You Get?

...Rod got to Germany on the 16th of February and we started getting everything down by the 18th. We rehearsed the songs that the keyboards were on. The next day Rod, Jimmy and Mick rehearsed four songs without the keys and recorded them. They weren't done right, so the next day we went in and re-did them to our liking. The next day was the big day with the keyboards. We got all that done without a hitch and so the last day was just doing two or three songs.

The next day, Rod and Jimmy went home and Mick finished up on all the overdubs and mixing.[26]

Touring 2006

After that, the annual spring tour of the UK with the Muffins. Jimmy then met Eugene Chadbourne...in Brest, France for a wonderful 5-day festival that turned out great.[27]

In May, Jimmy and his lovely wife, Monika, went back to Nancy, France, for the "free-jazz" festival and the project: "Chadfest". Jimmy played on the "Tribute to Johnny Paycheck" part of the fest and also the last night "Monster" part of Chadfest.[28] Eugene got to put six different shows together and invite 30 musicians from all over the world to do the "Chadfest". It was truly the wildest thing Jimmy ever did with him.

Eugene, Pat, Jimmy, and the lovely Monika then went down south to Marseille, France and played another festival that turned out great and then back home. Him and his wife had a very nice holiday!

[29]"When I played that festival with "Dr. Chadbourne" in France..., I met and played with Steven De Bruyn who is a harp player from Belgium. He later asked me if I was interested in coming to Brussels and recording a CD with him and a guy named Jos Steen in the Belgium National Radio studio.

I said sure, so I went and recorded with them. The pay was good and they paid all my expenses from Germany. It is a very interesting recording that fans would enjoy.[30]

Jimmy did a U.K. tour in the summer with Mick Pini under the name The Jimmy Carl Black Band to promote the new CD. It was Great!! He has played several gigs in the fall with Pini and that is the update of his biography.

IN CONCERT

JIMMY CARL BLACK BAND

FEATURING

MICK PINI GUITAR AND VOCALS
JIMMY CARL BLACK DRUMS AND VOCALS
UWE JESDINSKY   BASS & VOCALS
PLAYING 60 S, 70 S, R & B, BLUES, AND
ORIGINAL MUSIC

Jimmy is about 85% done (finally) with his autobiography *For Mother's Sake*. It will be published ... SOON!!!!

Notes to Chapter 20

[1] See further: [Chapters: 10 - Inkanish Music; 13 - Inkanish Records]

[2] Released 2002

[3] Recorded Oct. 26, 2001 at concert in Reggio Emilia, Italy; released as CDR by Inkanish Records, 2001; called *Jimi 2* when re-released in 2002 by Inkanish Records, again as CDR

[4] From sleeve notes to *Jimi 2*

[5] *Mercedes Benz* was released in April 2002.

[6] The 2nd paragraph is from CD Cover Notes, written in 2001, when the CD *Mercedes Benz* was released

[7] Two different Grandmothers touring bands were being promoted for 2002 in Europe, a USA based line-up and JCB's. JCB was being touted as playing in both, without his knowing. The European line-up collapsed as a result and ended JCB's involvement with the Grandmothers. However, JCB played at Zappanale 13 with the Lewinskys and with Grandmothers West, as well as guesting with Thana Harris, the Ed Palermo Band and Lennon/Tabacco/Zappa. [Ed] See further: [sandroliva.com]

[8] Nov-Dec

[9] Both CDs release on Inkanish Records, 2002

[10] *The Early Years*, The Jack & Jim Show, and *Live All Star's* (sic), The Route 66 All Star's (sic), both released as CDR, by Inkanish Records, 2001

[11] Extracted from sleeve notes to *Hamburger Midnight*

[12] Drawn from "Uncle Jimmy's Little Online Record Store", last update April 17, 2007. The document contains contradictions. For example, unitedmutations has *Drummin' The Blues* released 2000.

[13] Released as a Double CDR in 2004 in the USA

[14] Released as CDR by Inkanish Records, 2003

[15] If the recorded date of this interview is correct - 2003 - it would be 44 years

[16] [Ref: JCB interview with Claus Biegert, 2003, Siegsdorf, Germany]

[17] In the old website version of this passage of text, JCB continues: "I wish I would have done something different in the work-field like teaching or something like that."

[18] [From: JCB interview with Andrew Greenaway, for idiotbastard.com, Aug 7, 2008]. *The First Album* was released in 2004

[19] Written by JCB for the sleeve notes accompanying the CD which was released in 2005

[20] Boogie Stuff and JCB began working together in Sept. 2003 which resulted in some gigs, a tour of Eastern Germany, and the CD. Their association lasted about a year. [Ref: Horst Tolks]

[21] "The Muffins are the best band I've ever played with; they take the music and turn it into something else, something new!" [Ref: JCB comment printed in Cropredy 2005 Program]

[22] By "The Jack and Jim Show Plus The Artist Formerly Known As Black Paddy"

[23] Pat Thomas aka "Black Paddy"

[24] [From: written answers that JCB gave to questions posed by Robyn Flans for *Modern Drummer*, Dec 31, 2007]

[25] Drawn from "Uncle Jimmy's Little Online Record Store", last update April 17, 2007

[26] JCB's sleeve notes for the CD

[27] "In early April I am back in France to work both alone and with Jimmy Carl Black at the new Festival Invisible in Brest, France." [From: eugenechadbourne.com]

[28] "...and the Horror Part Nine finale during which Jimmy Carl Black read The Raven out loud..." [From: eugenechadbourne.com]

[29] [From: JCB interview with Andrew Greenaway, for idiotbastard.com, Aug 7, 2008]

[30] "It took about five or six hours to do everything and since it was a live recording in the studio, there were no overdubs. That was the beauty of this recording. It was totally spontaneous and on the spot. Jos is a great player and has some good tunes and Steven is one of the best harp players in Europe. EXCELLENT GUYS!!!! [From: JCB's "liner" notes to the CD]

2007 Newsletter[1]

Hi Everyone,

I hope you will forgive me if this letter isn't right. I have never written a newsletter but I think it is about time I started. After all, I do care about all of you. To start [with], my health is not too bad at the moment although I will never get rid of this leukemia, but I am still able to go on tours and record new products…

I have a few new products out now:
How Blue Can You Get is the new CD from my band The Jimmy Carl Black Band.

The second new CD I have out is with my old friend Eugene Chadbourne. The band is called The Jack and Jim Show and the CD is *Hearing Is Believing* and features Pat Thomas on keyboards… This CD will be released on the Boxholder label very soon in the States. The title says it all with this one…

…all the CDs we do (We have 21 CDs out now) are a mix of all kinds of music… but mostly comedy music. We do quite a few political songs like 'The Only Kind of Rice I Don't Like is Condeleeza Rice'.[2]… It is usually done with humor. Actually this is a pretty funny band.[3]

The third product I will have out soon is a re-make of a CD I did in the 1990s called *When Do We Get Paid?*… It will be coming out in the States soon. This is a compilation of material I recorded over the years that has not been released properly [before]…

I am still touring as often as I have work…

Strange News From Mars

[4]…a very interesting recording by Jon Larsen, who is a very talented guitarist and songwriter. I went to Oslo, Norway[5] and went into the studio the second morning and did my talking parts and a little percussion on a few tracks. He then took the tracks to Los Angeles and got Arthur Barrow, Tommy Mars, and Bruce Fowler to play on most of the songs. I really like the sound of the recording, as it sounds very Zappa like.

[6]...This year has been one of the busiest years for me that I have done in a while. The Jack and Jim Show played over 50 gigs this year.[7] The tour was called the Think 69 Tour since that is my age this year...

Live at The Merlin: Feb 23rd 2007

This was the first time that The Jimmy Carl Black Band has played at Merlin-Kultur and it was a great experience for the band. It is really the first time to play there for Mick Pini. Uwe and Jimmy have played there many times before with The Farrell/Black Band. The whole concert started by being sold out. The audience was extremely loud and the vibe was just right for the makings of a wonderful evening. The band didn't disappoint anyone that night. The weather outside was great and the people didn't smoke inside the concert.

...I did a few festivals with the Italian band I play drums with. They are great players.

Tempest Jazz

This band I played with recently[8] is a Jazz band. It's called the Tempest Quartet[9] - two saxophones, a Hammond organ and drums. I play drums in the band and I sing a couple of songs. I've had three gigs with these guys in the last three weeks, three festivals[10]...and the guy, I've known the guy since I first moved here, he's the first musician I played with in Europe. His name is Bruno Marini. He's quite a famous musician. He plays Hammond organ but...his main instrument is saxophone. Baritone Sax, Tenor Sax and Flute.

He played with Steve Lacy for years. (Steve's dead now of course, pretty famous Jazz guy.) Bruno's a phenomenal musician, Man! He's also on the "Disco" record, [Freedom Jazz Dance].

[11]Bruno called me up[12]...and asked me to come to Verona, Italy and go into the studio and record this CD[13]... I have never done anything like it before. I really enjoyed playing with all the players that participated on the recording.[14]

...Bruno arranged all the horn parts, which sound great, and he also played flute and Hammond organ.[15]

[16]We call it a Disco record but it's the only Disco record that's got all real instruments, no electronic instruments on it, drums are all real, percussions all real, the three horns are all real. It's called the Heavy[17] Metal Band. We've got this girl, 25 year old singer, the name she goes by - Valentina Black - I don't know why Black and I don't really know what her last name is but she's 150 percent Italian. So her name wouldn't be Black!

But two years ago she was Miss Verona. She's really a beauty queen, Man! She's so fucking beautiful it'd knock your eyes out, and so sweet a girl, and sexy. The whole package is there and not only that she can actually sing and she actually plays keyboards. She's a good keyboard player as well so she's our business, as we call it. We know we'll get a lot of guys buying the record and [it] sounds good, Man! There are four songs on the record and each one's 20 minutes long.[18] It's just Disco shit for dancing. They paid me to go play 8 bars of 10 different grooves. I'd never recorded this way ever, 1st time, they didn't use all the grooves, they only used four but he's got six for possibly the next project. He just loops it - it's like I'm playing that beat for 20 minutes. I hope we don't have to play any live gigs. I don't know if I could play that beat for 20 minutes or not. That's normal! The discos want the records long, they want the people dancing...they'll dance for 20 minutes, that's not a problem...they're on Ecstasy...or on something![19]

...I had a festival with The Jack and Jim Show in Germany.

JULY 27-29

"The Jack and Jim Show was asked to perform there... [this] year and it was a wonderful Festival. We had a great time playing there and the audience was wild. We had them dancing in the street, so to speak. If you want to hear very good avant-garde music then I recommend this festival. The food is good and the people are great. ROCK ON."[20]

...Back to Oslo and another recording with Jon and the CD is called *The Jimmy Carl Black Story*. ...I basically went into the studio one night and told my life story. It took me about one and a half hours to do it. He then used some blues players from Oslo and also some of the guys from the Strange News CD for the background music.

[21]...Then the States on the 27th of August until the 23rd of October with Eugene. We are the Dynamic Duo and have been playing together since 1991 mostly in Europe. We have 22 CD's out now and the music is pretty wild. We do a lot of Zappa and also a lot of Beefheart.

We didn't make it to Texas this time although I spent 11 days in Anthony with my family. It was great to visit my kids and grandkids. We took a little break in the tour so I could do that. I hadn't seen them in 7 years.

The gig at the Outpost [Albuquerque] was great. My whole family was there. The only one that didn't show up was Geronimo.

We played 40 gigs. The tour was very successful and we will be doing it again next year and probably until I can't do it anymore. I don't know how long I can keep playing the drums although I am playing better than I have in a long time. It's easier to just sing. Jack (Eugene) says we will do Texas next year and then the west coast. We did mostly the east coast and mid-west this last time.[22]

Photo: Jimmy at home in Siegsdorf, Bayern, with some Muffin men

I made it through that tour pretty good and then when I came home to Germany I had four days off and then went again for nine days with The Muffin Men from Liverpool. That tour started on the 27th of Oct. and finished on the 3 of Nov.; back home on the 4th. It was a short (thank God) but great tour of Germany.[23]

Kimo![24]

I have been going to my doctor for treatments for this Leukemia that I have and in fact, I must start chemotherapy on Monday for four days this month [Nov]. I will have some more next month and then I don't know. My illness isn't a very strong one so the Kimo! isn't very strong. I don't lose my hair or anything (I hope). At least that is what the doctor says.

Bop 'Til I Drop

[25]...I do have my memories and they are nice. My Moto is, "Have Drums, Will Travel" if the bread is right. I am playing with my own Blues band called The Jimmy Carl Black Band; [with] The Jack and Jim Show; [with] the Tempest Quartet; with Sandro Oliva in Italy; [and with] the Muffin Men from Liverpool, England (a Zappa tribute band and a good one). In that band I am the lead singer and [play] some percussion. I have been with them for 13 years so I still get a chance to play the music of Frank Zappa, which I do love, MUCHO.

I will be 70 years old on February 1st and this is going to be my 50th year as a professional musician. That is a long time in my book. I have made well over 100 CDs in those 50 years and if my health holds out...

...I have Leukemia that I have been dealing with this last month... It has been a rough month for me although I am coming back because I plan to "Bop 'Til I Drop". I feel I have gotten better the older I get because I have learned some tricks that help me play better without hurting myself. I am not as fast as I used to be but I know how to compensate for that.

To The Idiot Bastard

Saturday, June 28, 2008

Hey Andy,

Japan was GREAT and also very successful for Jack and Me. I am getting ready to start working on the interview. I just had to get over the trip somewhat. I probably went on that tour too early since I wasn't in the best shape over there. I am finally coming back to my old self. I think another couple of weeks and I will be OK again.

…

August 5, 2008

I [have] been in the hospital again and have to go back on the 20th of August for an operation on my lung. Here are the answers to the questions that you have sent to me so far.

…

Aug. 7, 2008[26]

Here is the second installment and I want to thank you again for doing it: (I am doing that interview this afternoon in my house with Alex.[27])

IB: You've been battling leukemia for a few years now?

JCB: I have had leukemia since 2001[28] and have gone through five months of chemotherapy and this April I started and completed 10 weeks of radiation therapy, which was a drag. The therapy wasn't bad; it was the after-effects that weren't good. I am still reeling from that shit. Three weeks, ago the doctors found a pretty big tumor on my right lung

that looked like cancer to them. I went into the hospital two weeks ago and had three biopsies done on that tumor. All three tests came back saying that the tumor wasn't cancerous. The doctors can't believe it. On the 20th of this month, I am going back into the hospital and having an operation to either remove it or something. I have to say that this has not been a good year so far for me health-wise. I hope it gets better from now on…

Photos: Top, J&J with Captain Trip; Above, Jimmy with Geronimo & Darrell in Bayern; 2008

IB: Dr Chadbourne mentioned a story that *WOIIFTM*[29] didn't actually feature the Mothers, but a bunch of session musicians. What was that all about?

JCB: That wasn't a story that he said. That was from an e-mail he got from Gail about us trying to release 'Mom And Dad' and 'Willie The Pimp' on the CD, *Hearing Is Believing*. She told the guy from Boxholder Records that I wasn't even on 'Mom And Dad', and in fact wasn't even on [the] *WOIIFTM* album. The good Doctor then asked her if Frank had hired Rich Little (a famous comedian, who does impressions) to do "Hi, boys and girls - I'm Jimmy Carl Black, and I'm the Indian of the group." Well, that stopped her in her tracks. It is ironic that she could say something like that when she wasn't even allowed to come down to the studio. I was there almost at every one of them [sessions] that happened at Mayfair Studios.

IB: Have you heard the *MOFO* CD set? Any surprises for you?

JCB: I have heard the CD as Roddie Gilliard gave it to me as a birthday present on my 69th birthday. I have to say that I really enjoyed the whole CD...

IB: How was Japan?

JCB: Japan was a wonderful trip for me, although I wasn't feeling very well. I had just finished 10 weeks of radiation treatments about three weeks before I left for Japan. Actually, that was way too soon for me to go. Man! That shit really knocked the piss out of me! Here it is in August and I am still not completely recovered from that shit. Anyway, we were in Tokyo for eight days and played three gigs. The first gig was a Captain Beefheart night, and so we played mostly Beefheart songs. The second gig was a Zappa night, so we played mostly Zappa songs - and, by the way, we made sure that the equivalent to the GEMA[30] in Japan paid the songs. The fourth gig was in Nagoya, and we got an excellent recording of that show which is now out on CD. I really enjoyed the food over there and was surprised to find so many Mothers of Invention fans at every show. It really made me feel good to know that I am still loved for the music that I was a part of. The tour was a short one, which I was grateful for...and my best friend, Eugene Chadbourne, was patient with me and did take pretty damn good care of me. I would like to go back sometime but, as you know, I don't know how much more time I have with all the shit medically going on with me. I hope a few years. When I pass on, maybe people will start buying my music and that way help my sweet little wife through hard times...

IB: How do you come up with the songs you cover in the Jack and Jim Show - DMX's 'One More Road To Cross', for example?

JCB: Jack usually just starts playing a new song and I pick up on it within a couple of bars and we have a new song in the set. We will then try to play it on every gig of that particular tour until it is the way he likes it. We have a new CD out called *Think 69*[31] from our very successful tour of the USA last year that has a new song called 'Mr. Spooky'. That song came from my little granddaughter, Lisa Maria, here in Germany. She's five years old and that is what she calls me, Mr. Spooky.

It is a very funny song and the people love it...

IB: What are your feelings about the Zappa Family Trust's recent "aggressive action" against tribute bands?

JCB: ZPZ says that Dweezil is the real thing but in reality Frank is the real thing and everything else is tribute bands, period...

IB: A video clip by John Cline of you performing with Frank in Albuquerque in October 1980 has just appeared online - can you tell me a little about that?

JCB: John Cline is a good friend of mine from Albuquerque. I was living up there at the time I went to California and Frank's studio and recorded 'Harder Than Your Husband'. When they did the 1982 tour, one of the first gigs on the tour was in Albuquerque at the university. Frank asked me if I would sing the song live and, of course, I said I would. John then asked Frank for permission to videotape the song and, to my surprise, Frank gave him permission. It really is a good video. I had never seen it until it came on YouTube...

IB: I understand you're about to be interviewed for a new documentary on FZ & [the] Mothers of Invention in the 60s...

JCB: Yeah, the boys are coming this afternoon to my house where we will do the interview...

IB: Do you know what prompted Walter Becker's lobbying of the Rock and Roll Hall of Fame to get you included as a founding member of the Mothers?

JCB: I have no idea why except that I am very grateful to him. I am a big fan of Steely Dan. I wished all of the Mothers of Invention could and should have been inducted at the time Frank was inducted.[32] I am sure that Gail was very happy that we weren't and, in fact, I wouldn't be surprised if she had something to do with it....

IB: Finally, can we talk a little bit more about your private life - how did you meet Moni?

JCB: I was playing a gig in Traunstein, Germany,[33] with the Farrell/Black  Blues Band, and she was in the front row just staring at me. At the time, I didn't know just how big of a fan of the Mothers she was. She had been looking at my picture on all those album covers - she has all the original albums - for the last 25 years. She was absolutely beautiful and I couldn't believe such a beautiful woman would be interested in an old fart (I was 58) like me.

I tried to get to know her after the concert but she didn't speak any English at that time and, of course, I didn't speak any German. So that was the beginning of our relationship. I have to say that 11 months later that year, I married that girl and am the happiest I have ever been in all my life - STILL. She takes very good care of me and she still loves Zappa music. She loves going to the Zappanale and hopefully we will go next year. That would be a finale of my career as a guy that was fortunate enough to play in the best band in the world from the 1960s. I really believed that, and still do.[34]

[Shortly afterwards, Cancer was found to have spread throughout Jimmy's body. He died on Nov 1st, at home, with Moni, family, and close friends.]

Notes to Chapter 21

[1] JCB started work on this Newsletter on Oct 17, 2006 but the content is looking forward to 2007. For example the three CDs mentioned are listed as having been released in 2007.

[2] The Secretary of State under President George Bush Jnr.

[3] [From: written answers that JCB gave to questions posed by Robyn Flans for *Modern Drummer*, Dec 31, 2007]

[4] [From: JCB interview with Andrew Greenaway, for idiotbastard.com, Aug 7, 2008]. *Strange News From Mars* was released in 2008 on Zonic Entertainment.

[5] Late January 2007

[6] [From: written answers that JCB gave to questions posed by Robyn Flans for *Modern Drummer*, Dec 31, 2007]

[7] "...we began the year [Feb] with gigs in Switzerland, Italy and Croatia...I spend a few days with Jimmy Carl Black and then we go to the north of Germany to play the annual festival organized by members of Faust, held on the guitarist's farmhouse in the tiny village of Schiphoorst. This is simply a blast!" [From: eugenechadbourne.com]

[8] JCB is talking in Aug of 2007 to Calvin Krogh in Oslo.

[9] The Tempest Trio are Bruno Marini, Danny D'Agaro and JCB.

[10] Including the Clusone Jazz Festival on July 15, without Christina Mazza, as the Tempest Trio, and with Christina, as the Tempest Quartet at the Solerno Zappa Festival Aug 4, 2007 (Vallo della Lucania) [Ref: Event Poster & Program]

[11] 1st paragraph [From: JCB interview with Andrew Greenaway, for idiotbastard.com, Aug 7, 2008]

[12] In fact, he seems to have emailed JCB: "Hi Jimmy! I'm Bruno Marini, organ and saxophone player from Verona (Italy). Do you remember me? We played together when you was in Vicenza with John Kanady and bass player Silvio Galasso." [Ref: JCB files]

[13] Recorded on May 7/8, of 2007, in Verona, Italy at T-studios, and released on the Italian Azzurra Music label.

[14] JCB was "guesting" in Roma, on May 7 2007, at Teatro Ambra Jovinelli, for the "1967/2007: 40 years of Sandro O-Live!" concert. This is tight scheduling for JCB: recording in Verona and playing in Rome on the same day and then recording back in Verona the next day.

[15] ""I really DIG the version of Freedom Jazz Dance. Right on! Tell Mr. Marini his organ is dripping with pesto." This was a direct quote from Eugene Chadbourne about the first time he heard that song." [Ref: JCB]

[16] JCB is talking in Aug of 2007 to Calvin Krogh in Oslo

[17] This is a slip on JCB's part. He means "Happy" Metal Band, as he recalls elsewhere. The 1st song is titled Happy Metal.

[18] The CD ends up with five long tracks, but all shorter than 20 min.

[19] "Maybe I have been going about this music business all wrong. I should have done Disco a long time ago and maybe made some money out of it." [From: written answers that JCB gave to questions posed by Robyn Flans for *Modern Drummer*, Dec 31, 2007]

[20] Jimmy wrote this review in response to a request from the avant-garde Festival organizers [Ref: avantgardefestival.de, 2008]

[21] Remaining text this page drawn from several emails JCB wrote when he returned from the States.

[22] "...Chadfest starts in New York City...climaxing in Jimmy arriving and playing with me over three nights with guests Tony Trischka, Thomas Heberer and Brian Jackson....

The "Think 69" American leg moves through North Carolina, Massachusetts, Florida, Kentucky, Illinois, Indiana, Minnesota, New Mexico, New York, Missouri, Kansas, Iowa, Nebraska, Wisconsin, Louisiana, Maryland, Washington DC, Michigan and let's not forget Ontario, where I rode the trains for free as a "senior companion.""
[From: eugenechadbourne.com]

[23] The 2nd tour of the year with the Muffins?

[24] [Ref: JCB interview response to Richie Unterberger, Nov. 30, 2007]

[25] [From: written answers that JCB gave to questions posed by Robyn Flans for *Modern Drummer*, Dec 31, 2007]

[26] Extracts from JCB's last written interview, for the idiotbastard.com, follow.

[27] Prism Films

[28] Diagnosed Oct 2000, as JCB notes previously

[29] *We're Only In It For The Money*, MOI's 3rd album, released March 1968

[30] GEMA is the organization that administers artists' royalty payments in Germany

[31] An Inkanish CDR in 2008

[32] Of course...I think I deserve to be in the Hall of Fame although I really don't think it would ever put any food on my table ...to put it mildly, I HAVE PAID MY DUES IN THIS BUSINESS. Next year will mark my 50th year as a professional musician. I don't think there is anything that I could do to get myself put in the HOF but you never know. I will say that Liverpool, England thought of me as a good enough musician to put my brick in the Cavern Wall outside of the famous Cavern Club in that lovely city. All the greats are in the wall if they played at the club. At least I made that ...Wall of Fame. Thank you very much! [Ref: JCB response to a question posed in an email, June 2007]

[33] Jan 31, 1997

[34] "I would like to thank Andy Greenaway for doing this interview, as I always do. Thanks MUCHO, Andy!!!!!!!!"

[JCB finishes the written interview with this statement. He did one other "live" interview - that same day - for the Prism Film production: *Zappa & MOI*. He did no further interviews, to my knowledge. Ed]

274

Dedication

Jimmy Carl Black dedicated his book to family, friends and fans. He said –

**Don't be sad-
Be happy!**

Photos: Top, Jimmy's kids: Kim, Gabbie, Jina, Darrell, Gary, Geronimo, Tom & Mellie;
Middle, Jimmy and two fans; Below, friends & family gathered near La Mesa, NM

Jimmy Carl
Black
* 1.2.1938
† 1.11.2008

When I pass over
The prairie retains my tracks
As long as the wind sleeps*

*Wake of a Choctaw

References:

We would like to acknowledge hereunder the authors that have been consulted and the web-based resources that have been utilized to complete or complement Jimmy Carl Black's Memoirs and Recollections.

We would like to express our thanks also for the work these authors and websites have done in recording the history and events of the times written about by Jimmy, by providing reminiscences for the Recollections, and enabling us to proof his Memoirs thoroughly so they in their turn may become a resource to be consulted.

Online Resources (≈ In order of reference)
1. Chikasaw Nation Marriages Register
2. globalia.net/fz/donlope/fz/chronology
3. members.shaw.ca/fz-pomd/giglist/
4. Prism Films
5. rockprosopography102.blogspot.de
6. unitedmutations.com
7. nashtheslash.com
8. wikipedia.org
9. eugenechadbourne.com
10. sandroliva.com

Books (By print year)
Frank Zappa &Peter Occhiogrosso,1989, *The Real Frank Zappa*
Michael Gray, 1993, *Mother! The Frank Zappa Story*
Mark Brend, 2002, *Rock & Roll Doctor*
Billy James, 2005, *Necessity Is...*
John French, 2010, *Beefheart Through The Eyes of Magic*

Interviews (By Interview date)

Ron Young, *Boogie Magazine*, St. Antonio, Texas	1987 Interview given by JCB
killuglyradio.com	1990 Interview with Dick Barber
Axel Wünsch and Aad Hoogesteger Printed in *T'Mershi Duween*, 1992, #24-25	1991 Interview given by JCB
Radio Ohr, Germany	1993 Interview with JCB
Stefan Kleiber Printed in *Trust* magazine, Issue 69 1998	1997 Interview given by JCB
Steve Moore	2000 Interview given by JCB
	2003 Interview given by JCB
Claus Biegert	2003 Interview given by JCB
Horst Tolks (Boogie Stuff)	2004 CD Liner Notes by JCB
Calvin Krogh	2007 Interview given by JCB
Robyn Flans, Printed in *Modern Drummer*	2008 Interview given by JCB
Andrew Greenaway (idiotbastard.com/Interviews)	2008 Interview given by JCB
	2010 Interview with Lorraine Belcher Chamberlain

Photographs, Drawings and Illustrations

Together with Roddie Gilliard, Jimmy originally planned a "multi-media" presentation of his autobiography: text, illustrations, recordings, live interviews. Jimmy's original oral account was transcribed by Roddie Gilliard for these Memoirs - the original tapes were not otherwise useable. (An oral account of part of Jimmy's story has since been recorded by Jon Larsen and is available on CD.) *

Jimmy assembled a collection of photographs and artwork for his book, though the task was unfinished. To apply his visual concept to unfinished parts of the book, we have added to this collection. Indeed some pages in the last part depend on these photos and graphics. We gathered these photos from Jimmy's family albums and from his large collection of photos and other memorabilia such as concert flyers and original drawings. Jimmy's fans, family and other musicians sent him many of these, often for his book. We have accredited all contributions where we know the provenance and welcome any additional information readers can give us. The table on the following page lists those photos for which we have no credit details, those photographers we have not been able to reach, and those who are not accredited in the body text (where size or layout is an issue). We have only included photos we firmly trust were Jimmy's to use in his book, if he chose too. We would be grateful to hear from photographers, artists or copyright holders if they have any concerns.

However, it would be disingenuous of us to leave the reader with the assumption that Jimmy largely completed the illustration and layout of his book. He did not, so critical appraisal of this should be directed at the editors. We have added illustrative graphics where the text has inspired us to do so. Images in the public domain have sometimes inspired us. These graphics do not reflect any editorial opinions nor is there any derogatory intent in their use. We hope they largely fit with Jimmy's view of matters and his overall concept for the book.

In the meantime, we beg your tolerance of what has been, for us, a labor of love and not an exercise in making money. Jimmy's book wasn't finished on his behalf before now because, to quote a writer in this field: "no one saw any profit potential."

The Papillon

Jimmy's second home was the Papillon bar and restaurant, just a few hundred yards from home. He was often there when wife Moni was at work or biking up a mountain. Chatting to the owner, the young girls working there, and the young musicians that came there to meet him, gave Jimmy a lot of pleasure. He also got lots of free drinks, when Moni wasn't looking!

Moni says thank you to all, for taking such good care of Jimmy.

The Jimmy Carl Black Story on Hot Club Records, 2008

Contributors*

We are indebted to at least the following: Helmut King, Roddie Gilliard, Art Tripp, Jay Tripp, Clark Inkanish, Monika Black, Cal McLeish, Slingerland, Gretsch, Julian Smith, Dennis Gillund, B. Mundi, Geronimo Black, Peter Mackay, Mick Pini, Trans-Media Inc., Tom Leavey, Steve Brown & Goldust Records, Lo Boys, ConSafo Records, Phil Applebaum, Helios Records, Tony Young, Junior Franklin, The Golden Echoes, Arthur Brown, Peter Butcher, Mannish Boys, Eugene Chadbourne, Peter & the ARF boys: Andre Sudmann & Thomas Jung; Reinhard Preuss & Muffin Records Productions, Miro Zupa, Ener Bladezipper, Sandro Oliva, Fireant, Divine Records, Behind The Mirror, Stormy Monday Records, Inkanish Records, Fritz Records, Blue Orchid, Walter Schreiber, Roald Weinstock, Richard Ray Farrell, Ulli Schaefer, Arf.., Nigel.., Jerry Ford, Smoking Jack Oozi, Horst Tolks, Mark Hadley, Jos Steen, Steve De Bruyn, Zjakki Willem, Thomas Atzinger, Boxholder Records, Jon Larsen, Bruno Marini, Christina Mazza, art-errorist.de, Captain Trip, Ferdinand Huber, and last but not least, Grandmothers, Muffin Men, and all their many fans, for photographs and artwork.

We are also indebted to all those artists, designers and photographers who contributed to the covers of the LPs and CDs that graphically illustrate the pages, who may not be listed in the table below:

Page	Location	Source (In addition to those credited in the body text)
141		From original photo by Peter Mackay
146	Bottom	From original cartoon by Helmut King
153		JCB collection; photographer unknown
154	Bottom	Design & Photo: A. Watson; © MCA Records 1972
156		From original photo by Albert Watson
172	Bottom	Cover design: Scott Goodman & Gary Israel
176		Original art by Paul Mitchell; courtesy Helios Records
182		JCB collection; photographer unknown
187		JCB collection; photographer unknown
206	Top	From original cartoon by Miro Zupa
210	Top	© Muffin Records Productions; courtesy R. Preuss
211-2		From original cartoon by Miro Zupa
214		Courtesy T'Mershi Duween
217		Original photo © Muffin Records Productions; courtesy R. Preuss
222	Both	Original photos © Muffin Records Productions; courtesy R. Preuss
224	Top	Photo taken by E. Bladezipper; © Sandro Oliva
233	M. Left	Original art by Katharina Stock; courtesy Behind The Mirror
234	Bottom	Tom Kastermans, 1998. Courtesy of Foto Studio Kastermans
239		Photo courtesy Robert Reidt

*Roughly in order of 1st appearance on the pages of the book, and including contributors to the text not mentioned in Acknowledgements – I on page 6

Page	Location	Source (In addition to those credited in the body text)
241		JCB collection; photographer unknown
243	Top Left	JCB collection; photographer unknown
244		JCB collection; photographer unknown
245		JCB collection; photographer unknown
254	Top Left	The Indian - original cartoon by Helmut King
255	Bottom	Artwork by Helmut King
256	Top	Cover art by Don Preston
256	Middle	Artwork by Helmut King
258	T. Right	JCB collection; photographer unknown
258	B. Left	JCB collection; photographer unknown
259	Bottom	From original photo by Herbet Gruber; courtesy: Horst Tolks
260	Lowest	From original photo by Mark Hadley
264	M. Left	Artwork: Joel Levicke, Charlotte James; courtesy E. Bladezipper
266	Top	Cover Design: Damiano Frix; courtesy Azzurra Music
267	Top	Illustration: Bjorn Melbye; courtesy Jon Larsen
269	Top	Courtesy Captain Trip Records
270		Courtesy Captain Trip Records
280		Photo: Simon Danby © VG Bild-Kunst, Bonn 2012; Poster courtesy of Böller und Brot
292	B. Right	From original cartoon by Helmut King

So we thank all those we've mentioned and all those we haven't for your contributions to what is a small but relevant piece of Rock music history. Finally –

Where's the Beer and when do we get paid?

Böller & Brot present a movie featuring Jimmy on the road with Eugene Chadbourne in 2007. Go to wheresthebeer.de for more information on future showings.

280

Index

Index

Index

Keep in touch?

Visit jimmycarlblack.com for...

Music

A
r
t

News

'ographies

Made in United States
North Haven, CT
06 March 2023

33695025R00163